Pentecostal Manifestos

James K. A. Smith and Amos Yong, *Editors*

PENTECOSTAL MANIFESTOS will provide a forum for exhibiting the next generation of Pentecostal scholarship. Having exploded across the globe in the twentieth century, Pentecostalism now enters its second century. For the past fifty years, Pentecostal and charismatic theologians (and scholars in other disciplines) have been working "internally," as it were, to articulate a distinctly Pentecostal theology and vision. The next generation of Pentecostal scholarship is poised to move beyond a merely internal conversation to an outward-looking agenda, in a twofold sense: first, Pentecostal scholars are increasingly gaining the attention of those outside Pentecostal/charismatic circles *as* Pentecostal voices in mainstream discussions; second, Pentecostal scholars are moving beyond simply reflecting on their own tradition and instead are engaging in theological and cultural analysis of a variety of issues from a Pentecostal perspective. In short, Pentecostal scholars are poised with a new boldness:

- Whereas the first generation of Pentecostal scholars was careful to learn the methods of the academy and then "apply" those to the Pentecostal tradition, the next generation is beginning to interrogate the reigning methodologies and paradigms of inquiry from the perspective of a unique Pentecostal worldview.
- Whereas the first generation of Pentecostal scholars was faithful in applying the tools of their respective trades to the work of illuminating the phenomena of modern Pentecostalism, the charismatic movements, and (now) the global renewal movements, the second generation is expanding its focus to bring a Pentecostal perspective to bear on important questions and issues that are concerns not only for Pentecostals and charismatics but also for the whole church.
- Whereas the first generation of Pentecostal/charismatic scholars was engaged in transforming the anti-intellectualism of the tradition, the second generation is engaged in contributing to and even impacting the conversations of the wider theological academy.

PENTECOSTAL MANIFESTOS will bring together both high-profile scholars and newly emerging scholars to address issues at the intersection of Pentecostalism, the global church, the theological academy, and even broader cultural concerns. Authors in PENTECOSTAL MANIFESTOS will be writing to and addressing not only their own movements but also those outside of Pentecostal/charismatic circles, offering a manifesto for a uniquely Pentecostal perspective on various themes. These will be "manifestos" in the sense that they will be bold statements of a distinctly Pentecostal interjection into contemporary discussions and debates, undergirded by rigorous scholarship.

Under this general rubric of bold, programmatic "manifestos," the series will include both shorter, crisply argued volumes that articulate a bold vision within a field as well as longer scholarly monographs, more fully developed and meticulously documented, with the same goal of engaging wider conversations. Such PENTECOSTAL MANIFESTOS are offered as intrepid contributions with the hope of serving the global church and advancing wider conversations.

PUBLISHED

James K. A. Smith, *Thinking in Tongues: Pentecostal Contributions to Christian Philosophy* (2010)

Frank D. Macchia, *Justified in the Spirit: Creation, Redemption, and the Triune God* (2010)

Wolfgang Vondey, *Beyond Pentecostalism: The Crisis of Global Christianity and the Renewal of the Theological Agenda* (2010)

Amos Yong, *The Spirit of Creation: Modern Science and Divine Action in the Pentecostal-Charismatic Imagination* (2011)

Nimi Wariboko, *The Pentecostal Principle: Ethical Methodology in New Spirit* (2011)

The Pentecostal Principle

Ethical Methodology in New Spirit

Nimi Wariboko

WILLIAM B. EERDMANS PUBLISHING COMPANY

GRAND RAPIDS, MICHIGAN / CAMBRIDGE, U.K.

© 2012 Nimi Wariboko

Published 2012 by
Wm. B. Eerdmans Publishing Co.
2140 Oak Industrial Drive N.E., Grand Rapids, Michigan 49505 /
P.O. Box 163, Cambridge CB3 9PU U.K.

Printed in the United States of America

17 16 15 14 13 12   7 6 5 4 3 2 1

Library of Congress Cataloging-in-Publication Data

Wariboko, Nimi, 1962-
    The pentecostal principle: ethical methodology in new spirit / Nimi Wariboko.
        p.   cm.   — (Pentecostal manifestos)
    Includes bibliographical references.
    ISBN 978-0-8028-6697-4 (pbk.: alk. paper)
    1. Pentecostalism.   I. Title.

    BR1644.W37   2012
    270.8'2 — dc23

                                                2011029918

www.eerdmans.com

To my wife, Paemi: Ibierebo, Deinbo, Ibakam!

Contents

Preface

There was one Easter; there are millions of Pentecosts.

José Comblin, *The Holy Spirit and Liberation*[1]

This book is first and foremost an engaged pentecostal-theological intervention in the methodology of social ethics. Arguing that the pneumatological dynamic is central to ethical methodology, it brings pentecostal experience and ideas into dialogue with the broader academy, with mainstream theological and philosophical scholarships, and other voices outside the tradition. It follows the recent efforts of leading pentecostal theologians to expand the horizon of pentecostal scholarship and to invite those outside the movement to seriously consider pentecostal voices, perspectives, and proposals in their theologies, philosophies, and ethics.

This study formulates the central pneumatological dynamic as the pentecostal principle — the capacity of social existence to begin something new. The pentecostal principle is a synthesis of both the Protestant principle and the Catholic substance and the animating force toward a theonomous connection of culture with the divine depth of existence. On the basis of a rigorous elucidation and defense of the pentecostal principle, I formulate a method of ethics that explicitly thinks through and out of the pentecostal reality. I show how the pentecostal experience and spirituality can be brought into the field of ethical methodology with a serious en-

1. José Comblin, *The Holy Spirit and Liberation* (Maryknoll, NY: Orbis, 1989), p. 184.

gagement with major conversational partners at the vanguard of public theology, social ethics, political theology, philosophy, and ethics in general. In particular, the book is a creative and constructive work on ethical methodology, yet clearly informed by pentecostalism as understood not only in terms of the global movement but also in terms of the Day of Pentecost symbol, and it is consistent with the major thrusts of recent pentecostal academic theology.

The book argues that ethical methodology (engagement) must assume the mode of cultural criticism, social creativity, and political engagement in which we should resist commitment to any knowledge-machinery that only works to understand the world but not to change it, and instead we must provoke moral development, and enact constituting and constituted social practices of human flourishing. An ethics faithful to the pentecostal principle does not allow itself the luxury of bathing in the blithe air of the problematic and vocabulary of past eras and their spirits (specters), but must continuously work to invent its own analyses and language, to speak in new tongues.

This study is also philosophical in its basic outlook, addressing the issue of the social ontological truth of the concrete religio-cultural order of historical expressions of pentecostalism. This work attempts to lay bare the "inner greatness," the "historical-ontological essence" of Pentecostalism as a phenomenon of our epoch without conferring ontological dignity on any pentecostal movement on the ontic level. We are in an era governed by the worship of bold, rapid, abundant energies. From gushing oil wells to chain reactions of atomic explosions, from race cars to space shuttles, from action movies to bungee jumping, from supersonic chats of cell-phone text messaging to the profound instantaneous and infinite speed of the Internet, everything is in the mode of explosion and detonation. As Peter Sloterdijk puts it, we are all "fanatical adherents of explosions, worshippers of that rapid release of a large quantity of energy."[2] Pentecostalism (in its fury, abundant energy, and rapid growth) is the religious archetype of the impetus of our age. Energy is a *pure means* and pure endedness, if not actually only a pure means (pure mediality).

The notion of energy as a pure means opens up another perspective for comprehending our epoch: economy, politics, and religion. The philos-

---

2. Peter Sloterdijk, "Conversation with Fabrice Bousteau and Jonathan Chauveau," *Beaux Arts Magazine*, October 2004, p. 192, quoted in Nicolas Bourriaud, *The Radicant*, trans. James Gussen and Lili Porten (New York: Lukas and Sternberg, 2009), p. 177.

opher Giorgio Agamben argues that the current phase of capitalism is "a gigantic apparatus for capturing pure means, that is, profanatory behaviors."[3] Politics does not operate as pure means; it principally refers to activities determined by preset ends of late capitalism — debates about the efficient means to accomplish closed ends. Today's politics (co-opted and emasculated by late capitalism) is about administration of projects and order maintenance and not about creating and sustaining a platform for debating and contesting different ends; is not a means toward an open end.[4] Pentecostalism portrays religion as pure means, a pathway of *profanatory* (not pejorative: in the sense Agamben uses the term) behaviors. Religion as a sphere of openness, pure means, is profoundly and qualitatively different from religion as an end. Pentecostalism displays the structure of aesthetic categories and the "logic" of play. Pentecostalism is the sacred in a *playful* mode.

Play is the signature of all things. It is the signature of creativity, resistance to social formatting, and struggle against any finite form claiming the status of the infinite. True play has no end — it is non-instrumentalized — and is governed by *non-zero-sum* dynamics. It is a *pure means*, totally given to its freely evolving potentialities. Play as the intrinsic nature, potentiality of Pentecostalism is also threatened by the instrumental logic of capitalism.

In this book I attempt to grasp the nature of the pentecostal principle and that of the playful character of pentecostalism and to use the knowledge so gained to craft an ethical methodology in a new key. It is a methodology to undergird an ethics that resists absolutism, provokes creative possibilities, and forges alternatives to any *given* world. The project is unfinished. It awaits you, the reader's creative philosophical and theological reflections, spiritual imagination, and collaboration to be complete. I have no body of knowledge to pass on to you from the onset of our cooperation. Together we will create the body of knowledge into which we go. Our minds create their own common knowledge space and expand into it. The two of us are partners in a pedagogical dance.

We start the dance by responding to the drumbeats of Paul Tillich in the rhythm of the *Protestant principle*. As we get better at the dance and as our knowledge grows into the spaces that will illuminate the pentecostal principle we will abandon the Tillichian sounds — which are classical in

---

3. Giorgio Agamben, *Profanations*, trans. Jeff Fort (New York: Zone Books, 2007), p. 87.

4. Giorgio Agamben, *Means without Ends: Notes on Politics*, trans. Vincenzo Benetti and Cesare Casarino (Minneapolis: University of Minnesota Press, 2000), pp. 115-17.

basic tenor — and create our own sounds, that of jazz which is improvisational, experimental, revisable. The sound of jazz, always not fully scored, is a free play of embellishment and enactment. It always actualizes its potentials in the very process it stores or re-creates them. Jazz captures something basic about existence. Existence is potentiality. Existence does not exhaust potentials; existence ignites its potentiality retroactively. And the pentecostal principle is the rhythmic pattern of the sounds made by the jazzy mobility of existence. It is when we grasp or *repeat* the play quality of our existence that we find, discover, and reveal the chord structure of human flourishing. Jean-Paul Sartre tells us in *Being and Nothingness,* "as soon as a man apprehends himself as free and wishes to use his freedom . . . then his activity is play." Friedrich Schiller, on the other hand, says in *Essays Aesthetical and Philosophical,* "Man only plays when in the full meaning of the word he is a man, and he is only completely a man when he plays."

The Kalabari of the Niger Delta in Nigeria have a saying: *"Tikiri ane Omekwe tari nnam fiye."* Literally, it means it was at the playground that Omekwe was first called a "daddy-husband" (lover, darling). Philosophically, it means that it is at play that a man or woman first finds, discovers, and reveals him- or herself. This is similar to how the sixteenth-century German Christian mystic and theologian Jacob Boehme conceptualized "becoming." He likened it to a play, a love-play of energies freed from purpose. For him, play is the essential mode of activity of those regenerated and perfected by grace.

We once moved over from the theology of work to the theology of grace. Perhaps, it is now time to move over to the theology *of religion as play,* as the *deactivation* of law and *radicalization* of grace.[5] Pentecostalism appears to be playing the role of a "vanishing mediator" between the theology of grace and that of play. But I must also quickly add that it is not clear to me if pentecostals are the true bearers of the pentecostal principle today.

At the beginning of this preface, I wrote that this book is both theological and philosophical. I need to quickly warn that this does not mean that there are two distinct parts to the book or two discernible arguments running side by side. Rather, the theological is philosophical and the philosophical is theological. Actually, what I consider as the philosophical ("the historico-ontological essence" of pentecostalism) is a thread woven into

5. See the introduction and chapters 4 and 5 of this book for a discussion on grace in the light of the pentecostal principle.

the fabric of the theological. The preceding paragraphs about play have brought the philosophical thread into greater colorful relief than is generally visible in most of the book. This highlighting of the philosophical thread is raised a notch in chapter 5. But as it is with the conception of this book, the philosophical — the pentecostal penchant for play — quickly morphed into a preliminary philosophical theology of religion as play.

This book was written in four countries (the United States, Nigeria, France, and Jamaica) as I traveled around lecturing, preaching, consulting, and visiting family members. And at least four contexts frame the ideas in this book. First, as a theologian I have principally worked on Tillichian theology and the intersection of theology and economics. This book has arisen out of my response to Tillich's Protestant principle. Second, in the spring of 2010 with two other scholars I edited the papers of the late theologian Professor Ogbu Uke Kalu for publication. It was in the process of writing the introductions for the three volumes of his work that the idea of formulating the pentecostal principle occurred to me; one of the volumes is on African pentecostalism. Third, I am a pentecostal Christian worshiping with one of the largest pentecostal-charismatic denominations in the world, the Redeemed Christian Church of God. As the reader shall see throughout the book, such an identity has not been allowed to detract from rigorous academic thinking on the pentecostal principle. In fact, it added a fillip to the quest for the proper formulation of the pentecostal principle. I need to know what that identity means in terms of ontological existence, unfolding world history, and God's relation with humanity. Finally and more importantly, it is an attempt to properly understand and examine the methodology behind my theological-ethical thinking. All this, I hope, will enable me to formulate an ethical methodology in a new spirit.

NIMI WARIBOKO
Westwood, Massachusetts

Introduction

The pentecostal principle is the capacity to begin. It encapsulates the notion that no finite or conditioned reality can claim to have reached its destiny. The movement of every existent to its destiny (full realization of potentialities) remains ever incompletable because it is "rooted" in the abyss of divine freedom. Every end has only one option: to be a new beginning. Hannah Arendt puts it in this way:

> Beginning, before it becomes a historical event, is the supreme capacity of man; politically, it is identical with man's freedom. *Initium ut esset homo creatus est* — "that a beginning be made man was created," said Augustine.[1]

Because of the demand of new beginning, more is expected from every moment and every life, and there is a radical openness to alternatives and surprises. The restlessness of all en-spirited life is recognized, understood, and grasped. What remains of this text is a further elaboration and interpretation of the first sentence.

The opening definition is informed by Hannah Arendt's theory of action[2] and *a* pentecostalist-evental interpretation of grace. Action, according to Arendt, is the only way to bring something new into the world, to initiate a new beginning in an automatic or continuous process. Action

---

1. Hannah Arendt, *The Origins of Totalitarianism* (New York: Schocken, 2004), p. 616.
2. Hannah Arendt, *The Human Condition* (Chicago: University of Chicago Press, 1958).

has no telos which must justify it and no end which must call it into cessation. It is characterized by unpredictability. Its telos is in its own means; it is a pure happening. It is not oriented to specific outcome. It is in a sense a *pure means,* a pure mediality in the *in-between world* of human coexistence. This is quite unlike *work,* which must have a goal and must be executed only for this end. To the extent that work has final product, final cause outside itself, and an endpoint it is predictable. The new in Arendt's understanding is unpredictable; is the act of initiating fresh beginnings, and it can only be brought into the in-between world by human action. Thus, action corresponds with the human capacity to begin, a capacity that is decisively rooted in *natality,* birth and rebirth, the originality of each new human being entering into an ongoing social process. Insofar as each human being entered into this world in utter originality and uniqueness, as a new beginning, he or she has the capacity to act and to start something new, to enact new beginnings. To act, to initiate something new, to exercise the capacity to begin is to be born-again.[3]

According to the popular pentecostal mindset grace is an event. Pentecostals view grace as disruptive. God's grace radically challenges and unsettles our human presumptions of self-sufficiency and self-complacency, and warmly embraces and *settles* us in salvation, service, our identification with Christ, and as beings indwelled by the Holy Spirit. Grace is an appearance of something new into creation, human life, human condition — which breaks into the order of things. It allows freedom to appear, to flourish as such. It is a movement toward openness to future possibilities, dislocating human lives and situations toward their future forms, nudging them toward full actualization of their potentials. In its dislocating movement, it has a *novum* character signaling it as a response to the current order of things which potentialities exceed the current structuring of individual and social existence. Grace expresses the hidden potentials of a situation, existence, or life as well as transcends them.

Grace as the evental movement of God (Holy Spirit) is full of novelty, possibilities, and potentials. In the pentecostal way of thinking the so-called "big," "serious" purpose of grace is the freedom to play in salvation for freedom. Grace is characterized by play, and not by any purpose at

---

3. One thing that makes Arendt's thought interesting to me is her deliberate effort to turn philosophy away from the focus on death and defining life over against death. She focuses on engendering more intense life and possibilities of new creation. (See Arendt, *The Life of the Mind,* Volume 1: *Thinking* [San Diego: Harcourt, 1978], pp. 79-80. See also pp. 83-84.)

all.[4] Grace is to exuberantly embrace the Holy Spirit as the spirit of play. "The spirit that animates humanity is the spirit of play. This spirit is the source of our capacity to actualize our potential and to honor God fully. We are able to actualize our potentials because we have freedom."[5]

Grace as an event is both continuous and discontinuous. This is the sense that though one can grow from glory to glory in its participation and reception (or grow in terms of one's participation in the triune life), it cannot be "practiced," *habituated* (possessed as habitual disposition) as it is always a gift and not a virtue.[6] Grace is renewed every morning. The baptism of the Holy Spirit is not once and for all, but continual; it is evanescent and perdurative. Grace is disruptive, yet it perdures within God's relationship with human beings and the rest of creation as characterized, sustained, and energized by the Holy Spirit.

This understanding of grace arises largely from a charismatic conviction that it is "an empowerment toward creative transformation, generally in terms of human being in-the-world." Another dimension of this charismatic conviction or pneumatological imagination is the notion that "life is a gift, generally in terms of its awareness of the contingency of all things. . . ."[7] Third, grace is also an effect, a manifestation of the indwelling Spirit of God in human beings.[8] Finally, the pentecostal worldview affirms the "surprises" of the Holy Spirit as a central and non-negotiable aspect of the understanding of reality.[9] The new is a manifestation of the Spirit's presence in the world and in nature. The new is a result of intense coopera-

---

4. Later in the book, the "purposeless character" of grace, grace as a "pure means," will be explained fully.

5. James H. Evans Jr., *Playing* (Minneapolis: Fortress, 2010), pp. 70-71.

6. There is a "depoliticized and destabilized" reading of the regnant genealogy and interpretation of virtue that renders it "disruptive" and liberatory. This particular conception of virtue (aretē, excellence) renders it suitable to the pentecostal notion of grace as disruptive and as a gift given over and over again within the God-human relationship. See Nimi Wariboko, *The Principle of Excellence: A Framework for Social Ethics* (Lanham, MD: Lexington, 2009).

7. Amos Yong, *Spirit-Word-Community: Theological Hermeneutics in Trinitarian Perspective* (Eugene, OR: Wipf and Stock, 2002), p. 136.

8. Frank D. Macchia, *Justified in the Spirit: Creation, Redemption, and the Triune God* (Grand Rapids: Eerdmans, 2010), pp. 18-29.

9. James K. A. Smith, "Is There Room for Surprise in the Natural World? Naturalism, the Supernatural, and Pentecostal Spirituality," in *Science and the Spirit: A Pentecostal Engagement with the Sciences*, ed. James K. A. Smith and Amos Yong (Bloomington: Indiana University Press, 2010), pp. 43-47. See also his *Thinking in Tongues: Pentecostal Contributions to Christian Philosophy* (Grand Rapids: Eerdmans, 2010).

tion and collaboration of human beings in action even as the Holy Spirit *intensely* displays God's presence in creation so as "to refocus our attention on the 'miraculous' nature of the ordinary."[10]

The evental character of grace has great implications for how we formulate the pentecostal principle or interpret pentecostalism. Pentecostalism is not only a movement *under* grace, it is also a movement *of* grace, struggling to trace and track the pentecostal principle.

The pentecostal principle predates pentecostalism and is likely to outlive it as a complex shared set of practice, discipline, and spiritual orientation.[11] Pentecostalism is a fast-growing religious phenomenon today and books have been written on it as a form of Christianity, religious movement, and spirituality. But what is the meaning of pentecostalism within the world-historical process? Is the pentecostal principle likely to provide models for grasping and guiding the dynamics of modern life in its various spheres? What do its meaning and existence hold for ethical methodology? What are the fundamental, practical, and social issues pertinent to ethical methodology in the event of the Pentecost? Can it structure the way we think about governance in the complex, contingent, networked, adaptive global world of today?

In this book I want to respond to these pertinent questions within the context of pentecostalism as a "special [fragmentary] historical embodiment of a universally significant principle."[12] This principle is what I have named as the pentecostal principle and it expresses the fluid dynamics of spirit and the conditions of creative emergence in the infinite fabric of life. It also gestures to a radical openness to the operations of the concrete Spirit in history.[13]

The pentecostal principle is the expression of the general will of existence (life): the name of the process of creative emergence that figures and disfigures biological and social life. It affirms the vision of transformation implicit in the doctrine of the incarnation, discernible in the in-dwelling Spirit, and manifest in the outburst of the divine on the Day of Pentecost (Acts 2). This is to say the *real* can be embodied in persons and social practices in time and space, and therefore social existence and history are themselves subject to the dynamics of life, to the impulse of transformation.

---

10. Smith, "Is There Room for Surprise in the Natural World?" pp. 46-47.

11. Here I have relied on James K. A. Smith for the definition of pentecostalism. See his *Thinking in Tongues.*

12. Paul Tillich, *The Protestant Era* (Chicago: University of Chicago Press, 1948), p. vii.

13. To learn more about this openness, see Smith, *Thinking in Tongues.*

Does the formulation of pentecostal principle at this point in history mean that we are living in the Pentecostal Era? To attempt a response to this question let us resort to Paul Tillich, who grappled with a similar concern when he formulated his Protestant principle early in the twentieth century. Believing himself to be living in the last days of Protestantism he once asked, "Will the Protestant Era come to an end?" He responded that it was likely to happen and in fact he looked to a form of Christianity that would synthesize the Protestant principle and what he called Catholic substance in a religion of the concrete Spirit. For he writes that "Protestantism as a principle is eternal and a permanent criterion of everything temporal" and can pass a negative judgment on Protestantism as a historical period and a form of religion.[14]

Tillich is right in identifying the Protestant principle as eternal and a permanent criterion of everything temporal, but it would be a mistake to consider it as principle of existence. It is primarily a religious principle, an expression of "one side of the divine-human relationship."[15] It has to be applied to the other side of the divine-human relationship to be realized and expressed. The more interesting and important principle to focus on is the pentecostal one. The pentecostal principle as a religious principle is a *synthesis* of both the Protestant principle and the Catholic substance and the animating force toward a theonomous connection of culture with the divine depths of existence.

ℵ The Synthesis and Theology of the Third Article[16]

This synthesis may remind readers who are familiar with D. Lyle Dabney's "theology of the third article," which combines the first article (Catholic and Orthodox theologies) and the second article (Protestant and christological theologies). Strictly speaking, my synthesis refers to Paul Tillich's Catholic substance and Protestant principle. Nonetheless, there are points of convergence: each type of synthesis analyzes its subject matter "in terms of priority of possibility, not in terms of the priority of being or the real."[17]

14. For the quotes see Tillich, *Protestant Era*, pp. vii-ix.

15. Tillich, *Protestant Era*, p. vii.

16. This notation is used to mark off strategic interventions in the flow of arguments in each section or chapter. It flags ideas that are well connected to the discourse at hand to deter posting them to the notes, but require a set-apart textual space to reveal their inner synchronicity with the ongoing development of an argument. In general, each aside aims to flesh out, deepen, and broaden key ideas and concepts in the book.

17. D. Lyle Dabney, "The Nature of the Spirit: Creation as a Premonition of God," in

In addition, both syntheses are primarily informed by the need to transcend Protestant theology (second article) and make pneumatology (the third article theology) as the starting point for theology. The third article is about the Spirit of God that harbors and undergirds the *possibility* that brings the real into emergent being. The focus on possibility offers a triadic lens to do theological analysis. The God of Exodus 3:14 who says "I shall be what I shall be," *"Eheyeh Asher Eheyeh"* is a God of possibilities, surging potentialities.[18] Jürgen Moltmann tells us in his book *The Coming of God* that possibility underlines the self-description of Jesus Christ in Revelation 1:8. According to him, when Jesus says, "I am . . . who is and who was and who is to come . . . ," he does not have stasis in mind or even the new that flows from the trajectory of the past and the present. It is the new that asks for, creates, and sustains the alternative possibilities, the unexpected path.[19]

With an engaging focus on possibility resources for addressing the theological-ethical issues of today are sought not in comprehensive, totalizing conceptualities but rather in "'emergent' processes and realities — novel, unexpected and unforeseeable events and developments which represent new possibilities of understanding and creating continuity within the profoundly fragmented and fragmenting world in which we find ourselves."[20] In chapter 2, I examine the science of emergent processes and social ethics to further explore this possibility.

And there is even more to the pentecostal principle than being a synthesis. When properly understood it is a universal dynamic principle of ex-

---

Starting with the Spirit, ed. Stephen Pickard and Gordon Preece (Hindmarsh, Australia: Australian Theological Forum, 2001), p. 101. Dabney's analysis of the synthesis can be further studied in pp. 3-110 of this book. See also D. Lyle Dabney, "Why Should the Last Be First? The Priority of Pneumatology in Recent Theological Discussion," in *Advents of the Spirit*, ed. Bradford E. Hinze and D. Lyle Dabney (Milwaukee: Marquette University Press, 2001), pp. 238-61; D. Lyle Dabney, "Otherwise Engaged in the Spirit: A First Theology for a Twenty-first Century," in *The Future of Theology: Essays in Honor of Jürgen Moltmann*, ed. Miroslav Volf, Carmen Krieg, and Thomas Kucharz (Grand Rapids: Eerdmans, 1996), pp. 154-63; D. Lyle Dabney, *"Pneumatologia Crucis*: Reclaiming *Theologia Crucis* for a Theology of Spirit Today," *Scottish Journal of Theology* 53, no. 4 (2000): 511-24, and Amos Yong, "A Theology of the Third Article? Hegel and the Contemporary Enterprise in First Philosophy and First Theology," in *Semper Reformandum: Studies in Honour of Clark H. Pinnock*, ed. Stanley E. Porter and Anthony R. Cross (Carlisle: Paternoster, 2003), pp. 208-31.

18. David Birnbaum, *Summa Metaphysica II* (New York: J. Levine/Millennium Classics, 2008).

19. Jürgen Moltmann, *The Coming of God: Christian Eschatology*, trans. Margaret Kohl (Minneapolis: Fortress, 1996), pp. 23-28.

20. D. Lyle Dabney, "Starting with the Spirit: Why the Last Should Now Be the First," in *Starting with the Spirit*, p. 10.

istence, of life. As a principle of existence, it is a precondition for them (both Protestant principle and Catholic substance), and has an excess that cannot be incorporated into the synthesis. It remains both inside and outside the sum of their parts. It refuses capture by the two sides of the divine-human relationships that Tillich has identified, and challenges them. This book will attempt to transform Tillich's Protestant principle into a principle of creative restlessness, emergent creativity in the fabric of life, and the focus of spiritual striving in today's globalizing world. But does it also translate Tillich's Protestant Era into Pentecostal Era?

The pentecostal principle in a certain sense captures the spirit of our current era. The era's basic orientation is dominated by flexibility of experimentation and creative freedom. The times we live in reflect an increasing legibility and recognizability of the pentecostal principle. The implacable restlessness of life, that call to go beyond any extant creativity, figuration, is felt more acutely today than ever before. Pentecostalism (which is not the same thing as fundamentalism) expresses the provisional, improvisational character of modern civilization, "always responding to, adapting, and experimenting with new challenges."[21] Its energy gestures to the basic restlessness of life, to the incomplete, protean, and dynamic achievements and doings of human beings. Its consciousness is also dominated by a strong commitment to drawing from a source stronger, greater, and more powerful than human beings. There is a strong communal consciousness of divine and inexhaustible creativeness to which men and women ought to relate their autonomous activities. This is the faith of a frame of mind that gravitates toward the scientific impulse to tinker, yet always in acknowledgment of what is more-than human.[22] This is the tension of negotiating the old and new as religion moves forward in our age of scientific culture where faith is not in retreat; rather, it is growing.

The basic impulse of an era is not only given or identified, it must also be received (embodied). These are the objective and subjective dimensions

21. Cornel West, *The American Evasion of Philosophy: A Genealogy of Pragmatism* (Madison: University of Wisconsin Press, 1989), p. 143. West, based on W. E. B. Du Bois's insight, uses these words to describe African-American music. This music, jazz, captures something of the spirit of the people and of the United States. The practice of pentecostalism as we know it today cannot be adequately understood without noting the stamp African-Americans and blacks all over the world have put on it. See also Harvey Cox, "Jazz and Pentecostalism," *Archives des sciences sociales des religions* 84, no. 4 (October-December 1993): 181-88.

22. Smith, *Thinking in Tongues,* pp. 86-105.

of every universally significant principle. So the answer to the question whether we are living in the Pentecostal Era depends on the identification of a critical mass of true, authentic, and faithful bearers of the principle. The bearers of this principle are those who are vocationally conscious of the principle and are willing to interpret and transform society in its light, and they are not limited to pentecostals. They (pentecostals) arguably have the form of it but are yet to grasp and express the "substance."

From Protestant Principle to Pentecostal Principle

Since both Protestant principle and pentecostal principle share a common word, "principle," let us start from there. What is principle? A principle is the power and logic of history — an expression of humankind's essential being as historical reality — that has been grasped and formulated as a practical (existential) idea and thus stands in judgment of all spheres and aspects of historical reality. The task of all those who are vocationally conscious of the principle is to interpret and transform society in the light of the principle.

Now add the word *Protestant* in front of *principle* and we have *Protestant principle*. The Protestant principle is the name Paul Tillich gives to the force or tension that is in a constant struggle with form as a limit-actuality, as what can never be surpassed. It relativizes all forms, resists and conquers their closure, and intimates to them of their insufficiency at the same time that it orients them to the open future, the to-come time. The form on which this tension is to strain forward is produced on what he calls the *Catholic substance.*[23]

The Protestant principle is the moving and self-critical principle of the church and even generally of all human sociality. It opposes the absolutizing of any particular form of sociality, human arrangement, and ethos. In its lights, every cultural form, the relative, can become a vehicle for the absolute, the unconditional, but nothing can ever become absolute, unconditional itself. The cultural form which bears the divine presence he

23. The catholic substance in a positive sense is "the concrete embodiment of the Spiritual Presence." In the negative sense in which Tillich uses the syntagma it refers to the pretentious immobility and timelessness of sacramentality (the presence of the divine in cultural forms, actions, objects, or finite creation). For the quote see Paul Tillich, *Systematic Theology,* Volume 3: *Life and the Spirit; History and the Kingdom of God* (Chicago: University of Chicago Press, 1963), p. 245.

calls the catholic substance and the reaction against the absolutization of the vehicle he calls the Protestant principle. As Tillich puts it:

> The Protestant principle is an expression of the conquest of religion by the Spiritual Presence and consequently an expression of the victory over the ambiguities of religion, its profanization, and its demonization. It is Protestant, because it protests against the tragic demonic self-elevation of religion and liberates religion from itself for the other functions of the human spirit, at the same time liberating these functions from their self-seclusion against the manifestation of the ultimate.[24]

Tillich holds that it is only Jesus as the Christ who in history has the perfect combination of Catholic substance and Protestant principle in him. Jesus (the incarnation) is the fundamental symbol of the catholic substance (divine presence in history, the divine and human in New Being) and the preeminent expression of the Protestant principle (via the cross). By sacrificing himself on the cross he embodies the Protestant principle. The "yes" of the divine presence ("the uninterrupted unity with God") was subjected to the "no" of the cross ("the continuous sacrifice of himself as Jesus to himself as the Christ").[25]

The question that we need to ask about the Protestant principle is this: What causes it to react against the substance, and when? What causes it to react, as we have already stated, is the elevation of something finite and

---

24. Tillich, *Systematic Theology,* vol. 3, p. 245.

25. Tillich regards the symbol of the cross as absolute owing to its self-negating character. This assertion is based on his understanding of the absolute criterion of all symbols of divine presence. "A revelation is final if it has the power of negating itself without losing itself." Paul Tillich, *Systematic Theology,* Volume 1: *Reason and Revelation, Being and God* (Chicago: University of Chicago Press, 1951), p. 133. Or as he states in *Dynamics of Faith* (New York: Harper and Row, 1957), p. 97, "The criterion of truth of faith, therefore, is that it implies an element of self-negation. That symbol is most adequate which expresses not only the ultimate but also its own lack of ultimacy."

In Jesus as a person in history we saw two outstanding characteristics that made him the New Being: "uninterrupted unity with the ground of being and the continuous sacrifice of himself as Jesus to himself as the Christ." Paul Tillich, *Systematic Theology,* Volume 2: *Existence and the Christ* (Chicago: University of Chicago Press, 1957), p. 137. Because of this, according to Tillich, the cross is the only symbol in history to satisfy the criterion. This assertion has led many theologians to criticize him for disregarding his own principle. See, for example, Terrence Thomas, "On Another Boundary: Tillich's Encounter with World Religion," in *Theonomy and Autonomy: Studies in Paul Tillich's Engagement with Modern Culture,* ed. John J. Carey (Macon, GA: Mercer University Press, 1984), p. 237.

conditional to the status of infinite and unconditional. When is the reaction triggered? It is at a kairotic moment. This is a moment in which the criticism occurs and it leads to the creation or transformation of existing institutions or situations. There is an in-breaking of kairos from outside the substance (the sociality, the specific manifestation of the spiritual presence in history) into it. The principle, which provides a "guardian position" against the pretensions of finite and ambiguous institutions, is born of kairos. Kairos, as Tillich puts it in his book *The Protestant Era*, "describes the moment in which the eternal breaks into the temporal, and the temporal is prepared to receive it." When the break-in occurs it makes the creative omnipresence of the divine in the course of history concrete. So the idea of kairos "unites criticism and creation."[26]

א PROTESTANT PRINCIPLE: SIGN OF A SIGN[27]

The Protestant principle is a *sacrament* of a sacrament. It is a sign of a sign. It is not only the sign of the spiritual presence in a finite reality (unconditional import), it also points the sacrament (Catholic substance, which is itself a sign) to its abyssal depths. Unlike an ordinary sign it also is efficacy. In addition to signifying dynamism and spiritual import, it confers that of which it represents (via kairos, an "instrumental cause," an active principle that each time animates the sacrament) on the Catholic substance.

There is a hidden aporia implicit in the Protestant principle. Consider the case of a cultural form that has lost all its spiritual content — void and empty. If so, how can the divine import break through it? If you say there cannot be any circumstances under which a cultural content becomes void and empty, then it means that its first reception of the spiritual presence and (or) impact of kairos left an indelible imprint on it. (*It gave it character*, to use the medieval theological language relating to sacrament.) The imprint is a sign produced by a sign of a sign marking now an "expired" event. It is thus a sign itself marking excess signification. Accepting this position amounts to also accepting that the indelible imprint exceeds the proper relational nature of Catholic substance to the kairotic evental kiss.

With regard to the relation implied by the indelible imprint, what is the basis for it? You may say kairos. The kairos exceeds the relation and also grounds it. But if as we have learned the kairos is from outside, occasional, and independent of the

26. Tillich, *Protestant Era*, p. xv.

27. This discussion section is inspired and informed by Giorgio Agamben, *The Signature of All Things: On Method* (New York: Zone Books, 2009).

operations of immanent entities,[28] how can it ground what is always there? If you are to argue that the kairos or the Protestant principle is permanently there in the substance then, contrary to Tillich, you will be saying the entity or cultural form is holy. (Note that the Protestant principle and Catholic substance constitute a form of dualism.) Now again if there is perfect coincidence between the form (immanent bearer) and the principle (kairos) without the slightest parallax then the immanent loses its identity at best and at worst becomes idolatrous. There is a paradox here: Protestant principle as a system of signs blocks dynamics from finding a home within the fabric of concrete life. In truth, in the world of signs there is no easy passage from bearers to kairos/Protestant principle. A gap separates them and we must situate the pentecostal principle precisely in this gap. It "dwells" in this gap because it is not a structure (either substance-principle, or sides of divine-human relationship) but a function of existence, the *signature* of existence. The pentecostal principle is a "passion of being"; every life has it for the sheer fact of being, existing.[29] Thusly, the pentecostal principle interrupts the false alternatives of permanent and transient kairotic protestant principle.

The articulation of the Protestant principle may appear at first to be profoundly alien to nonprofessional theologians, but it is actually a retrieval of familiar themes in Christian history and doctrine. The Protestant principle is a manifestation of the prophetic spirit. It is in a sense Tillich's

28. For further analysis of the problems relating to Tillich's conception of kairos see chapter 1 below.

29. The phrase "passion of being" is used here to designate a general attribute of being and not emotion or affection. It is part of the eros of being. I mention this because some fine pentecostal theologians have named right affections *(orthopathos* or *orthopathy)* as the core of pentecostal spirituality. See Steven J. Land, *Pentecostal Spirituality: A Passion for the Kingdom* (Sheffield: Sheffield Academic Press, 1993); and Samuel Solivan, *The Spirit, Pathos and Liberation: Toward an Hispanic Pentecostal Theology* (Sheffield: Sheffield Academic Press, 1998). But this is not what I have in mind as I am dealing more with the ontological dimension of the pentecostal principle than with pentecostal spirituality. As it will be clear in this study, the Pentecostal principle is not an exclusive property of pentecostals as a group or groups of Christian believers.

It will take us too far afield to work out the possible connections between the affections and pathos of pentecostal spirituality and the passion of being we are identifying here as the pentecostal principle. For instance, Land treats affection as a kind of virtue — almost as an Aristotelian virtue. If Aristotle has as his telos, eudaimonia, Land sets his own as the apocalyptic vision, which is the yearning for the consummation of the kingdom of righteousness (Land, *Pentecostal Spirituality,* pp. 136-37, 173-75). Given enough time one may try to address the question: how does this yearning for consummation of the kingdom of righteousness relate with the pentecostal principle as the unfolding of potentialities?

way of renaming prophetic critique, the power of social criticism, the protest against injustice, especially by biblical prophets. The biblical prophets resist any finite person, group, or institution ("sacramental demonries") that regards itself as the holy, absolute, and ultimate. The Protestant principle names this notion of prophets' protest, critique, and resistance to the finite and particular which is claiming ultimacy as the inherent dynamic power of all cultural forms and functions and of history itself. Julia A. Lamm deepens our understanding of the ancient roots of Tillich's Protestant principle when she writes:

> Religiously speaking, Tillich's "Protestant Principle" is a manifestation of the ancient prophetic tradition; theologically, it is a retrieval of the *via negativa* of the Pseudo-Dionysius; philosophically, it is an observation of the limits of human understanding.[30]

The Protestant principle is not only rooted in the three "traditions" that Lamm mentions, it is also based on the Pauline-Lutheran theology of justification by faith. This doctrine implies such a radical corruption in human nature and institutions that any claim of finality, perfection, or lasting value is tantamount to arrogant pride and denial of God's dynamic and liberating grace. The social-ethical implication of this is that persons in whatever vocation they may find themselves are called upon to reform existing patterns to create the social space for the outworking of godly duties.

Another critical element of Protestantism is the exposure of absolutism. Tillich also extends the notion of criticism and resistance to absolutism to the culture as a whole. His principle is drawn from the idea of paradox in divine presence in cultural forms: applying the principle of justification to theology of culture. However much a human institution or product bears the presence of the divine (the spiritual presence) it is not absolute and is always relative to its time, culture, and place. A finite medium of the infinite divine grace always and everywhere retains its finitude and remains estranged. And thus its determinate form is always subject to the breakthrough of the unconditional import *(Gehalt)* for the emergence of new *gestalt* of grace, a new theonomy.

---

30. Julia A. Lamm, "'Catholic Substance' Revisited: Reversals of Expectations in Tillich's Doctrine of God," in *Paul Tillich: A Catholic Assessment,* ed. Raymond F. Bulman and Frederick J. Parrella (Collegeville, MN: Liturgical Press, 1994), p. 59.

א Pentecostal Principle: From Justification to New Creation

As already noted, Tillich derived his Protestant principle from the Protestant doctrine of justification. The sinner is justified by grace; life is constantly reformed and regenerated. In addition, the notion of justification is based on the idea that Jesus Christ died for us. Justification focuses on what God does for us, what is conferred on us from outside. More importantly, it is backward-looking (forgiveness) and its sight is not trained on new creation of life. To transform Tillich's Protestant principle, we need to graft onto it Martin Luther's idea that to go forward one has to continually begin afresh. For in the pentecostal experience of the Spirit there is always justification and new creation.[31] So the pentecostal idea of change or transformation is about new life — not regeneration, but new beginning. Christ not only died for us, he rose and sent to us the Spirit (the *fons vitae*), who is capable of opening potentialities (both exterior and interior) in any historical situation as the Spirit lives with us in history. The Spirit that was poured out at Pentecost is the Spirit of Christ that manifested after the resurrection (a positive referent of the power of creation and new creation).

On reading Frank D. Macchia's new, penetrating book on theology of justification, *Justified in the Spirit,* at a time when this project was largely completed, I was inspired to notice another "fault line" in Tillich's Protestant principle. Tillich's Protestant principle opens a breach between the cross and Pentecost. The whole question of the infinite reacting (protesting) against the finite for "usurping" the place of the infinite has an unintended Anselmian undertone. (This is in spite of the fact that Tillich understands justification not in a forensic or exchange sense, but as an embrace of ambiguous life by the indwelling Spiritual presence.)[32] We find in the protest somewhat of a necessity to assuage divine wrath and to restore honor, balance, and finitude. The logic of this kind of protest has the logic of punishment (the wages of wrong claim and behavior is forceful reminder of sheer creaturely finitude). This is not the logic of surplus and excess that characterizes Pentecost — God's self-giving, self-imparting embrace of humanity. This is not the logic of resurrection — the divine possibility of new life, renewed creation indwelt by the Spiritual presence.

The pentecostal principle attempts to heal the breach between the cross and resurrection/Pentecost hidden in Tillich's Protestant principle. The heart of the pentecostal principle is not protest, but rather new creation, which is the work of

---

31. See Jürgen Moltmann, *The Spirit of Life: A Universal Affirmation* (Minneapolis: Fortress, 1992), pp. 144-60. This theme of justification and new creation has also recently been systematically developed by the eminent pentecostal theologian Frank D. Macchia, in his *Justified in the Spirit: Creation, Redemption, and the Triune God* (Grand Rapids: Eerdmans, 2010), especially pp. 256, 292.

32. Tillich, *Systematic Theology,* vol. 3, pp. 222, 226; Macchia, *Justified in the Spirit,* p. 71.

the life-giving Spirit. Pneumatic existence is new, life-renewing existence. Now, a perspicacious interlocutor may raise a protestation and say that the pentecostal principle as already noted in this essay incorporates in its conceptualization an element of protest. How do I respond to this charge? The reaction or protest of the Protestant principle releases the deep waters of the infinite to entomb the finite beach-sand castles of humanity's hubris. But the pentecostal principle goes further to insist that the tomb becomes watery womb for the renewal of life. The pentecostal principle is about transformation of life, new beginning, newness of enspirited life.[33]

If the incarnation and the cross, creative and critical edge of prophecy, and the paradox of divine presence in history point us to the Protestant principle, Tillich reasoned in 1965, in his famous last lecture, that a turn to the Spirit (concrete Spirit) can point us to and bring forth a new paradigm that synthesizes sacramentality and critical openness to reform and future. He called this synthesis a "new form of Christianity." The pentecostal principle this book is addressing not only points to this synthesis and its *telos*, but it is also the engine of motion of the synthesis. The pentecostal principle is not a thing, but a demand; it directs cultural forms to experience their unlimited possibilities; it is a directing concept.

The Demand of Inconsumable Potentiality

Each existing cultural form is always and above all an actualization of human creativity itself, an event of dynamics that exceeds every structuration and is, nevertheless, animated by two opposing tensions. The first, which Tillich calls the Catholic substance, attempts to capture, encode, and encapsulate the excess by articulating it in traditions and normative practices. The second is oriented, on the contrary, toward keeping the cultural form open and beyond any determinate structuration. The former is a way of grounding obligations and subjection to established cooperative human practices; the latter is an expression of the freedom of human beings (their freedom to always find alternatives to any extant form). The Catholic sub-

---

33. The reader who is familiar with Macchia's *Justified by the Spirit* will have already noticed that I am connecting my conception of the pentecostal principle to his notion of Spirit-and-Spirit baptism as the starting point for a proper trinitarian theology of justification. See *Justified by the Spirit*, pp. 237-38, 287-88.

stance tends to lead to the absolutization of *nomos* (in the sense of the ways, norms, divisions of human cooperative activities). Where nomos is an absolute force it leads to the diminution of vitality, denial of essential change, and non-recognition of new forms of potentiality. When this happens origin dominates and end (destiny, the goal and limit of actualization of potentialities) suffers. Tillich's Protestant principle is about making end to dominate over origin, making freedom to dominate over absolutizing nomos.

The question that animates the pentecostal principle is this: Can end and origin live in tension with each other in the exigency of fulfillment of human creativity? How can end and origin, Protestant principle and Catholic substance, be synthesized as the moving force of history? Can such a synthesis be conceived in such a way that its kairos is not always breaking in from outside, but it is also immanent? Such a synthesis, such a dynamically tension-filled existence, is conceivable if we think of potentiality in the two ways as Aristotle did in *De anima* (417a21ff). There is generic potentiality that exhausts and destroys itself in actualization. The second figure of potential, according to Aristotle, is not consumed in the act; potential conserves itself in the act and gives *itself to itself.* Potentiality exceeds the act of actualization itself and its signification. If the Catholic substance is not potentiality that has exhausted itself in the act, but if it is, rather, potentiality that is not consumed and is conserved and dwells in the Catholic substance, then the opposing tensions of origin and end abide in it. (Potentiality is a presence, and not an object, and as such cannot be objectified; cannot be taken as something tangible and fixed. It can be actual — the actual as a gestalt of potentiality — but not objective; it is present in all objects but always transcends them.)

This is the thought of the pentecostal principle. It is not that what is, past and present (nomos), resists what is not-yet, or what is to-come casts its light on what is in order to expose its demonic nature; rather, it is all-*figuring.*[34] Figuration is where the nomos comes together in a disfiguration with the not-yet to form a new constellation. Figuration is a dialectics in deferral. But this deferral is not infinite, as the unconsumed potentiality soon turns back on itself, fulfilling (coming forth to full legibility, recognizability) the figuration and deactivating the dialectics at a standstill.

---

34. Mark C. Taylor, *After God* (Chicago: University of Chicago Press, 2007), p. 20.

Pentecostalism and Pentecostal Principle

Tillich's Protestant principle came out of Protestantism and judges it as well as every other religious and spiritual experience. He writes that "Protestantism as the characteristic of a historical period is temporal and subjected to the eternal Protestant principle. It is judged by its own principle, and this judgment might be a negative one."[35] Now how is the pentecostal principle related to pentecostalism as a philosophical outlook or power and logic of history? How is the pentecostal principle related to pentecostalism as an *emergence* from the qualities contained within the Catholic-Protestant fabric? While pentecostalism is fed by the Catholic substance and the Protestant principle, it not only transcends them in quality, but includes them in its grasp. It represents in its character the goal of their existence, releases them from their isolation as two extremes of thought about the church, and sustains them and gives them a directionality and importance which as mere separate qualities they do not possess.

Pentecostalism springs forth from the restlessness of the Catholic-Protestant fabric. It is the empirical quality of their development. Catholic substance and Protestant principle have no reality apart from each other. They are dimensions or aspects of one reality, church, body of Christ, kingdom of God, Catholics-Protestants. Their interactions generate various qualities and relations of past and future, stasis and dynamism, tradition and reversibility. In the hierarchy of qualities, elements, and relations the next highest quality to the highest attained is pentecostalism (as power and logic of history). It is always the next empirical quality, never fully actualized. It is the forward-tendency of the Catholic-Protestant fabric. It is the emergent quality of substance-principle. It is the process in which the whole kingdom of God is engaged. It is a variable quality and as the church grows it changes with it. Pentecostalism is not so much a quality that belongs to church (some churches, if you like), as church is the body that possesses pentecostalism.

It is a step beyond the Protestant principle. The pentecostal principle is Protestantism but something different from it in kind. Church, the communion[36] that possesses pentecostalism, must also be protestant, for

---

35. Tillich, *Protestant Era*, p. viii.

36. Communion is used here in Jean-Luc Nancy's sense. See his *The Inoperative Community*, trans. Peter Connor, Lisa Garbus, Michael Holland, and Simona Sawhney (Minneapolis: University of Minnesota Press, 1991).

Pentecostalism presupposes Protestantism, just as Protestantism presupposes in its possessor the Catholic substance and Catholic substances social practices. Though pentecostalism must be protestant in the same way as it must be catholic and socially relational, its nature is not protestant. To think so would be like thinking Protestantism is purely Catholic substance. Pentecostalism is something new and while it is also protestant, it is not merely protestant.

Catholic substance, Protestant principle, and pentecostal principle are aspects of the same communion. Tillich names a part or dimension of the communion as a substance; another part that he thinks is more alive with dynamism, he calls the Protestant principle. The pentecostal principle, however, is the principle of growth of all the dimensions. The pentecostal principle is sustained by the communion and all its aspects to which it belongs. Pentecostalism is the name for the highest order of existence of the communion as we know it today.

The church is a communion engendering within itself the empirical qualities of Catholic substance, Protestant principle, and other features of which pentecostalism is one step beyond Protestantism. But this possessor of pentecostalism is not actual, but an ideal. As an actual entity it is the proleptic relationality with its nisus toward pentecostalism, or is in travail with the pentecostal principle. As actual, no church or denomination possesses the quality of pentecostalism, but instead is a communion tending to that quality. This is in the sense that the present manifestation of the body of Christ is straining toward pentecostalism. As a principle it is directionally infinite, incompletable and unrealizable to any body of believers. If it were attained there would be in turn another directional infinity. Pentecostal churches as actual existents are always becoming pentecostal but never attaining it. Pentecostalism is a nisus and never a done deal. A true pentecostal movement is an ideal pentecostalism in embryo. The Catholic substance represents an attempt to secure pentecostalism in finite forms. The Protestant principle attempts to be the communion of next order of finites. The pentecostal principle compels us to think of the whole communion as straining toward pentecostalism, tending toward infinity, endeavoring toward the new. It compels us to think of the restlessness of the Catholic-Protestant fabric. The pentecostal principle is ultimately not only about the church, but also about the spread of freedom and emergent creativity across the world and the free relation of such to the divine.

Pentecostal Principle as Ethical Methodology

At this juncture, it is germane to mention that the pentecostal principle is not a metaphysics but a method of social historical analysis. We must avoid interpreting it as an appearance of an essence, spiritual force, or transcendental idea. In this respect, it fits in with Tillich's idea that the Protestant principle is decisive for interpreting history. As he states it:

> The Protestant principle demands a method of interpreting history in which the critical transcendence of the divine over against conservatism and utopianism is strongly expressed and in which, at the same time, the creative omnipresence of the divine in the course of history is concretely indicated.[37]

This book attempts to bring together three vital elements in pentecostal thinking for the interpretation of history. These three elements are: universality, particularity, and excellence. The universal element demands for global civil society (koinōnia, spiritual community) through a ceaseless restructuring of all spheres of existence as the Spirit decreases exclusion and increases embrace. What is the right global ethos for dealing with the pluralism of cultures under the influences of the non-confinable Spirit? The particular aspect is an expression of the Catholic substance, the nomos of each historical manifestation of the Spirit in specific context. How can the ultimate meaning of existence shine through it? How can it be transparent to the divine depths? The third aspect is the imperative that drives and balances the two toward their theonomous depths. This is the principle of excellence; the kairotic combination of criticism and creation moves everything finite, the nomos, the vessels of spiritual content to drive beyond itself.

Thus, this is a book about methodology rather than a traditional subject of social ethics or any particular point of theology. It is, however, not a methodology conjured up in the arid, thin air of rootless thought, not a metatheory floating above the diversity of concrete studies. The methodology laid out here is developed out of the analysis of major social issues of the twenty-first century. So we are learning about the methodology of social ethics as we explore the issues of political governance, emergence and ethics, public theology, and pentecostal spirituality. The methodology is a

---

37. Tillich, *Protestant Era,* p. xiii.

set of fruits plucked from trees of analysis planted in the garden of concrete life issues. It is a plucking rather than a new planting because each of the essays is crafted to show not only how a particular subject matter is treated, but also more importantly the method behind the analysis that sustains the treatment. Each of the essays is an exemplar of the overall methodology put forward by this book. Each gives us an understanding of the fundamental issues of the methodology and a clear direction of thought as to how the pentecostal principle is useful in understanding reality.

There are two elements running through them: a perceptive view of the currents of the present, that is, the conceptual expression of reality, the rigorous treatment of a subject matter which I will designate as thought element. Then there is the practical element, which consists of the methods of ethical analysis. This fusion of the two elements in each chapter expresses a distinct characteristic, namely that the treatment of an ethical or theological matter has value only as they set forth or affect a methodological outlook. In this union, the treatment of theological-ethical issues aims at that which is meaningful for the development of a methodology, a way of approaching the study of social issues. With this approach, ethical analysis is a methodology and ethical methodology an analysis.

The Day of Pentecost

The founding event of pentecostalism is the rupture, the singularity described by Luke in Acts 2 and whose effects are still legible today. The current forms of pentecostalism are immense echoes of this founding event. The event in itself is an image of and announces the dynamic I am naming in this text as the pentecostal principle. Let us "return" to this event to retrieve some insights for the task of elucidating the pentecostal principle:

> When the Day of Pentecost had fully come, they were all with one accord in one place. And suddenly there came a sound from heaven, as of a rushing mighty wind, and it filled the whole house where they were sitting. Then there appeared to them divided tongues, as of fire, and *one* sat upon each of them. And they were all filled with the Holy Spirit and began to speak with other tongues, as the Spirit gave them utterance. And there were dwelling in Jerusalem Jews, devout men, from every nation under heaven. And when this sound occurred, the multitude came together, and were confused, because everyone heard them speak in his

own language. Then they were all amazed and marveled, saying to one
another, "Look, are not all these who speak Galileans? And how *is it that*
we hear, each in our own language in which we were born? Parthians
and Medes and Elamites, those dwelling in Mesopotamia, Judea and
Cappadocia, Pontus and Asia, Phrygia and Pamphylia, Egypt and the
parts of Libya adjoining Cyrene, visitors from Rome, both Jews and
proselytes, Cretans and Arabs — we hear them speaking in our own
tongues the wonderful works of God." So they were all amazed and per-
plexed, saying to one another, "Whatever could this mean?" (Acts 2:1-12,
New King James Version)

Many scholars and Christians readily agree that the event on the Day
of Pentecost was new. But exactly in what sense can we say it was new?
There may be many reasons you, the reader, can proffer. For my limited
purposes in this book I interpret the new, the event, as an interruption in
ongoing situation — especially, as interpreted by Peter: the absurdity of
life bent toward death, spiritual death, automaticity of obedience to law
without Christ, and without the possibility of new beginning. This rupture
signified by the tongues of fire and the wind that blew created a new space
for Peter and the other believers to begin anew. The 120 or so believers
gathered at the Upper Room became diverse incarnations of the power of
the new — their diversity and universalism inescapably captured by the
multiple languages they spoke under the power of the Holy Spirit. Their
number and the diversity of the tongues point to the irreducibly pluralistic
nature of the power of the new. No one individual, entity, or institution is
capable of incarnating it alone. No human being can be self-sufficient in
holding the force of creativity, in storing the wind in his or her bosom. No
one person can incarnate creativity, because, as Hannah Arendt once informed us, "Not man but men inhabit the earth and form a world between
them." There is no weakness on the part of any human being that he or she
is dependent on others for help, but only a reflection of the irreducible
pluralistic nature of existence, serendipitous nature of creativity, and restlessness of becoming which does not have a bus stop. The event of Pentecost is an affirmation of the miraculous nature of human action, that capacity to begin something new, the articulation of *natality.* According to
Arendt,

The miracle that saves the world, the realm of human affairs from the
normal, "natural" ruin is ultimately the fact of natality. . . . It is in other

words, the birth of new men and the new beginning, the action they are capable of by virtue of being born [and born again]. Only the full experience of this capacity can bestow upon human affairs faith and hope, those two essential characteristics of human existence which Greek antiquity ignored altogether, discounting the keeping of faith as a very uncommon and not too important virtue and counting hope among the evils of illusion in Pandora's Box. It is this faith in and hope for the world that found perhaps its most glorious and most succinct expression in few words with which the Gospels announced the "glad tidings": "A child has been unto us."[38]

An analysis of Peter's reaction to the accusation of early morning drunkenness leveled against the disciples by the crowd observing the disciples' ecstatic behavior succinctly reveals the pentecostal principle as defined in the opening paragraph. We stated above that it is the capacity to begin, adding that every end has no place to go, but to begin again.

ℵ The Pentecostal Principle and Revelation 1:8

This idea of end as a beginning might even be discerned from Revelation 1:8 where Jesus is described as the Alpha and Omega, the beginning and the end, and the one who is to come. This description suggests that that beginning and end coincide and that this single, double-edged process is the to-come, the not-yet that is always coming. The poet T. S. Eliot once wrote that "The beginning is often the end / And to make an end is to make a beginning."[39]

Peter retrieved the eschatological prophecy of Joel that stated that in the last days the sons and daughters of Israel will prophesy, her young men will see visions, and her old men will dream dreams. Peter said what they were seeing was the fulfillment of the prophecy. The last days have come right on the first day of the founding day of the church community. Quoting Catherine Keller here will be very helpful:

---

38. Arendt, *Human Condition*, p. 247.

39. This little intervention is inspired and informed by Catherine Keller, *On the Mystery: Discerning God in Process* (Minneapolis: Fortress, 2008), p. 170. For T. S. Eliot's poem see his "Little Gidding," the last of the *Four Quartets*, in *Collected Poems 1909-1962* (New York: Harcourt, Brace & World, 1970), p. 207, quoted in Keller, *On the Mystery*, p. 170.

In other words it turns out that *those last days were really first days.* Pentecost is, after all, considered the founding event of the church. But the point is larger than ecclesiology: the message of Pentecost is that the end is really the beginning: the eschaton is an opening end, an end that opens the new beginning. "For the first time and forever."[40]

Let us examine more closely some of the features of what happened on the Day of Pentecost. There is the sound of rushing wind. We have tongues of fire alighting on each of the disciples; the speaking of many languages, and Peter's daring hermeneutics. How can we philosophically exegete these features? In addition, there is the fellowship in the Spirit: they were gathered together in one accord and subsequently they even form a strongly bonded community, sharing food and property together.

Wind and Sound

The wind *(ruach, pneuma)* as model or metaphor of spirit is well known and need not delay us here. Sound will delay us a little. In the beginning was the ~~word~~ sound. In a certain sense, sound is the basis of existence. The word (controlled sound), the sound precedes light in both Genesis 1:1-3 and John 1:4-5. Sound is life also. Quantum physics has it that sound (vibration, the finest aspects of movement) is the source of light; light gives color and energy, and light as energy sustains life. Biblically, life is also related to sound. The creation comes after (with) the word, the sound of God's breath. In Genesis 1 Adam is sounded (structured breath) into existence; and in Genesis 2 he is ("un-structurally") breathed into existence: the life-giving breath is blown into him (clump of clay). So wind and sound point to life-giving force and its enveloping and pervading power. They point to the air as the medium between the divine and humans, which fired imagination across many ancient cultures, which associated the wind with spirit, breath, and life, and with the breath of God that permeates all existence. The wind that blows anywhere it wishes cannot be confined and thus it analogically points to abundance of alternatives and possibilities.

The combination of the all-pervading wind and sound is a very powerful symbol of universalism. Sound or wind has no particular object

40. Catherine Keller, *On the Mystery,* p. 163.

(considered specifically radiant and valuable) as its focus of attention. Sound and wind both ultimately point toward existence itself and hence are not graspable as objects either. Their relation to space, in a certain sense, resembles the way being-itself relates to the world. They occupy the whole space they are in; they are omnipresent. Consider for instance what theologian of music Jeremy S. Begbie says about sound:

> This feature of sound-perception, in which our attention to sound can be severed from attention to objects and entities, is exploited in music. . . . Sound is employed largely in a way which opens up a spatiality which does not depend on discrete location and mutual exclusion of entities. In the world I see, an entity cannot be in two places at the same time, and two things cannot occupy the same place at the same time. Visual experience and discrete location become inseparable — seeing this lamp "here" means I cannot see it "over there." But in aural experience, although a sound may have a discrete material source whose discreet location I can identify . . . , the sound I hear is not dependent on attention to that "place." It surrounds me, it fills the whole of my aural "space." I do not hear a sound "there" but "not there" — what I hear occupies the whole of my aural space.[41]

The sound and the wind filled the whole house, we are told. This can be interpreted to mean that the coming (immanence) of the Spirit is not a partial response to the human existential situation or predicament. It is an effort to remake existence and release the full potentials of human beings; and in doing this none will be excluded. Sound by its nature comes to a person, to all persons, from all sides. Sound in this way suggests an opening toward others in a movement that does not have a final object or destiny. It surrounds the person in its space in totality. It is not "here" or "there" like an object, filling the person's "space and time." This quality of sound, making the person the center toward which it flows from all sides, situates particularity in the flow of universalism. This point will become clearer if we learn more about the working of the major bodily organ that relates sound to persons, the ear; and about how "to hear" discloses participation. Victor Zuckerkandl, philosopher of music, explains the difference between seeing and hearing:

---

41. Jeremy S. Begbie, *Theology, Music, and Time* (Cambridge: Cambridge University Press, 2000), p. 24.

The eye discloses space to me in that it excludes me from it. The ear, on the other hand, discloses space to me in that it lets me participate in it. The depth that I hear is not a being-at-a-distance; it is a coming-from-a-distance. . . . Where the eye draws the strict boundary line that divides without from within, world from self, the ear creates a bridge. . . . The space experience of the eye is a disjunctive experience; the space experience of the ear is a participative experience.[42]

The phenomenon of sound suggests total participation of both Spirit and humans in the event; "spirit and matter" (or en-spirited matter) ordained toward one purpose, *world-remaking*, showing the possibility of how human beings can be in-the-world differently.

We are not done with the sound and wind. Let us press on further that we may lay hold of some philosophical-theological insights. The sound came *suddenly!* This means it was totally incalculable, a pure and simple event, nothing leading up to it even though we are told the disciples were gathered in a room in one accord (praying and praising God). It came "underivably" and unconditioned.[43] "The birth of the new," according to Paul Tillich,

is just as surprising in history. It may appear in some dark corner in our world. It may appear in a social group where it was least expected. It may appear in the pursuit of activities which seem utterly insignificant. It may appear in the depth of a national catastrophe, if there be in such a situation people who are able to perceive the new of which the prophet speaks. It may appear at the height of a national triumph, if there be a few people who perceive the vanity of which the Preacher speaks.[44]

This "suddenly" indexes the "exemplary matrix of the link between" social existence and the pentecostal principle. Let me unpack this. What is the use of telling us that they were gathered in one place in one accord (tarrying in praying) and saying suddenly the sound came? No particular point here,

42. Victor Zuckerkandl, *Sound and Symbol: Music and the External World* (London: Routledge and Kegan Paul, 1956), p. 291.

43. I have here borrowed Alain Badiou's description of event to tell the story of the sudden appearance of the sound of the violent wind. See his *Saint Paul: The Foundation of Universalism* (Stanford: Stanford University Press, 2003), p. 17.

44. Paul Tillich, *The Shaking of the Foundations* (New York: Charles Scribner's Sons, 1948), p. 183.

you may say; it is just Luke's way of linking this portion of the narration with its earlier parts. So let us move on. And yet, no, let us tarry instead. The combination of suddenly-and-prayer (praise, one accord in one place) points to the way the new comes into social existence. Novelty may come in a dialectical fashion, incorporating something of the old (the site of the old) by exceeding it. It conserves and sublates. It may also come independent of the site. It appears Luke endows this portion of his narrative with "a twofold principle of opening and historicity," "eventuality and immanence." He seems to be saying: "that the event is new should never let us forget that it is such only with respect to a determinate situation wherein it mobilizes the elements of its site."[45] As we will see when we begin to discuss kairos in the next chapter, the tension of "eventuality and immanence" is the key to understanding how the pentecostal principle plays out in history.

"And suddenly there came a sound from heaven." Here the word "came" is our point of focus. The word *came* has been customarily used by the Old Testament prophets — as in "Now the word of the Lord came to Jonah" — to open their addresses, to mark, to gesture, and to underline external intervention. It announces a new beginning and an incursion of the supernatural into human life. It is a divine intervention that either negates, interrupts, human culture and automatic social processes or (inclusive "or") positively claims such for a task. In either case, it marks a new beginning, *inter-venir*. This view of God's word regards the coming of the word as an *event*. The Acts 2 event of immanent divine presence symbolized by the *came* is not only an *inter-vention* (a coming among two-existing things, including past and future time segments), but also marks human beings as initiators of new beginnings amid the continuum of time and the automatic, ongoing processes of social existence.

On the whole the wind-sound phenomenon profoundly captures an aspect of miracles or grace that characterizes pentecostalism as a social practice or pentecostalism as a principle. It represents excess that cannot be fully incorporated, institutionalized, or controlled by a system or used as a basis for sovereignty of governance. As a miracle and as the opening miracle, it has implications for political theology or it compels thought along this line since Carl Schmitt opens up this line of inquiry to support his theory of sovereignty. Unlike Schmitt who in his *Political Theology* regards miracles as analogous to state of exception of the law,[46] the miracles

---

45. For the quotes see Badiou, *Saint Paul,* pp. 17, 25.
46. "The exception in jurisprudence is analogous to the miracle in theology." See Carl

in pentecostalism cannot be used to instantiate or found the connection between power and law, authority and obedience. Grace and miracles represent an irreducible excess which cannot be captured to legitimate state power or theory of state power. The promise of grace "exceeds any claim that could supposedly ground itself in it. . . . Grace does not provide the foundation for exchange and social obligations; it makes for their interruption."[47] Miracles do not found, they fulfill or actualize potentialities that cannot authorize the definition of the normal.

Flames of Fire

Tillich argues in *The Shaking of the Foundations* that the fire represents the creative Spirit and gestures to the particularity and universality of all existence:

> In the story of the Pentecost, the Spirit of Christ shows its creativity in both directions, the individual and universal. Each discipline receives the fiery tongue that is the new creative Spirit. Members of all nations, separated by their different tongues, understand each other in this New Spirit, which creates a new peace, beyond the cleavages of Babel.[48]

Jürgen Moltmann reaches the same conclusion, linking the fire to creativity.[49] The flaming fire is "an image for the new creation of the world," adding that the images of the tempest and fire point to the experience of eternal love which creates and energizes life. This energy, he states in another place in the same text, is an "eroticizing energy." By eros he means

---

Schmitt, *Political Theology: Four Chapters on the Concept of Sovereignty*, trans. George Schwab (Chicago: University of Chicago Press, 2006), p. 36.

47. Giorgio Agamben, *The Time That Remains: A Commentary on the Letter to the Romans*, trans. Patricia Dailey (Stanford: Stanford University Press, 2005), pp. 120, 124. See also Ruth Marshall, "The Sovereignty of Miracles: Pentecostal Political Theology in Nigeria," *Constellations* 17, no. 2 (2010): 197-223, for the connection between pentecostal miracles and sovereignty.

48. Tillich, *Shaking of the Foundations*, p. 138.

49. The fire may also symbolize a continuous, burning passion in the disciples for the realization of the kingdom of God in the midst of time. Another perspective is that fire symbolizes the cleansing of the "primitive self," the "old man," so that its excluded possibilities and desires do not come back to soil or haunt the "new man."

the force which holds the world together and keeps it alive, anthropo-
logically and cosmologically; the power of attraction which unites, and
the individual weight which simultaneously distinguishes. The rhythm
of attraction and distance, affection and respect is the power of eros. So
"in the Spirit" we experience both community and the diversity of the
Spirit: unity in diversity, and diversity in community. We experience at
one and the same time our socialization and our individuation. "In the
Spirit" we come to know the love that binds and the freedom which
makes our own individual, separate selves.[50]

In sum, one can use the words of Catherine Keller to encapsulate the meaning of the flames of fire that sat on each of the disciples: "possibility dances
like flame along the edges of our finitude."[51] The Spirit alights, flows, and
pours forth newness and vitality for the actualization of new possibilities.
"The Spirit of God acts in the same way as the rain which, coming down
from heaven, enables an entire landscape with the most varied living beings
to burst into new life together, full of freshness and vitality."[52]

We find a lot of "movement metaphors," as Moltmann puts it, on the
Day of Pentecost: rushing wind, flaming fire, and speaking in other
tongues. They all, in one way or the other, point to the creativity of the
Spirit, the restlessness of becoming. The Spirit (the breath of God,
Yahweh's *ruach, pneuma*) comes upon the disciples as fire (creativity), after
a gale of tempest (wind, breath, *ruach*) and they spoke (words are controlled breath). This dramatic display, interplay, and interpenetration of
word and breath point to the principle of creativity, the initiation of the
new in a very moving way. Moltmann captures the significance of this intersection of word and breath when he writes in another context these illuminating words:

> If the *ruach* is associated with God, and God with the *ruach*, then
> Yahweh's *ruach* and Yahweh's *dabar* — his word — are very close to one
> another. Ruach is thought of as the breath of God's voice. . . . If this
> unity of breath and voice is carried over to God's creativity, then all
> things are called to life through God's Spirit and Word.[53]

50. Moltmann, *Spirit of Life*, pp. 278-82, 196.

51. Keller, *On the Mystery*, p. 176.

52. Michael Welker, *God the Spirit*, trans. John Hoffmeyer (Minneapolis: Fortress,
1994), p. 126, quoted in Keller, *On the Mystery*, p. 162.

53. Moltmann, *Spirit of Life*, p. 41.

Genesis 1 tells us that God created by speaking — uttered in God's voice, breath, the energies of the *ruach*. So the quintessential example of creativity is also combination of word and breath. "The masculine Word *(dabar)* and the feminine life force *(ruach)* necessarily complement one another."[54] These also point us to the Son and the eternal Spirit and their unity, according to the image of Word and Breath.[55]

At the level of concrete human existence, the interpenetrating relationship between the Spirit and Word as described above presupposes the existence of community and impulse toward communality (increasing connectedness). The community receives, practices, promotes, and sustains the Word even as it is nurtured and guided by the Spirit. The Spirit enables self-transcending response from those who receive the Word, constituting them into a community, *communio*. Thus, Moltmann's dyad of Word and Spirit calls to mind the pentecostal theologian Amos Yong's Spirit-Word-Community which puts the Word and the work of the Holy Spirit together with the community of believers in mutual interplay. For Yong there is a community that courageously and charismatically engages with God's Word and Spirit in its spiritual discernment, imagination, hermeneutics, and relationship with the world. Yong writes:

> The dialectical relationship between Spirit and Word is played out in the context of Community. The dialectical relationship between Word and Community is mediated by Spirit. The dialectical relationship between Spirit and Community is anchored in Word. Spirit implicates Word and Community; Word implicates Spirit and Community; Community implicates Spirit and Word. None of these three are subordinate to either of the other, and all assume and require each other.[56]

Tongues

Now let us look at speaking in tongues *(glossolalia*, not *xenolalia)* and the fellowship. The phenomenon of glossolalic utterances has been generally interpreted as reversal of Babel, unity in diversity, the same message heard in different individual languages. In the next chapter I will offer a rigorous

---

54. Moltmann, *Spirit of Life*, p. 42.
55. Moltmann, *Spirit of Life*, pp. 71-72, 283, 307.
56. Yong, *Spirit-Word-Community*, p. 18.

philosophical engagement with ecstatic religious speech; here it will suffice to offer an alternative (additional) interpretation based on information theory for consideration. I think the glossolalia on the Day of Pentecost arguably points to information dispersal: that is, the development, distribution, and decentralization of information as the key to human creativity and productivity in the age of the Spirit or of the Pentecostal Era. On the Day of Pentecost (Acts 2), the Spirit was not taken from one person and given to others as when the Spirit that was on Moses was distributed to the seventy elders (Num. 11:24-25).[57] From the beginning, there was decentralization and dispersal as symbolized in the multiple flames and languages. The two different formats for distributing the Spirit compare well with the old vertical industrial and corporate model and a horizontal network model that characterizes the information economy; or with the broadcast network model (one fixed point of emission and multiple points of reception) and rhizome.

ℵ PENTECOST, MOUNT SINAI, AND PLURALISM

In Genesis 1, the breath of God is the bridge between "nothingness" and "somethingness." This Spirit (*ruach*, the breath of God) and the pronouncement of "let there be light" (controlled breath as sound; latent potentiality lighted, set on "fire") are the set of primal thrust that set potential and possibility surging forward toward greater and greater actuality. It marks the beginning of structuring the *tehomic* chaos.

The ancient Jewish tradition links the festival of Pentecost (*Shavuot*) to the giving of the law to Moses at Mount Sinai. The Ten Commandments were given with thundering, sparks of fire flying around, and every single word from God splitting into seventy languages. The giving of the law points to the nomothetic organization of an infant civilization and conditioned the development of Jewish ethos. So one can say that Pentecost is when the divine presence in history ignited into sparks of creativity (nomos, ethos, kairos all involved at once) — the yearning force of ever accumulating folds of potentiality breaking into open reality, springing into actualization, straining forward into the future.

There is another point to the metaphor of multiple languages or many tongues that characterizes the Pentecost tradition in Judaism and Christianity. It prioritizes a pneumatological approach to pluralism that invites us to honor multiple voices in

---

57. Also consider Exodus 3: one big fire that was burning the bush and two voices, divine and human, as the source of sound. But in Acts 2, several small equal fires and over a hundred human voices. The divine voice was silent, rather uttered in human voices, transcendence being borne by the immanence.

discerning and solving the problems of common social existence. Michael Welker, a Reformed theologian, has argued that the miracle of Pentecost

> lies not in what is difficult to understand or incomprehensible, but in a totally unexpected comprehensibility and in an unbelievable, universal capacity to understand. . . . This difference between the experience of plural inaccessibility to each other and of enduring foreignness, and unfamiliarity, on the one hand, and of utter commonality of the capacity to understand, on the other — this is what is truly shocking about the Pentecost event. . . . An astounding, indeed frightening clarity in the midst of the received complexity and variety, a dismaying familiarity in the midst of the received inaccessibility and unfamiliarity — this is what is miraculous and wonderful about the revelation at Pentecost. The Pentecost event connects intense experiences of individuality with a new experience of community.[58]

And Amos Yong, a pentecostal theologian, adds that Pentecost "knows no boundaries, whether such as conceived politically, socially, linguistically, racially, or ethnically, or otherwise."[59] The event of multiple languages that characterized Pentecost cannot be just interpreted as diversity of tongues. Insofar as the 120 disciples engaged in translation and communication (those observing them were no longer mere observers, but active participants in what was going on) there was an "energetic engagement with diversity" to use Diana L. Eck's words. It was this kind of engagement that created the first church, "the common society from all that plurality."[60] Luke did not just mention tongues, he took time to name the cultures that produced the tongues, and I interpret this to mean that their identity, their differences, and angularities were worth noting and maintaining as they came into the common society not based on one essence but on each gift.

The ethical implication for this is that at the minimum the participation of citizens in the public space should not entail the shirking of their religious and other commitments, but movement from there to context of plurality and active engagement with the diversity of other voices (including those of science) in bridge-building dialogue for the sake of common flourishing. As Eck puts it:

> [P]luralism is not relativism, but the *encounter of commitments*. The new paradigm of pluralism does not require us to leave our identities and our commit-

58. Welker, *God the Spirit*, pp. 230-31, 233, quoted in Amos Yong, *The Spirit Poured Out on All Flesh* (Grand Rapids: Baker Academic, 2005), p. 172.

59. Yong, *Spirit Poured Out*, p. 173.

60. For quotes see Diana L. Eck, "What Is Pluralism?" *The Pluralism Project at Harvard University*. Accessed August 3, 2010 at http://pluralism.org/pages/pluralism/what_is_pluralism, and "From Diversity to Pluralism," *The Pluralism Project at Harvard University*. Accessed on August 3, 2010 at http://pluralism.org/pages/pluralism/essay/from_diversity_to_pluralism.

ments behind, for pluralism is the encounter of commitments. It means holding our deepest differences, even religious differences, not in isolation, but in relationship to one another. . . . Pluralism is based on dialogue. The language of pluralism is that of dialogue and encounter, give and take, criticism and self-criticism. Dialogue means both speaking and listening, and that process reveals both common understandings and real differences. Dialogue does not mean that everyone at the "table" will agree with one another. Pluralism involves the commitment to being at the table — with one's commitments.[61]

In chapter 3, I explore the development of an ethical methodology to enable citizens to engage in public policy debates in ways that honor their religious commitments as well as engage in dialogue in a pluralistic public space.

Fellowship

The gathering was a community of creative possibilities. The waiting and coming of the Spirit affirm existing connections, and create and widen the network of social relationships. Relationship is the fount of life and no life survives without the experience of relationships.

The new birth, the freedom in the Spirit, is also an impulse to create new community. As Catholic theologian José Comblin argues:

Freedom does not drive one away from others. Human newness consists in friendship with other people. Human newness is to find human relationships. The new things we create are not merely material realities, but above all social realities. Freedom creates the new community.[62]

In this new community, we see also freedom in another sense, the distinction of individual "who," and this freedom is signified by the diversity of gifts (languages and flames on each person). Individual distinction is the basis for the initiation of the new. This kind of freedom that flows from mutual participation in life and allows the individual to be all that he or she can be with a "creative passion for the possible" Moltmann calls "freedom as sociality."[63]

---

61. Eck, "What Is Pluralism?"

62. José Comblin, *The Holy Spirit and Liberation*, trans. Paul Burns (Maryknoll, NY: Orbis, 1989), p. 139. See also pp. 88-99 for further elaboration on community. In another place (p. 181), he writes, "each new community is a new creation, a new beginning, a new Pentecost; what happens in Jerusalem happens once more."

63. Moltmann, *Spirit of Life*, pp. 71-72, 118-20, 196, 226.

In the light of Arendt's theory of action, the disciples' acting and speaking before the gathered Jerusalem group are powerful indicators of freedom and expression of individual "who." According to Arendt, actions enable human beings to distinguish themselves from mere bodily existence. It is through actions that human beings achieve individuation, distinction, and outstanding achievements. It is through actions that they rise up to the level of heroism and outstanding performance that are recounted in generations to come and thus achieve social immortality. It is by action that a human being becomes a "who" (in contradistinction to "what") and attains identity: "In acting and speaking, men show who they are, reveal actively their personal identities and thus make their appearance in the human world, while their physical identities appear without any activity of their own in the unique shape of the body and the sound of the voice."[64]

Finally, this is an interesting community or fellowship if we look at it from the perspective of one of the other key features of the Day. The "essence" of this fellowship or community is *partagé:* divided and sharing. (For instance, sharing divided tongues of fire.) This essence exposes each of the 120 to the limit of their being, the singularity of Being, the limit of singular/common being. It is in this exposure that the community is brought into play and the meaning of the political as such becomes at stake. The political is "the site where being in common is at stake," and "having access to what is proper to existence, and therefore, of course, to the proper of one's own existence." This power of the fellowship as "an exposition in common and to the in-common" is both imaged and abandoned in the common sharing of resources in the primitive community that formed on the wake of the Pentecost.[65]

Touch

One feature we have not yet mentioned is the set of senses at play and at display on the Day of Pentecost. On that eventful day, the senses of the body were also in action. People saw the flames of fire and heard the rushing wind and the spoken words. Some of them who did not hear their own languages spoken mistakenly thought Peter and company had tasted some wine too early in the day. We are not clear what they smelled; Luke is silent

---

64. Arendt, *Human Condition,* p. 179.
65. For quotes see Jean-Luc Nancy's *Inoperative Community,* pp. x, xxxvii.

on this point. Yet given the festivities, temple sacrifices and burning incense in the temple environs, the excitement, and the huge number of bodies gathered at one place, the olfactory nerves were also on active duty. Then there was touch (feeling).

Not only human bodies brushing against one another, but the Spirit touching physical human bodies: flames sitting on heads. What do we make of this touch? It is an experience of embodiment, realism that resists idealism. The touch reveals immediacy and continuity between the one who is touched and one who touches. They are exposed to each other. There is also distance. The toucher and the touched are not the same. The *touching-distance* between them is more complicated than one will immediately suppose. The touch touches the sense at the site of the body. But at the same time, the body as material existence is not exactly the incorporeal senses. So touch here is not only about immediacy, proximity, and continuity between two "surfaces," but also rupture, distance, and separation. May we say the touch is both inside and outside? The flame of fire is at the point where the Spirit situates itself outside of the body it inscribes in as the signature of fire. In the gap that the touch creates (touch-separation) there is an excess of signification and symbolization. It is thus a place of restlessness and non-rigidity.

This particular touch on the Day of Pentecost also reveals a relation to the untouchable. There is a point the touched cannot ultimately possess. We know that the relation to the untouchable happens at the limit — an event at the limit of the sense, bodily finitude. But, as Jean-Luc Nancy has argued, the point of touch, tact, or contact is where an opening of world occurs. If we follow this idea of touch as philosophized by Nancy, the touch of flame points us to another important feature of Pentecost. The touch is symbolic of the meeting of transcendence and immanence within history that pentecostals celebrate. This meeting is of a certain kind in Nancean thought. In general for Nancy, touch (the touch of senses altogether, sensing, *"fait corps avec le sentir"*) "is neither a transcendent principle governing the senses, nor an immanence which underpins their ultimate unity or homogeneity, but rather, according to the logic of contact in separation, it is both a transcendence and an immanence, a 'transimmanence' of the senses or of sense."[66]

This touch on the Day of Pentecost was a fluid movement. It lived only in the movement that the Spirit enacts. It was first initiated by the rushing

---

66. Ian James, *The Fragmentary Demand: An Introduction to the Philosophy of Jean-Luc Nancy* (Stanford: Stanford University Press, 2006), p. 216.

mighty wind, *omni-presently* touching everything and everyone in the house ("it filled the whole house"). Call this *omnipresence*. The touch of wind then transformed into the touch of fire on every individual in the house.

The touch of fire is of *particular presence,* a touch of the union of power and meaning as temporal-spatial sharing of a meaningful world at the limit of touch. If the *presence* only stood in the universal, it would be without validity for human existence, which is always concrete, as the presence will be valid only for the Spirit enacting it and it has no part in existence. If the *presence* stood only in the particular it would be without sharing, opening of space, movement-to, being-toward the world, for existence is a singular-plurality. The combination of both types of presence in the fluid movement of the Spirit points to the space-time of existence.

> The passage from one place to another *needs time* [*D'un lieu à l'autre,* il faut temps]. And moving in place [*du lieu à lui-même*] as such also needs time: the time for the place to open itself as place, the time to space itself. Reciprocally, originary time, appearing as such, *needs space* [*il lui faut l'espace*], the space of its own distension, the space of the passage that divides [*partage*] it.[67]

And as Ian James, an astute interpreter of Nancy, explains: "the opening up of spaces can occur only as temporality, and temporality can occur only as the opening up of spaces, that is, space-time."[68]

Finally, there is what I call the touch of *manifest presence.* The touch of particular presence led to the outpouring, the manifestation of the bubbling interior energy outward in the way of utterances that now touched the ears of the people as sound (controlled breath) and tugged at their heartstrings. This is the manifest presence: the particular presence that is breaking forth into reaching others in the services of language translation and hermeneutics of Peter. The presence leaves the confines of the 120 and reaches beyond to the gathered public onlookers. This manifest presence is not about revealing the power of truth proper to the unity of spiritual content and sensuous form the disciples have experienced, but the putting to work of truth as unconcealing of world. Peter's art of hermeneutics unconceals a world open to surprises. James K. A. Smith argues that Peter's

67. Jean-Luc Nancy, *Being Singular Plural* (Stanford: Stanford University Press, 2000), p. 61. Italics in original.

68. James, *Fragmentary Demand,* p. 105.

courage in offering a hermeneutic that deftly responds to the advent of surprise is a mark of radical openness characteristic of Pentecostalism. "I think Pentecost is really about radical openness to divine surprises — especially an openness to a God who exceeds our horizons of expectation and comes unexpectedly. . . . [This openness] lies at the heart of being pentecostal, and so at the root of a pentecostal worldview."[69]

IN A SENSE this study builds on Steven G. Smith's *The Concept of the Spiritual: An Essay in First Philosophy* (1988). Smith lays down that interpersonal relationships as the ground and norm of meaning — the "spirit" — are the first philosophy, the most fundamental issue in all of philosophy. This is what we must speak first if we want to speak about anything. We should not start from ontology (the question about being itself), epistemology (the ground and limits of human capacity to know), or language (conditions and rules about all meaningful sentences). The current, regnant focus on language in philosophy cannot constitute the basic approach. Language cannot be the fundamental issue of philosophy because, Smith argues, "it is essentially interpersonal, or to be more specific, essentially an activity of creating and maintaining forms of commonality among persons. Interpersonal commonality is not just what language is *for*; it is *in* language, and in it more than anything else."[70] The issue of relationship comes first and the language of relationship is the language of "spirit" and "the term 'spiritual' remains uniquely suited to bear an adequate conception of the original situation where the order of priority in questions begins."[71]

One need not agree completely with Smith's definition of spirit to note the power of his philosophical insight for understanding the pentecostal principle. In chapter 1, I begin with his concept of rectification as the dynamics of the spiritual to elucidate the pentecostal principle. More important, this study undertakes to lay bare the fundamental dynamics, the guiding principle of relationships, social coexistence. By deftly using ontological analyses and the concept of the spiritual, this book carefully develops the pentecostal principle as a pneumatological methodology of ethics. What would it look like if we began an ethics with a methodological prolegomenon based on relational reality (coexistence) and its associated na-

69. Smith, *Thinking in Tongues*, p. 34.

70. Steven G. Smith, *The Concept of the Spiritual: An Essay in First Philosophy* (Philadelphia: Temple University Press, 1988), p. 4.

71. Smith, *Concept of the Spiritual*, pp. 4-5.

ture, logic, and dynamics? In the remainder of this book I begin the process of thinking through some of the possibilities raised by this question.

Summary of Arguments

I will close by offering a tabular summary of the key points of Tillich's Protestant principle and the pentecostal principle. The features, which are stated below, not only encapsulate the foregoing arguments, but also look forward to developments ahead in the remaining chapters of the book.

Protestant Principle	Pentecostal Principle
All systems are perpetually reforming and are always transformable.	Yes
The principle keeps every structure and system inescapably open.	Yes
If a system which is finite claims to be infinite and ultimate, it will engender a negative reaction that will counter its claims.	Yes, but the negative reaction is turned into the womb of new creation. We need to add that Tillich thinks that this oppositional force comes from outside (such as the kairos, masculine force; we will make a case for an internal, feminine kairos in the next chapter). Without denying this tendency, the notion of pentecostal principle points to an *excess* that is within every structure and system: a something it can never fully assimilate, incorporate, or comprehend. This inherent incompleteness is what engenders emergent creativity.
The Protestant principle serves to correct, ameliorate hubris, rejection of dependence on God, the refusal to properly acknowledge the divine depths of cultural functions, a denial of finitude.	Yes and much more. The pentecostal principle also serves to point humanity to the call of full actualization, maximization of human potentialities. It simultaneously affirms finitude and natality, dependence and *ekstasis,* depths and possible heights.

Tillich's casting of the principle is dyadic: to reform or not to reform: substance and principle. Managers of the structures and systems *consciously* keep them static; but there are always unconscious drives, forces from the divine depth that keep them dynamic.

It is triadic. The pentecostal principle acknowledges the conservative power in social existence as well as the dynamics. But there is a third element: the relation between the two that contains an aporia, an excess. There is no substance apart from the dynamics, and there can be no dynamics apart from the substance. Neither can function on its own. The constitutive interrelationship between them is the condition of possibility of the operation of each of them — resistance and change.

In the way Tillich presents the Protestant principle as an interplay of catholic substance and dynamics it gives the wrong impression that variation, dynamics is accidental (kairos must be imposed from outside) and not inherent to any system. But with the pentecostal principle dynamics is valued as "a defining reality," as an emergence. Transformation then is an interplay of external and internal pressures. The pentecostal principle is the Protestant principle caught on the wing.

There are bearers of the Protestant principle. The bearing is all ethical, but not religious.

Yes, and more. First, in pentecostalism there is a choice to be made. Since there is no certainty of faith or assurance of faith the individual must make a temporal choice that has eternal consequence. To believe or not to believe: the bearer defines the self and appropriates the event of Pentecost only through decisions. Second, there is fidelity to the event, the event of the Pentecost. Third, it is a religious commitment — as well as an ethical commitment.

ℵ THE TRIADIC METAPHOR AND PNEUMATOLOGICAL IMAGINATION

We neither have the time nor the space to explore the methodological and hermeneutic implications of the triadic metaphor. The knowledge of fitting ethos and relevant levels of flourishing that pertain to and undergird the quest for actualization emerge only semiotically by way of what Amos Yong has called "pneumatological imagination" ("human imagination with specifically pneumatological feature"). The semiotic process, according to him, is inherently triadic; so is the pneumatological imagination, which has three moments — Spirit, Word, and Community. His book *Spirit-Word-Community* has explored the "hermeneutic and methodological implications of this triadic metaphor in an attempt to develop a pneumatological and trialectic approach to the knowledge of God."[72]

Even what we have said earlier about linking human actions to its divine depths (theonomous process) requires a deep rooting in the creative faculty of imagination, specifically pneumatological imagination, as constrained normatively by the pentecostal principle. As Amos argues, "pneumatological imagination is empowered actively by the divine breath, is attuned especially to the spiritual components of reality, and is structured normatively according to her christomorphic shape and trinitarian character."[73]

I am grateful to Yong for bringing to my attention his brilliant book on theological hermeneutics after reading the first full draft of the manuscript of this book. He graciously pointed out to me that my intuition about the triadic nature of the pentecostal principle parallels and complements the triadic hermeneutic in *Spirit-Word-Community*. On reading his book, I realized that the triadic nature of the pentecostal principle resonates with his triadic hermeneutics. Even my suggestion about the "aporia" or "excess" element is thematized pneumatologically in his book as the pneumatological imagination (vis-à-vis a trinitarian epistemology), as foundational pneumatology (vis-à-vis a trinitarian ontology) and as the pneumatological dynamic that undergirds the interpretive process.

Outline of This Book

This is a slim volume. It contains only five chapters and a *recursive* epilogue. In chapter 1, I further develop the theory of the pentecostal principle by offering a critical analysis of Tillich's Protestant principle. This serves as a clearing to make the case for the pentecostal principle as a

---

72. Yong, *Spirit-Word-Community*, p. 217; see also pp. 311-16; Nimi Wariboko, "Imagination: Source of Self and Religion," in *Ethics and Time: Ethos of Temporal Orientation in Politics and Religion of the Niger Delta* (Lanham, MD: Lexington, 2010).

73. Yong, *Spirit-Word-Community*, p. 216.

framework for interpreting history and a methodological approach to social ethics. More importantly, in a rigorous philosophical manner it illuminates the phenomenon of pentecostalism as a historic force and principle of pure existence and creative emergence.

In chapter 2, "Emergence and Ethics: The Ethos of Pneumatological Methodology," I examine creative emergence and its possible impact on ethics. This chapter explores the ethical implications of the core concepts of emergence in societal management. In investigating the connections between emergentist philosophy and ethics, I imaginatively construct a "model" of an emergentist social world characterized by contingency and possibilities. The model is then used to investigate the interplay between emergentist phenomena and ethics and to map out some of the possible decision-scenarios managers of societies (large-scale systems) characterized by contingency and possibilities may face. More specifically, it examines how policy makers, guardians of society's stability and norms, will react to perceived threats if they think that they are living in an emergentist world and have adopted the emergentist philosophy as a policy framework. It also outlines a form of social ethics that is necessary for citizens to cope with the character of the emergentist world. Together, these two angles of vision — leaders' and citizenry's — are used to map out the ethical framework of an emergentist social world.

This framework suggests that we may need to rethink some of the fundamentals of social ethics. A commitment to an emergentist worldview obliges us to embrace the *prophetic-pentecostal spirit.* It calls forth a citizenry that can sense the unprecedented, identify opportunities and threats, and craft the appropriate responses rooted in their creative and prophetic power. We need to fashion an ethics that will enable individuals to cope with *emergence,* to rely on the *spirit* rather than on rules and predetermined ethical codes for navigating what is and what must be a bewildering world.

The third chapter, "Many Tongues of Pentecost: Ethical Methodology as a Paradigm of Pluralism" develops an explicit procedural method of ethical analysis relevant to public policy decision-making. The chapter proposes an ethical methodology as a form of public discourse, a meta-ethical model showing how themes, concerns, and insights of public theology can be systematically organized into practical policy arguments. It provides a robust "mechanics" to aid public theologians to prepare ethical analyses for public policies. The method the chapter sets forth flows from a conception of ethics and ethical analysis that are rooted in the pentecostal principle. Ethical analysis is conceived as *faith seeking resistance.* This seeking aims to overcome resistance to the common good in the name of the ultimate concern of society. So every genuine ethical analysis aims at the overcoming of resistance.

Ethics points us to ends beyond the existing forms of human sociality. It insists that an existing order can find those ends beyond itself only when its agents rise beyond themselves. In this quest for fulfillment our brains, voices, and bodies are all involved in both resisting existing orders that absolutize themselves and in forging and straining toward a new window of "else-where" and "else-when." This idea of window points us toward both what is present and what is absent in an extant order. In ethics we are trying to paint a portrait of our community and/or the subject of our focus. The portrait becomes a space through which the community or the subject is seen. But it also provides the lens, perspective to see what is absent in the community and to initiate something new. Like all windows, an "ethical window" marks the boundary between what is inside the house (what is currently obtained) and what is outside, what we can strive for in the open, unconfined space.

Theological-ethical reasoning is, in large part, an attempt to provide a window on creativity and an avenue to show how the creative principles at work in human coexistence and the larger cosmos can be harnessed for human flourishing. It is an ordered speech that attempts to link forms of human sociality to perceived[74] inner thrusts of God's liberatory activity in the world. In other words, ethics attempts to relate the inner life of social institutions to the invisible rhythms and creative force that sustain and move the universe.

Based on the foregoing, what do we discern as the pentecostal spirit? What is the spirit of the era that is upon us today? How does all this affect the way we do social ethics? The fourth chapter, "The Pentecostal Spirit: Way of Being for the Pentecostal Principle" responds to these pertinent questions by formulating a notion of the spirit that not only fits the pentecostal principle, but is also duly informed by the current pentecostal movement. It defines the pentecostal spirit as a way of being that is radi-

---

74. I carefully chose the word *perceived* to indicate that human perception of God's activities in the world is always a particular decision. "We *must* make decisions about where God is at work so we can join in the fight against evil. But there is no perfect guide for discerning God's movement in the world. Contrary to what many conservatives would say, the Bible is not a blueprint on this matter. It is a valuable symbol for pointing to God's revelation in Jesus, but it is not self-interpreting. We are thus placed in an existential situation of freedom in which the burden is on us to make decisions without a guaranteed ethical guide." James H. Cone, *A Black Theology of Liberation* (Maryknoll, NY: Orbis, 1986), p. 7. Italics in original.

cally open to divine surprises, always at work resisting obstacles to human flourishing, and is committed to creating, broadening, and deepening new possibilities of life. The word "spirit" here means the totality of a group's creative self-interpretation of itself or its moral life. Put another way, it refers to the principle of self-consciousness or subjectivity. This particular understanding of spirit enables us to suggest new directions for ethical methodology in the light of the pentecostal principle.

One of the major insights that emerges from chapter 4 is the playful character of Pentecostalism. Our understanding of the pentecostal spirit will be inadequate if we do not reckon with the festival (Pentecost) nature of the pentecostal movement. In chapter 5 ("The Promise of the Pentecostal Principle: Religion as Play") I pursue this lead by investigating the connections between the pentecostal principle, the quest for actualization of potentials, and "theology of play" as a *radicalization* of grace. In the process a new understanding of play as *pure means* emerges as a theological-philosophical orientation to, perhaps, point pentecostalism to the fulfillment of its historic task.

The epilogue is titled "The End Which Is to Come" because it is befitting for a book that is about the open-ended process of life, a book that insists endings must be beginnings, and argues that the creative process does not have an end, to have an ending that is an opening end. So the ending part of the book encourages us to try to think and talk again. It first offers a summary of the main findings of the book and folds back on itself an end that opens a new beginning. The epilogue also locates the book within the context of my overall work: that is, puts it within the unending creative process that birthed it and shows how it unfolded into that which enfolds it. "Birthed" might not be the right word. In a certain sense, it was not birthed; it is the "logos" of the womblike chaos of the creative process itself. It shows how this slim volume sets forth and unconceals the methodology implicit in my work as an ethicist. So this work comes after its practical application and comes only as a reawakening or a reflection. As philosopher Giorgio Agamben puts it in his 2009 book on method, *The Signature of All Things*,

> Anyone familiar with research in the human sciences knows that, contrary to common opinion, a reflection on method usually follows practical application, rather than preceding it. It is a matter, then, of ultimate or penultimate thoughts, to be discussed among friends and colleagues, which can legitimately be articulated only after extensive research.[75]

75. Agamben, *Signature of All Things*, p. 7.

1 The Pentecostal Principle

The spiritual content of any culture is the imperative of infinite rectification, where rectification "is a movement of righting rather than a fixed position of being right."[1] It rejects any claim of an absolute, final form of culture, or of a determinate thing or order of things. Nothing is absolutely as it should be. Inspired by the Reformation and its famed paradox of justification by faith, Paul Tillich calls this imperative the Protestant principle. The principle as conceived by Tillich ultimately points us beyond all matter. This is exemplified by his resort to kairos, external and heavenly, which can only galvanize static or calcified forms to move forward, to rejuvenate their spiritual force, their restless rectification. Do we need to go beyond all matter to engage the process of infinite rectification?

Tillich draws his inspiration from the Reformation; but, as I have already noted, a turn to the New Testament gives us another inspiration. In Acts 2, we can identify and retrieve the pentecostal principle. Here we see that the spiritual content and its material bearers are combined or networked as the infinite restlessness of existence (life). The creative spirit becomes "incarnate" in 120 material bodies, just as spiritual form can become visible as it was in the Doric column Martin Buber admires in his *I and Thou*.[2] In Buber's reporting, the material column is occluded by the

1. Steven G. Smith, *The Concept of the Spiritual: An Essay in First Philosophy* (Philadelphia: Temple University Press, 1988), p. 124.

2. "Take the Doric Column, wherever it appears to a man who is able and ready to turn toward it. It confronted me for the first time out of a church wall in Syracuse into which it had been incorporated: secret primal measure presenting itself in such a simple form that

spiritual form it "incarnates," but on that fateful day of Pentecost in first-century Jerusalem we find the materialization of spiritual content. It was a moving-together of spirit and matter toward actualized goodness. Why a movement toward actualized goodness? Once we accept the materialization (or incarnation) of the creative fire we are bound to actualize (or at least reflect on) what counts as its true actualization in human sociality. How do we measure the adequacy of materialization?

Elsewhere I have stated that there is always a void between materialization and what our true self is, or its actualization. The movement to cover this void which really can never be covered I have called *excellence*.[3] Whereas excellence is a movement (process) that must have a "product" (material deposits), the pentecostal principle is like "a calling upon that movement, of its essence a provocation or solicitation, a kind of implacable restlessness that is superordinate to any impatience [excellence] might feel on its account."[4]

In this book, I intend to further develop the notion of the pentecostal principle in continuous conversation with Tillich's Protestant principle. My goal is to show that the pentecostal principle offers a better lens to view the dynamism of human social life and the spirit of the twenty-first century. Hopefully the analyses and discussions that pertain to the task of explicating the principle will help us to understand the pentecostal movement which claims to be the bearer of the spirit of the pentecostal principle. It will be clear at the end of this book whether pentecostals are the true historic bearers of the principle. Too, how should the pentecostal principle inform the way we do social ethics? What does the uncovering of this principle mean for ethical methodology? The rest of this chapter proceeds not by direct line of disquisition, but by weaving arguments around the fault lines of the Protestant principle and at the same time bringing forth the kernel of the pentecostal principle.

---

nothing individual could be seen or enjoyed in it. What had to be achieved was what I was able to achieve: to confront and endure this spiritual form there that had passed through the mind and hand of man and become incarnate." Martin Buber, *I and Thou*, trans. Walter Kaufmann (New York: Charles Scribner's Sons, 1970), p. 175.

3. Nimi Wariboko, *The Principle of Excellence: A Framework for Social Ethics* (Lanham, MD: Lexington, 2009).

4. S. G. Smith, *Concept of the Spiritual*, p. 243.

The Protestant Principle

Tillich's Protestant principle is about constant reform; it refers to the dynamism of social existence. Yet is this mere dynamism or dynamism that is life-giving? What is driving the reform? Is it merely the negative reaction of the infinite toward that which is finite claiming to be infinite, or is it an asymptotic striving toward wholeness in an open future?

The Protestant principle is a symbol of a protest, an outside force or energy reacting against the particular that raises itself to universal status and finality of form and content/dynamics. Can it be reconceived as something that exists or parallels the human tendency to idolatry and something that exists within the Catholic substance, within the structures of human sociality? The notion of pentecostal principle rethinks the idea of protestant principle as the spirit of creativity, the creative transforming energy that operates within the structures and throughout the processes of creation as its law of motion. The pentecostal principle is the power of emergent creativity that disrupts social existence, generates infinite restlessness, and issues in novelty.

א DUALISM IN TILLICH'S PROTESTANT PRINCIPLE

Tillich presents his Protestant principle as a transformation of the Catholic substance, implying a certain dualism in the becoming of human sociality, a tension similar to that behind mind and body. Are there two "forces" (principle and substance/substrate) in tension (dualism)? Is the principle ultimately reducible to substance? If one says no to substance, does that represent a triumph of — and a yes to — principle? Or is it both yes and no to substance and principle? To cut through this knot we need a perspective that represents a sensitivity to matter as both being and becoming. And this could be drawn from the philosophy of emergence. It will help us to see how the Protestant principle — a supposed higher power over substance in Tillich's thought — appears from and is constituted by the "lower-level" Catholic substance. This is to explore further the functioning of the higher and more complex principle which is not merely explicable in terms of the substance as it is capable of unpredictable novel properties.

The attempt to rethink Tillich's notion of the Protestant principle in terms of basic arguments in emergentist thought is just one way to view it with unfurnished eyes. It thus becomes easy to note a confusion regarding the principle. What is not very clear in Tillich's presentation of the principle is the response to this question: Is the Protestant principle an individual or group phenomenon? Does it pertain to the basic unit of life or does it depend on the emergence of sociality and relationality? I suggest it is an *emergentist property,* a property that arises as a result of the multiplicity of activities in a group. Failure to make this distinction can result in three errors. First, the Protestant principle may become reducible to basic ontological element. Second, its power will be thought to be borne by individuals rather than groups, when in fact it is also an interpersonal phenomenon. Finally, we may fail to note the paradox of the Protestant principle, namely, that though it is a group phenomenon, its originary power lies at the individual level. Cultural or interpersonal, networked systems are akin to what physicists call *nonlinear dynamical systems.* The effects of interactions among individuals are exponential and nonlinear and the influence of one event can have a profound effect on the whole system as time goes on. The bottom line of such interactions is a counterintuitive global behavior (such as the impulse for the Protestant principle that Tillich is talking about) without a common, cultural management unit. Individuals acting on their own can generate a system of complicated and coordinated global behavior.

What is the first question we should ask about the pentecostal principle? It is not "What is the pentecostal principle?" but "What is the *meaning* of the pentecostal principle?" — that is, "What can be said and understood of the pentecostal principle?" The pentecostal principle is the power of coexistence that perfects or maximizes actuality, which has an emotional attraction to the good. This attraction is visible as the restless search and realization of new forms and unions of form and meaning.

Tillich says that the fire that manifested on the disciples on the Day of Pentecost represents creative fire. But what does it really mean for the Holy Spirit to present itself as creativity alighting on human beings? One possible explanation is that it is creativity-in-and-for-itself. For divine creativity is no longer known merely as substance but also as subject. By demonstrating, reaffirming, or showcasing that human beings are carriers of divine creativity, two things happened at once on that day. On the one hand, divine creativity in ongoing social existence (in the concrete you-and-I sociality of historical being) that is not borne by human subjects (which is creativity-in-itself) is limited inasmuch as it is removed from the instantiation of creativity in which creativity has its reality. On the other hand, creativity that is purely human creativity for itself denies its divine depths. What recommends the Day of Pentecost as a moment when human creativity was linked to divine creativity is that those present saw that the spirit of creativity rejects both disincarnate subjectivity and pure autonomous creativity. Creativity, theonomous creativity, overcomes all dualism.

Following this perspective of creative spirit, Pentecost means that creativity constitutes the true nature of human beings and also the end which human beings need to realize in history. The essence of the spirit is to be free, to set us free from all obstacles, to initiate reconciliation and overcome alienation between human beings and God, and to enable us to be all that we can be. The activity of freedom is rooted in its drive to inclusiveness and expansiveness. The spirit universalizes love that particularizes caring: lifts up our intention, care, or commitment and extends it to the social whole. It wills for one as well as for all others the same thing in relevantly similar situations. A corollary of the spirit's freedom and inclusiveness is its creativity. All human beings who envision the new and act to realize it "necessarily intend that they be *free* and *able* to act."[5] In the absence of freedom, which is the condition of the possibility for creative actions as producers of novelty, human beings will be too determined and conditioned to produce the new. Freedom is the precondition for the exercise of creativity. Therefore a relationship of total and complete determination or domination in which no alternative is possible cannot be creative.

This creativity that constitutes the nature of human beings harbors a lack. Yet this lack is not of the sort that is bound to make us despair or to disapprove, but is rather a surplus of the sort that we should glory in. Creativity involves human beings realizing themselves by relating themselves to themselves and to their environment. What constitutes the whole relation? In relating themselves to themselves and their environment they must relate themselves to another. Thus, human creativity cannot possess itself. Finite creativity finds its peace in infinite divine ontological creativity.

א Rightness and Goodness in the Protestant Principle

The Protestant principle emerges by the act of first distinguishing Catholic substance and reactions against it, finite form and incompletable, infinite final form. The pentecostal principle is about what lies beyond, what cannot be incorporated into an extant form. This *something more* has become not only the condition of the possibility of existence, but also the condition of the meaning of existence. The category in which an institution, practice, or position is evaluated under the Protestant principle is "rightness" rather than "goodness" or "fitness." This is so because the point of such an evaluation is to determine how the institution, practice, or position stands with respect to the infinite, which constitutes an absolute, exterior stan-

5. S. G. Smith, *Concept of the Spiritual*, p. 141.

dard to all forms of human accomplishment or cultural functions. But the pentecostal principle is focused on the good toward which all cultural functions are drawn. The question here is how the institution, practice, or position fits with the movement toward the unconditional good of actualizing potentials in relation to the divine depths of existence. The good is actualized fitness; it is maximized existence. Is God satisfied with anything less than the full flourishing of God's creation?

The two principles are reconcilable. It is good for all things to exist maximally, to be moving toward unrealizable full actuality and toward the unreachable divine depths. It is *right* to serve this end, this good, and it demands that we should not regard any cultural form as final and infinite, but always ready to change, to move forward. Since Tillich also regards excellence as the actualization of potentials,[6] the deeper meaning of his evaluative category of "right" is *actualized rightness*. The pentecostal principle informs us about what is, what is going on, and what ought to be. It informs us about *norming*, a pattern or behavior to be followed, the ought-to-be. The pentecostal principle in this sense precedes, embraces, and transcends the Protestant principle. The good is an imperative that claims us and requires us to act in a particular way, to live in a certain manner.

In the attempt to avoid the absolutism of substance (system of eternal structures and essence, unchangeable element), Tillich's formulation of the Protestant principle tilts the weight of ethical analysis toward change itself as the ultimate principle. Yet this formulation fails Tillich's own test for the suitability of religious or theological terms. According to him, religious terms are more adequate the more they express and preserve the tension between the unconditionally real (the power of dynamics, "self-transcendence") and the conditionally real ("realism"). The Protestant principle as he articulates it does not adequately express this paradox in its depth and power.[7] The pentecostal principle, on the other hand, attempts to achieve a necessary balance between these two extremes. The basic idea is that existence ("substance," form), which points to the most general characteristics of all that there is, is used as the very notion which transcends every form that is. It points to substance whose realization depends on the continuous creativity of human beings in history. It calls attention to that unconditional command, the validity of ethics, which can penetrate concrete existence, adapting to the demands of history as well as transforming history.

6. Paul Tillich, *Systematic Theology*, Volume 3: *Life and the Spirit; History and the Kingdom of God* (Chicago: University of Chicago Press, 1963), pp. 67, 75, 85-87.

7. Paul Tillich, *The Protestant Era* (Chicago: University of Chicago Press, 1948), p. 79.

א Key Differences between the Protestant Principle and the Pentecostal Principle

Tillich's notion of substance and its interplay with principle is one difference that sets the conceptualization of the Protestant principle apart from the pentecostal principle. Substance, or reality, consists not of actualities but potentialities (that is, possibilities and probabilities). Tillich assumes that substances are actualities or essences that must not be allowed to be fixed, immutable, or absolute. They must be constantly disturbed or interrupted by the Protestant principle to move them forward even asymptotically to their final state. But from the point of view of the pentecostal principle the starting points are processes that enable the emergence of creativity and complexity in human networks or matter.

Another key difference between the Protestant principle and the pentecostal principle is the way in which each conceives existence as a motion. In conceptualizing the Protestant principle Tillich implicitly assumes that existence is "standing" plus "motion." In this view the Protestant principle gives institutions or cultural functions a kick that sets them in motion — only to stand again. But the pentecostal principle interprets existence as an issue of motion. Here it is germane to quote philosopher Steven G. Smith on the importance of interpreting existence as an issue of "motion, and actually one kind of motion or another":

> Better than standing for two reasons: first, because if I am already in motion my reasons for acting give me places to put my feet down (which reasons can indeed give me) rather than pushes or pulls to move me from a standing center (the kind of "motivation" that reasons as such cannot give); second, because if I am essentially one who stands I can meet another only by going forth from my place, which will uproot and alienate me. I will necessarily lose myself in having anything to do with others — which is absurd. (However, to achieve a positively significant stability, one that is not mere stasis or stagnation, it is both sufficient and necessary to parallel my motion with motion of others, in relationship.)[8]

There is much to be said about the primacy of motion as we conceive human coexistence and the imperative of infinite rectification, the pursuit of the good. The good of my existence and the good of others as others claim me, open up a space between me and my maximal actualization (flourishing), and set me in motion.

The in-breaking of the eternal Holy Spirit into history on that Day of Pentecost two thousand years ago both pronounces and exemplifies such an ethics. The speaking in tongues symbolizes a prophetic critique of and protest against the configuration of differences as well as an announce-

---

8. S. G. Smith, *Concept of the Spiritual,* p. 104.

ment of the not-yet gathering of all God's children across lines of separation, a definite gesture toward the hope of the to-come.

Pentecost is not a once-and-for-all occurrence. Difference in the interpretation of this event lies at the heart of the controversy between pentecostals and some mainline churches. Conservative theologians argue that the Pentecost, which happened two thousand years ago, is the only kairotic inbreaking of the Holy Spirit and is valid for all times — in the sense that it is not repeatable. Pentecostals argue that it is valid for all times — in the sense of an ideal for history as a whole — and does not belong to that time only. From this perspective, human destiny finds its end in the kairotic inbreaking of the Holy Spirit and life in a changing world must be understood as life of the spirit. The pentecostal principle must realize itself from spirit to spirit, engendering and supporting an ethics that is dynamic, open, and contingent. The spirit is the principle of ethics, and creativity (emergence) is the way it is concretely embodied in history. It is continuously taking forward (not destructively) the structures, experiences, wisdom, and laws of the past into the future in openness to the underivably new.

But the pentecostal principle transcends the religious and confessional character of pentecostals. The pentecostal principle is a principle that stands beyond all concrete realization and goes beyond pentecostalism as a religious or cultural form.[9] It is the dynamic power in the current worldwide pentecostal movement, but of necessity goes beyond it. It is also present in Catholicism and Protestantism, even as it transcends them. It is available in things that want to go beyond themselves to their depth, to dynamic ontological creativity, to the Spirit of creation. It is available in all forms of existence as the resident power of continuous outworking of possibilities and potentialities.

The pentecostal principle is the religious language of excellence[10] grasped by the power of the spiritual presence; or it is excellence appropri-

---

9. The idea here connects with Wolfgang Vondey's point about Pentecostalism moving beyond itself. In his recent book *Beyond Pentecostalism: The Crisis of Global Christianity and the Renewal of the Theological Agenda* (Grand Rapids: Eerdmans, 2010) he makes the case for pentecostal theology to move from classical pentecostal issues toward a global theological agenda and beyond, thus suggesting that the genius of Pentecostalism is to surpass itself. He writes, "I suggest that Pentecostal thought and praxis function as indispensable catalysts for the development of global Christianity that Pentecostalism perpetuates at the cost of its own particularity" (p. 2).

10. The reader who is interested in the philosophy and theology of excellence should see my 2009 book, *The Principle of Excellence*.

ated as a religious act or intuition. It is excellence grasped in ecstasy. The pentecostal principle is the dynamic union of excellence and ecstasy and it is at the heart of every religion (although manifested in different degrees) insofar as it is an approach to the unconditional and keeps alive the union of absolute (unconditional, infinite) and the conditioned (human, relative, finite object) powers of existence. As Tillich puts it,

> Religion tries to surpass the given reality in order to approach the un-conditional. The means for achieving this is rapture and ecstasy. Wher-ever we transcend the limits of our being, moving toward union with another one, something like ecstasy ("standing outside of one's self") occurs. Ecstasy is the act of breaking through fixed form of our own be-ing. In this sense of the term we must say: Only through ecstasy can the ultimate power of being be experienced in ourselves, in things and per-sons, and in historical situations.[11]

Pentecostals have gotten a sense of the dynamic union of excellence and ecstasy. The only problem is that often the ecstasy overwhelms the excel-lence, the demand to subject all to the endless actualization of potentiality.

The Protestant Principle and Kairos

Tillich's doctrine of kairos in the Protestant principle is principally fo-cused on the in-breaking force coming from above or outside. But the for-mulation of the pentecostal principle insists that there is also an elevating of human existence toward divine blessing. This supernal union is symbol-ized in the creative account of Genesis 1. The Spirit of God hovers over the waters, preparing and lifting them to receive the divine word, light flowing downwards from above. Pentecostalism understands serving God as not limited to grace coming down from above but also as grace elevating the earth and its fullness to God. In a fallen world, every person can potentially become a carrier of God's holiness and through prayers and good deeds and discipline (ethics) this potentiality can be liberated and made to serve God in spirit and in truth (in the power of the Holy Spirit and in the truth of Jesus Christ). Every person and every sociality is potentially a site of transimmanence, that is, of transcending that does not go beyond, yet passes and connects, always occurring.

11. Tillich, *Protestant Era*, p. 79.

This is made clear in a recent work by pentecostal theologian and philosopher James K. A. Smith. According to Smith, the pentecostal social imaginary, which he discerns from pentecostal practices, does not view the Spirit's care and activity in human sociality as exceptions or interruptions. This is so, he explains, because "pentecostal worship and practice are characterized by a kind of gritty materiality as space for work of the Spirit."[12] The Spirit is always involved in materiality, in human sociality animating and reanimating it to manifest and actualize maximum goodness. Transimmanence is an ethos in the social practices that constitute pentecostalism. The gritty materiality of pentecostalism is a complexly structured set of doings and being that rejects the opposition between transcendence and immanence; it is an existence that is radically oriented to continual opening and reopening. The inside always exposed to the outside.

The ontology (a participatory ontology that is *non*reductive and incarnational) implicit in pentecostal practice affirms that "matter *as created* exceeds itself and *is* only insofar as it participates in or is suspended from the transcendent Creator."[13] This ontology allows for intensities of participation at certain sites and moments. As he puts it, relying on the thought of another fine pentecostal theologian, Amos Yong, "while all that is participates in God through the Spirit, there are sites and events that exhibit a more *intense* participation."[14]

Let us further query Tillich's conceptualization of kairos as an inbreaking force coming into history from above and outside. As I have already stated, it is a downward-flowing power, eternity breaking into history. In this sense, it is a very masculine notion *(ho kairos)* of in-breaking, coming from above as a blade that thrusts into existing configurations. It is a giving force, coming down into a receptacle, the new bearing down on the old. My question is: Why can't there be another type of kairos that is generated within, from below? There must be ascending and descending kairoi. Why can't we think of a feminine version of kairos, especially in the light of Tillich's notion of God as "ground/abyss of being"?[15] Kairos as a blessing going up: a receiving force, elevating institutions upward to-

---

12. J. K. A. Smith, *Thinking in Tongues: Pentecostal Contributions to Christian Philosophy* (Grand Rapids: Eerdmans, 2010), p. 99.

13. J. K. A. Smith, *Thinking in Tongues,* p. 100. Italics in original.

14. J. K. A. Smith, *Thinking in Tongues,* p. 102. Italics in original.

15. The ground of being points to the "mother-quality of giving birth, carrying, and embracing, and at the same time, of calling back, resisting independence of the created, and swallowing it." Tillich, *Systematic Theology,* vol. 3, p. 294.

ward change, raising them up toward the new? Kairos occurring as congealing of conditions of history and culture, as in some from-below notion of transformation?

There are, indeed, two types of kairos — at least I am proposing them for consideration. They are not mutually contradictory. They are complementary aspects of the dynamic rhythm of life. In one case, we can conceive of kairos as ever present and in the other as a breaking-in. If the divine is the absolute ground of being, immanental, panentheistic, everywhere present and timeless, and underlying all human reality it can break through to consciousness and be expressed by actors as leading them to harmony, unity, and inclusiveness. The new comes in terms of the inner continuity of the given, the nomos undergirded by dynamic divine ontological creativity. The second sense of kairos sees the absolute, the divine as tearing into nature, into the breach of history as an active power to transform it. These two conceptions (inner-worldly and other-worldly, feminine and masculine) point to the simultaneous differentiation and interrelation that is the nub of life,[16] existence, and sociality. One points to our differentiation and gap from the divine; as for the other, our finite differentiation is overcome by penetration, interpenetration of the divine, the infinite in the finite.

The masculine concept of kairos that Tillich adapts compels us to wonder whether he was misled by its etymology and the Greek understanding of it. I raise this question because if we line up the two concepts of kairos against his two types of philosophy of religion (the ontological and cosmological arguments for the existence of God), his treatment of kairos runs against the grain of his thought and preference.

In the masculine concept of kairos, human beings meet a "stranger" when kairos is uncovered. The coming and meeting with kairos is accidental. But in the feminine concept, when human beings discover kairos they discover something from which they are "estranged, but from which [they never have] been and never can be separated." The feminine notion of kairos goes with the ontological type of the philosophy of religion that Tillich supports because of his understanding of God as power of being (Being itself). And knowledge of kairos is knowledge of love (movement toward the estranged) and the question of kairos presupposes knowledge of kairos.

---

16. On the one hand, the deepening of being, by directing it toward the infinite, figures, structures, and stabilizes the infinite fabric of life. On the other, it also disfigures, destructures, and destabilizes the stabilizing structures of socialities.

When taken together, the dual concepts of masculine and feminine kairoi provide useful insights into how emergent creativity disrupts structures to promote the *novum*. If kairos is conceived as purely a time phenomenon it lies at that dynamic in-between moment of transcendence and immanence. Spatially put, it is the mediating matrix of eroticized, creative energies that creates the space it inhabits. However useful, though, these masculine and feminine kairoi are ultimately inadequate for understanding the interrelationships between the old and the new that the pentecostal principle attempts to forge. The condition of possibility for kairos must include a synthesis of both perspectives — such a synthesis must be seen both as prior to and after them. Each instance of kairos presupposes their complex interactions. They are codependent and coevolve: the appearance of kairos is neither transcendent nor immanent. And to borrow the words of theologian Mark C. Taylor, kairos

> is something like immanent transcendence which is inside as an outside that cannot be incorporated. This interior exterior or exterior interior is the source of the endless disruption that keeps complex systems open and makes them subject to constant transformation yet also preserves them from disintegration and simple extinction.[17]

א Protestant Principle and Kairos from Below

Tillich's failure to develop a more explicit notion of kairos from below is perhaps linked to the larger issue of how Protestantism ignores the mystical element of religion. Mysticism, as Ernst Troeltsch informs us,

> aims at the immediate, present, and inward quality of religious experience, at the immediate relationship with God that leaps over or complements traditions, cults, and institutions. The historical and institutional is to mysticism merely a stimulus and a means towards the inner, timeless intercourse with the divine. Mysticism in this sense already found expression in primitive Christian enthusiasm, in the doctrine of the possession of Spirit that directly reveals or fulfills and continues the mysteries of the Godhead. Paul's religiosity, in particular, is deeply penetrated by a mysticism of this kind, which stands in deep inner tension with his ideas concerning redemption, salvation, and institution. But it was only with the assimilation of Neo-Platonic mysticism that the consolidation of Christian mysticism was achieved. According to the Neo-Platonic

17. Mark C. Taylor, *After God* (Chicago: University of Chicago Press, 2007), p. 41.

conception, a latent presence of God remains in the finite spirits as they ema-
nate from the Divine. This presence is a seed or spark of the divine essence
which, through the contemplation of the mysteries of this ground of being, carries the soul upward to substantial union with the divine, and back again.[18]

The whole issue of lifting up to God is banished in mainline Protestantism
and with it comes the neglect of feminine kairos or feminine waters, to use an old
terminology.

Another resource that we can use to formulate a notion of kairos from below is
the ascent of love and the desire from the earthly to the heavenly that Augustine
taught us, and which Martha Nussbaum has reintroduced to us.[19] Love can generate kairos from below and this much Tillich agrees with.[20] He even goes on to say
that love is able to appear in every kairos, realizing itself from kairos to kairos, and
that this "may demand a transformation of our kairos."[21] Love is a movement of the
estranged, a movement toward the ground of being, ultimately to end separation.
This movement can cause irruptions that can transform society from below, and
kairos may well be "the way of its embodiment in concrete contents,"[22] the tasks of
a special period, the strategic agonistic politics of the certain here and now.

Tillich came very close to theorizing ascending and descending kairoi. Yet he
consistently pulls back by way of his unrelenting focus on externality and eternity.
Tillich says love is "eternal, although it can create something new in each kairos."[23]
While kairos is the eternal breaking into history to transform it, love is the immanent eternal lifting up the concrete contents of existence, the forms and structures
of life, to kairos for transformation. Tillich even says that love is the creative and
basic principle that is actualized from kairos to kairos.[24] Love is the feminine
kairos, the creative depth of existence that is stirred by the kairos, by the masculine
love to advance communities toward God. (In the kairotic moment described in
Acts 2, we can arguably discern the two kairoi: the love represented by fellowship
of the 120 disciples gathered in Christ and the tongues of fire as the thrusting blade
inserting itself in this receptacle of love.)

18. Ernst Troeltsch, *Religion in History,* trans. James Luther Adams and Walter F. Bense
(Eugene, OR: Wipf and Stock, 2002), p. 326.

19. Martha C. Nussbaum, *Upheavals of Thought: The Intelligence of Emotions* (Cambridge: Cambridge University Press, 2001), pp. 527-90.

20. Tillich, *Protestant Era,* p. 156.

21. Tillich, *Protestant Era,* pp. 156-57.

22. Tillich, *Protestant Era,* p. 159. Here we see Tillich come very close to the notion of
kairos from below. He had it in his thought, but was never able to bring it out clearly.

23. Tillich, *Protestant Era,* p. 158.

24. Tillich, *Protestant Era,* pp. 159-60.

Based on the foregoing elucidation and critique of Tillich's notion of kairos in his Protestant principle, in our formulation of the pentecostal principle kairos is not treated as an exception to all the principles of human creativity, invoked to save their failure. Instead, human creativity is the chief exemplification of kairos. One can neither shelter kairos from human creativity, or human creativity from kairos; nor can one shelter either of them from the nomos that defines our sociality, nor the nomos from either of them. There is no shortcut to the pentecostal principle. Kairos is the dynamic that has been given form by human creativity in concrete existence. The pentecostal principle is the imperative of the forward moving process of life that synthesizes the feminine and masculine rhythms of life into a trinitarian system with itself as a part of but at the same time outside the triadic embrace both as an excess that cannot be incorporated and as immediate mediator/motivator.[25]

ℵ The Notion of Transimmanence

James K. A. Smith lays the groundwork for my claim that the Spirit is always involved in materiality and in human sociality, animating and reanimating it to manifest and actualize maximum goodness. I claim as well that this transimmanence is an ethos in the social practices that constitute pentecostalism. But this opens up key questions about the Spirit-world relationship. I cannot discuss all these here, but it is germane to shed more light on this idea of transimmanence, as well as introduce a related concept that we might call *immantrance.*

Transimmanence is a transcendence that moves across individual immanent lives, but does not go beyond, above, and outside finite human coexistence, does not exceed the manifolds and relations of immanence. But let us think about the way the word itself is constructed. By putting *trans* before *immanence,* it gives the impression that the spirit somehow becomes transcendental (though resident or born amid immanence, depending on one's perspective on whether it is an upper- or lowercase S/spirit) and moves *across* the space of immanence or can possibly

---

25. There is another perspective through which we may want to approach the idea of masculine and feminine kairoi. This is perspective taken from Slavoj Žižek's Lacanian psychoanalysis-philosophy. Insofar as the masculine kairos refers to the *big Other,* corresponds to dynamical antinomies, it follows the logic of *constitutive exception.* Masculine kairos always escapes the universal sway of the rule of human socialities. Kairos in the masculine perspective is the exception to the rule of the human social system. The feminine kairos is the *non-all (pas-tout).* The logic of non-all *(mathematical antimonies)* implies that a system is never complete and it is non-totalized. The feminine kairos or the non-all reflects the logic of the *Real.* See Adam Kotsko, *Žižek and Theology* (London: T. & T. Clark, 2008), pp. 46-51.

move outside of immanence if not properly anchored or can become *spectral* (and *trance-immanental*, if you like). In the notion of transimmanence as infinite finitude, the infinite which has no outside (other) world to go to appears like Walter Benjamin's angel of history poised to be blown outside by the wind. In addition, by putting the *trans* in front we are allowing ourselves to assume a purely external relation between transcendence and immanence in transimmanence. It implies that the *trans*, the moving power, could be conceived as ascending free of immanence before dropping down and confining itself to the immanent because there is no beyond to ascend to. The impression is unfortunately given that the energy, the catalyzing dynamic, for the movement comes from whatever is in transcendence that is relating to the immanence. But what if there is nothing relating to immanence, nothing crossing or underlying immanence other than itself? (That is, what if as we have noted, kairos is a function of the congealing conditions of history?) If the immanent is itself an active element in the genesis of transcendence and the-moving-across, then the idea of immanent-transcendence, immantrance, is more precise than that of transimmanence.

Putting the *trans* first in transimmanence may take the edge off the idea of transcendence as a beyond or outside, but it neglects the idea of transcendence as that which grounds or underlies human processes. These two senses of transcendence are coupled together in the transcendence-immanence debate in theology.

I would invite the reader to think of kairos as not transcendence or immanence but immantrance, as a moving and passing that is oriented to a whole, moving into some depth of the whole, but not out of the whole. It is a movement from the singular-plurality of whole into its outer regions of plural-singularity. It is a clearing within immanence, within *being-with*, within finite infinitude. The motion and crossings of the plurality create (open) a new modality of self-world that is sensate to all singularities and disappears when the manifolds and relations of immanence disappear. The spirit remains in-dwelling (Latin *im*, "in," plus *manere*, "to dwell") insofar as the group is together and the collective energy of its members moves within it. It is immanence that is moving, that is transitive. It is a movement within immanence to realize unfulfilled possibilities within it, touching its infinite range of excluded possibilities. Immantrance is an immanence that belongs to a certain dimension of immanence that is also a certain kind of transcendence.

James K. A. Smith's Analysis of Ecstatic Language

In the introduction I mentioned tongues-speech as one of the key experiences on the Day of Pentecost. I wish now to engage this with more philosophical rigor. The issue of tongues-speech opens the analysis of the pentecostal principle to the horizon of state of exception as it relates to both theology and politics in a global age. What can ecstatic language tell us about our being in the world as exposure to naked existence without recourse to normative frameworks, or tell us about the contingency of every order, including that of the language which expresses our encounter with reality? And what is it saying, if it is saying anything at all, about existence having recourse to divine framework wherein the meaning and course of life can be deciphered?

James K. A. Smith provides an interesting analysis of "tongues-speech as a liminal case in the philosophy of language." He subjects tongues-speech to three types of philosophical analysis of language: phenomenology, philosophical hermeneutics, and speech act theory. He is able to use tongues-speech as a limit case to illuminate new issues and questions and critique some old assumptions in the philosophy of language. His analysis shows that "as a kind of vocal utterance on the margins of language, tongues-speech" is resistant to the given categories in philosophy of language and calls for deeper philosophical engagement. It is such an engagement that the discussion below hopes to offer.[26]

Smith's analysis of ecstatic language struggles with a typographical question: is glossolalia outside or inside language? His analysis seems insufficient to adequately account for the phenomenon. If ecstatic language's characteristic feature is a total or partial suspension of meaning (communication) order, how can such a suspension still be embedded within it? How is such an anomaly ensconced within the communication order? And if ecstatic language is something external to communication, unrelated or contrary to communication, how can the communication order contain such a lacuna?

In truth there is no typographical opposition. Ecstatic language is not external or internal to communication. The problem of theorizing or defining it concerns seeing it as a threshold, its location between outside and inside, as a zone of indifference where inside and outside intermingle. It is a language of exception. This language of exception is inscribed within a communicative (linguistic) context. It is not total chaos; an order still exists in it even if it is not a (the usual) communication order.

What is inscribed within the communicative order is something that is exterior to it, suspends it. It is a placement of an outside within an inside by the originary constituting power of language. It is the power of ecstatic language that, though it is not constituted in the virtue of a meaningful

26. J. K. A. Smith, *Thinking in Tongues*, pp. 123-50.

language, it is nevertheless connected to existing language in such a way that appears as its constituting power, and for this reason it cannot be totally assumed and completely negated by a meaningful language. Yes, the norm of communication is suspended and yet the application is presupposed — the whole attempt at speaking presupposes the norm of communication. But this presupposing, this holding on to the nexus of norm and its application is carried out in the form of exception. "This means," according to Agamben, "that in order to apply a norm it is ultimately necessary to suspend its application, to produce an exception. In every case, the state of exception marks the threshold which logic and praxis blur with each other and a pure violence without *logos* claims to realize an enunciation without any real reference."[27]

Now, if we hold that the speaker is not totally possessed and completely taken over, then a certain decision-making inheres in ecstatic tongues-speaking. The speaker makes a decision to speak in tongues. In so doing, she suspends the norm of normal social communication and the language of exception reveals a formal element: decision. Both the suspension of the norm and the decision remain within the framework of communication. The human being, the languaged being, who can decide on the language of exception, to enter the state of exception, anchors it to the communication order. But precisely because her decision concerns the annulment of the norms of communication, she stands outside the normally valid communication order even as she belongs to it.

The state of exception in the communicative context that is instantiated by the language of exception is an anomic space in which there is a force of language without language. Such a force, "in which potentiality and act are radically separated, is certainly something like a mystical element, or rather a *fictio* by means of which [language] seeks to annex anomie itself."[28] How is this conceivable?

The student of political philosophy might have already recognized that I am engaging in the unenviable task of transmuting Carl Schmitt's theory of state of exception — as elaborated by Giorgio Agamben — into a theory of ecstatic language. I am not the first scholar to see a connection between language and law (exceptions inscribed within juridical context). Agamben has this to say:

27. Giorgio Agamben, *State of Exception*, trans. Kevin Attell (Chicago: University of Chicago Press, 2005), p. 40.

28. Agamben, *State of Exception*, p. 39.

The structural analogy between language and law is illuminating here. Just as linguistic elements subsist in *langue* without any real denotation, which they acquire only in actual discourse, so in the state of exception the norm is in force without reference to reality. But just as concrete linguistic activity becomes intelligible precisely through the presupposition of something like a language, so is the norm able to refer to the normal situation through the suspension of its application in the state of exception.

It can generally be said that not only language and law but all social institutions have been formed through a process of desemanticization and suspension of concrete praxis in its immediate reference to the real. Just as grammar, in producing speech without denotation, has isolated something like a language of discourse, and law, in suspending the concrete custom and usage of individuals, has been able to isolate something like a norm, so the patient work of civilization proceeds in every domain by separating human praxis from its concrete exercise and thereby creating that excess of signification over denotation that Claude Lévi-Strauss was first to recognize. In this sense, the floating signifier — this guiding concept in human sciences of the twentieth century — corresponds to the state of exception, in which the norm is in force without being applied.[29]

ℵ Tongues-Speech as Exception to Language

Tongues-speech (ecstatic religious speech, not *xenolalia*) as communication without order is in a space of exception. This exception consists in the fact that tongues-speech is, at the same time, outside and inside the language order. It traces a threshold between relation and the nonrelational, a zone of indistinction between chaos and normal language. Neither natural language nor gibberish,[30] it is the zone of indistinction in which bare language (vocal utterance) and natural lan-

---

29. Agamben, *State of Exception*, pp. 36-37.

30. Tongues-speech as a speech act effects or does something. It is also expressive. Though it is not communicative it nevertheless "says" something about "the Spirit's presence and activity within the believing community. . . . In this respect, we might say that tongues-speech is a kind of speech that functions as a *gesture*, but the kind of gesture that calls into question Husserl's exclusion of gesture from the realm of expression. Glossolalia (understood here as ecstatic religious speech), we might say, is a mode of *speech* that does not employ words (in Husserl's sense) but nevertheless is expressive." J. K. A. Smith, *Thinking in Tongues*, pp. 133-34. Italics in original.

guage constitute each other, including and excluding each other. Tongues-speech is a space of exception inhabited by bare expression. It cannot be subsumed under natural language, and it defies codification, but it simultaneously reveals formal elements of language: expression in absolute purity, and a pure potentiality to signify which is withdrawn or suspended from every actual, concrete reference.[31]

The verbal utterances of ecstatic speech are all elements of language; they belong to the set of utterances that constitute language (or *langue*). But they are not included in the sense that they cannot be re-presented in the metastructure of natural communicative languages in which all languages are counted as one term insofar as they are codified into a class of utterances (discourse) in which denotation is not (cannot be) maintained in infinite suspension. Thus, ecstatic religious language cannot be included in the whole of communicative languages of which it is a member and cannot be a member of them in which it is always already included.

Though tongues-speech is excluded from natural language in the state of exception it is not absolutely without relation to the rules of the "language game." Speaking is always a rule-governed action — albeit in the case of ecstatic language, as the philosopher James K. A. Smith has argued, it may be governed by rules "not identifiable as rules of a discernible *language*."[32] More importantly, it maintains itself with respect to the rules in the sense of the very suspension of the rules that define the normal case of discernible natural languages in its own realm of validity. As Agamben suggests, the rule of natural language applies to "the exception in no longer applying, in withdrawing from it." As he puts it, "The state of exception is thus not the chaos that precedes order but rather the situation that results from its suspension. In this sense, the exception is truly, according to its etymological root, taken *outside (ex-capere)*, and not simply excluded."[33]

The exceptional character of "speaking in tongues" can be pursued from another angle: as a potentiality that does not pass into actuality — in the Aristotelian sense of *dynamis mē energein*. Paul in 1 Corinthians 14:2-5 says that tongues can be interpreted or translated into known human language. He clearly calls for interpretation to make the speech communicative. One may then say that Paul is here gesturing toward the potentiality and actuality of ecstatic religious speech. The actuality of the translated religious speech is preceded and conditioned by the potentiality of the "unknown" religious language, but also seems to remain superordinate to it. Nonetheless, he appears to recognize the autonomous existence of the potentiality of "speaking in tongues." This "existence," this potentiality (to be or do) is capable of not passing into actuality. It can only pass into actuality by the act of choice that opens a horizon of meaning. Thus, ecstatic language on its

---

31. On language/langue see Giorgio Agamben, *Homo Sacer: Sovereign Power and Bare Life*, trans. Daniel Heller-Roazen (Stanford: Stanford University Press, 1998), p. 20.

32. J. K. A. Smith, *Thinking in Tongues*, p. 146. Italics in original.

33. Agamben, *Homo Sacer*, p. 18.

own is a potentiality that is im-potentiality *(adynamia)*. As Aristotle put it, "What is potential can both be and not be. For the same is potential as much with respect to being as to not being."[34]

For Aristotle the real question is how that which has the im-potentiality passes into actuality. The passage into act or the realization of act is possible only at the punctual determination when it sets aside its own im-potentiality, and its conditions of actuality demand that the creative actualization cannot exhaust the potentiality or destroy the im-potentiality. It is the giving of itself to itself.[35] In the same way, the ecstatic language can pass into translation (real known language) by the Spirit that gives the meaning and not by any automatic means of decoding. The potentiality of the language gives itself to itself through the power of the sovereign Spirit. Ecstatic language maintains itself in the state of exception precisely through its ability not to be, not to be translated, and can realize itself only by taking away its own potentiality not to be interpreted. And in doing this it is not preceded or determined by natural language. Presupposing nothing other than its own potentiality and doubled as both potentiality and potentiality not to be, at every moment of realization (interpretation) pure actuality is indistinguishable from pure potentiality. This is the kind of ambiguity that is characteristic of any state of exception, zone of indistinction as Agamben has taught us. And when ecstatic language is conceived in all its radicality, as we have done, then it ceases to be strictly speaking a matter of (philosophy of) language but becomes a category of ontology — potentiality and actuality are categories of being and concerns of first philosophy.[36]

Ecstatic Language as Bare and Pure Language

I want now to analyze tongues-speech as a "naked" language in order to further explore the pentecostal principle as a positive critique of the instrument logic of present-day society and religion, including pentecostalism. Tongues-speech, I suggest, is bare, pure language. The condition of its bareness and purity stands outside it. It is bare because it seems to lack the capacity of language to signify, to apply to, and to mark and map the self-world correlation. It is bare in a certain metaphorical sense — through a certain playful comparative lens that deploys Agamben's notion of *homo sacer* and turns it 180 degrees. Every person can kill the *homo*

---

34. Aristotle, *Metaphysics*, 1050b, 10. In *The Basic Works of Aristotle*, ed. Richard McKeon (New York: Random House, 1941). The quotation above uses the translation in Agamben, *Homo Sacer*, p. 45.

35. See Aristotle, *Metaphysics*, 1047a, 24-26 and *De anima*, 417b, 2-16.

36. Agamben, *Homo Sacer*, pp. 45-48.

sacer, the bare life, yet he cannot be sacrificed to the gods. Paul in 1 Corinthians 14 states that ecstatic religious language ("speaking in tongues") can be "offered" to God, but must be translated, "killed," severed from its ecstatic home. It is always exposed to death in the human realm in the sense that it is either translated immediately or instantly flees from human understanding, yet it is "sacrifice-able to God." What is captured from the godly realm is at the same time excluded and destined to be extinguished; and human verbal utterance confined in the no-man's land between communicative language and absolute gesturality, a refugee, is sacralized only through an abandonment to death. This is the bare, anonymous language that must be abandoned to die and yet belongs to God. But this abandonment, extinguishment, for Paul, creates the possibility for a re-presentation of its significance. Paul's insistence on interpretation (decoding) is illuminative about the peculiar danger of the state of exception of ecstatic speech. The suspension of the norms of usual communicability allows any gesture or utterance to potentially acquire the force of language — or rather, the force of divine message.

ℵ Translation of Tongues-Speech

I have just suggested that Paul's insistence on interpretation (decoding) casts light on the peculiar danger of the state of exception of ecstatic speech. I am here also tempted to ask: Is the translation (decoding) not an attempt to cover up a "troubling" gap too quickly? Is it not a hasty retreat from the ontological gap opened by the tongues-speech? The untranslated tongues-speech is a proto-speech, not yet actual, not yet explicit words, ambiguous, with unspecified and free-floating meaning. It is thus localizable in a primordial space between the phenomenon and noumenon. A gap separates the tongues-speech from symbolic registration, pre-ontological from the ontological (symbolically mediated), pre-synthetic imagination from synthetic understanding. According to Slavoj Žižek this kind of ontological gap is like the Hegelian "night of the world," "a momentary suspension of the positive order of reality [language]." And because of this ontological gap reality "is never a complete, self-enclosed positive order of being."[37] The gap whispers to us the void that necessarily exists in the midst of every being, every order from which springs *event,* the Badiouian truth.

What can cover this gap so we can move from tongues-speech to explicit words, translated statements? Can we be too quick to cover or prohibit it without

---

37. Slavoj Žižek, *The Ticklish Subject: The Absent Center of Political Ontology* (London: Verso, 2008), p. 69.

doing violence to subjectivity? Is this gap not "correlative with the pure void of the subject's absolute spontaneity"? Is it not in part a subject-language (à la Badiou) of the subject committed to the truth of an event?

Let us consider the issue from another angle. Translation serves the constitutive role of the exceptional. Tongues-speech is a gesture of radical negativity toward established language order. But we get the order back as mediated by the Spirit's will (the Spirit being the enabler of the translation). "The way a sovereign relates to positive laws involves the same paradox: a Sovereign compels us to respect laws precisely insofar as he is the point of the suspension of laws."[38] This act of "fulfilling" the language by simultaneously suspending and accomplishing it may well be "the violent gesture of asserting the independence of the abyssal act of free decision from its positive content."[39]

With regard to purity, it is important to note here that speaking is not a means to an end and is not evaluated in relation to the end that it is a means. (On what basis is the irruption or the use of ecstatic speech justifiable, you ask? It suggests that we do not consider the justness of the purpose of speech to evaluate the justness of the speech itself.) Ecstatic language stands as pure medium and its purity does not lie in itself but in its relation to something outside it. Every form of "conscious" speaking to God serves a purpose and the issue is, what is the proper purpose of such an act? What is the legitimate or illegitimate end it serves? Ecstatic speech is not about legitimate or illegitimate means to the ends of speaking to God but relates to the ends in a different way. It is a medium without end and "holds itself only in relation to its mediality."[40] Following Walter Benjamin, Agamben writes, "pure language is that which is not an instrument for the purpose of communication, but communication itself immediately, that is, pure and simple communication."[41]

Ecstatic language, while it exposes the limits of natural communicative language as such, exposes and severs the nexus between religiosity and ends. So at the end it is not a speech act that frames, advances, or defines any purpose, but a divine-human relationship that purely acts and manifests. Here, speaking is only a manifestation. It is a performance — and not performative. And in a certain sense, by refusing to be instrumental it ges-

38. Žižek, *The Ticklish Subject,* pp. 135-136.
39. Žižek, *The Ticklish Subject,* p. 136.
40. Agamben, *State of Exception,* p. 62.
41. Agamben, *State of Exception,* p. 62.

tures at a critique of the dominant instrumental logic that dominates organized, disciplinary religion from time immemorial. There is, ultimately,
dissolution of the relation between language and religion (spirituality, if
you like). It is a religion without its key, and it is no longer religion but life.
It is life as it is lived at the threshold of heaven.

The suspension of the rules of normal language practice that we have
just mentioned compels a thought that invokes a Kantian aesthetic judgment. The rupture of the nexus between means and ends corresponds to
an aesthetics of pure means. Ecstatic religious speech, insofar as it functions as a means, does so only subjectively — in that it causes the play of
the emotional and participatory powers of the subject. It does not function as a "fulfillment of an objective end" (since the real purpose is not to
cause this play).[42] In Kant's philosophy of judgment the notion of aesthetic object functions thusly:

> The aesthetic object is neither instrumental nor normative; it cannot be
> judged in its capacity as a means of an end or in its agreement with a
> preconceived concept of what it ought to be.[43]

This deepening of our thinking about ecstatic speech by way of the theory
of aesthetic judgment should not be construed as an aestheticization of it.
The aesthetic experience (interpretation) of tongues-speaking is not in the
form of *as if;* not a substitution of the fictional for the real utterance. "It is
not some functionality in our relation of [tongues-speech to real lan-
guage] that renders the experience of it aesthetic, but, rather, its suspension of the relation between means and ends."[44]

Based on the foregoing philosophical elaborations of tongues-
speaking, "What does it mean to act religiously, pentecostally for that matter?" It means to act aesthetically. Tongues-speaking, a pure means,
grounds the religious (spiritual) "on that moment in aesthetic judgment
when we appreciate something not because it is useful or because it fits
with our conceptual understanding of the world, but simply because we
have a relation to it, independent of its purpose."[45] This is the religious

---

42. Benjamin Morgan, "Undoing Legal Violence: Walter Benjamin's and Giorgio
Agamben's Aesthetics of Pure Means," *Journal of Law and Society* 34, no. 1 (March 2007): 48.

43. Morgan, "Undoing Legal Violence," p. 48.

44. Morgan, "Undoing Legal Violence," p. 63.

45. Morgan, "Undoing Legal Violence," p. 64.

space pentecostalism claims for itself in the name of divine encounter and for human action.

Reason and Will in the Pentecostal Principle[46]

There are other aspects of Tillich's overall theology that bear, in my opinion, unfavorably on the Protestant principle or limit how it can be appropriated in what might be called the Pentecostal Era. Take, for instance, the struggle between reason and will in his conception of God. On the one hand, the universe is guided by divine logos and therefore the orders of things are not contingent; on the other hand, the divine will is continuously active and the orders of things are contingent. God is both ground of being and abyss: all reality has its ground in God (the rational structure of reality, logos) and nonbeing, which allows for the possibility of contingent world. The two poles, which he calls form and dynamics respectively, exist in tension. The problem is that the dialectical tension is not maintained very well in his systematic, rational theology and he tilts the pole toward form. As he puts it, "being implies form. Even relative chaos has a relative form."[47]

Besides, Tillich argues in his essay "Two Types of Philosophy of Religion" that there are two conceptions of God: ontological and cosmological. In the ontological model, in which he locates himself, God is about the knowledge of truth and such knowledge is a priori rather than a posteriori. In this way, he also gives priority to reason/knowledge over experience, in spite of the substantial voluntaristic tendencies in his theology.

Tillich emphasizes the logos character of all reality. The logos of being is manifested principally in forms, and the excess in the rational structure of being is carefully guarded by the second Trinitarian principle. According to Tillich, the logos of being is "the rational word that grasps and embraces being, and in which being overcomes its hiddenness, its darkness and becomes truth and light." In other words, logos of being is the "form and structure in which meaning is manifest."[48] In spite of Tillich's emphasis on organization, we know that every structure is in continuous interplay with an excess. "System and excess are not opposites but are codependent: there

---

46. This section is inspired and informed by Mark C. Taylor, *After God*.

47. Tillich, *Systematic Theology* 3, pp. 50-51.

48. Tillich, *Protestant Era*, p. 90.

can no more be a structure apart from the supplementary excess that disrupts it than there can be an event of the disruption without the stabilizing structure it dislocates."[49]

All this emphasis on form is driven by the high value Tillich places on the logos (reason) quality of the divine and the universe and on "meaningfulness," and they betray themselves in much of his theology. This comes at the price of "checking" the endless restlessness that is in the fabric of life, which is the condition of the possibility of creative emergence.

In one of Tillich's earliest formulations of the Protestant principle, he applies it to questions of truth, ideology, and the ambiguity of all knowledge, deploying it to guard against the pretensions of knowledge.[50] Not surprisingly, then, Tillich's presentation of the Protestant principle is too much beholden to the model of God as reason, as logos. This is the idea of God's reason having priority over God's will: reason governing and determinative of will, and even "providence as the divine reason itself." The focus is on order; faith is a matter of knowledge and the telos of life is knowledge of God.

ℵ Tillich's Focus on Order

Tillich's focus on form and structure has implication for his ethics. Where is the revealing word, the logos of being in concrete situation? First, Tillich accepts that the logos of being appeared completely, full of grace and truth in Jesus the Christ. Where is the logos of being incompletely revealed in history today? Tillich believes it appears in cultural forms and functions — this is the orientation of the Protestant principle.[51] For the pentecostal principle, the appearance of the Holy Spirit as tongues of fire on each person gathered on the Day of Pentecost means that it appears (potentially) on all human beings who are in the spirit. The perspective provided by the pentecostal principle is that both individuals and cultural form and structure are equally sites for the manifestation of the logos of being, of the Spirit.

Why does Tillich principally limit the logos of being to cultural life and not include the individual lives of believers? Certainly it is partially due to his cultural context: given the general socialist temperament of post–World War I Europe it is understandable why Tillich will emphasize the common life and interpersonal and

---

49. Taylor, *After God*, p. 304.

50. Paul Tillich, "Kairos and Logos." In *The Interpretation of History* (New York: Charles Scribner's Sons, 1936/1926). See also Terrence M. O'Keeffe, "Ideology and the Protestant Principle," *Journal of the American Academy of Religion* 51, no. 2 (1983): 283-306.

51. Tillich, *Protestant Era*, p. 90.

collective consciousness as sites for the manifestation of the logos of being. By giving the cultural form and structure in which meaning is manifested priority over individual life, Tillich has — to use the words of Jürgen Moltmann in his critique of Friedrich Schleiermacher — "abolished the generic simultaneity of socialization and personalization. But the experience of sociality and the self are merely two sides of one and the same experience of life, and they come into being together and simultaneously. It is impossible to talk about priority here."[52]

There is another model of God in which God's will has priority over and is antecedent to and determinative of God's reason. God's will is not bound by reason; it is bound by nothing. This does not mean that God is irrational. It only means that God's creative and omnipotent will is the fount for both reason and unreason. God is not self-contradictory, though having the power to do what God wills God freely limits Godself. It is not that reason, order, knowledge are rejected; rather, the emphasis is that order is contingent, not necessary. Thomas Aquinas is an exemplar of the first model and William of Ockham of the second. Pentecostalism does not reject reason, but believes that God's will is unsearchable. The will of God cannot be comprehensively comprehended. Though the will of God is not completely knowable, pentecostals do not throw their arms into the air in despair. The will of God is readable through scripture, experience, and signs of the times — and even then only in part. Faith is not a search for certainty, for reason that reason cannot oppose, but believing in spite of uncertainty. (Pentecostalism affirms faith in its great ambiguity.) This is not a negative stance to reason, and it is not a negative faith as a matter of knowledge, but faith arises through the inability of the believer to fully comprehend God. Only when the subject realizes that there is nothing she can do to fathom God, to separate faith from uncertainty, does she become open to the possibilities of the creative will of God, to the unfinishedness of all existence, which are all rooted in the productive divine will which is the groundless ground of all existence.

Reason, the pentecostals insist, must begin with concrete experience rather than a priori principle. If faith is to be a matter of knowledge (and pentecostals do not reject this notion offhand), the supporting data must be a posteriori and inductive, not a priori and deductive. Pentecostals would easily agree that the structure of the world and the universe are or-

---

52. Jürgen Moltmann, *The Spirit of Life: A Universal Affirmation* (Minneapolis: Fortress, 1992), p. 225.

dered and function by reasons (rules, codes, and laws) put in place by God, but these are not themselves determined by reason, but by the productive will of God, by *potentia ordinata*. So pentecostal faith, or view of God-world interaction, includes or presupposes reason. It can never include it fully or exclude it fully.

Faith is believing on the One who can do exceedingly abundantly above all that we can ask or think. So faith, in a paraphrase of Jean-Luc Nancy's idea in another context, is always thinking, believing, and acting on the limit. The limit of believing and comprehending defines faith. Believing is always faith-ing "about the incomprehensible — about this incomprehensible that 'belongs' to every comprehending, as its own limit."[53] This willingness to presume something that it cannot fully assimilate, the existence of this aporia, is the condition of the possibility for the *novum*. And it is also the audacity and extravagance of the pentecostal faith.

This is an important insight for transforming Tillich's Protestant principle toward the pentecostal principle. This call for revision should not be construed to mean that theological voluntarism is not present in Tillich's thought. The only problem is that Tillich never formulates the idea that God (Spirit) is always active, willing, and acting wherever, whenever, and however God wills. Pentecostals do not limit the freedom of God. The freedom of the Holy Spirit (the power of creation, the dynamic power of all of reality) to rework and advance the structures of sociality and to re-create personal lives is premised on the abyss of freedom.

The pentecostal principle does not really negate the Protestant principle; it transforms it, transcending and including it in a creative advance. The Protestant principle properly understood and not made identical with logos, form is the dynamics in all existence, the restlessness of life, the drive toward actualization. So in the age-old tension in Western theological and philosophical development — that between will and reason, the Protestant principle fits well with the side of "will" and this much is clear from Tillich's account of it. But then he ignored his own insights and overemphasized reason, logos. The pentecostal principle is the "justification" of the Protestant principle; it is that through which Protestantism "meets its finite limits and also receives its infinite rights."[54] It is the Protestant principle expressing itself fully, expressing its own intrinsic character.

53. Jean-Luc Nancy, *The Experience of Freedom*, trans. Bridget McDonald (Stanford: Stanford University Press, 1993), p. 54.
54. Tillich, *Protestant Era*, p. 14.

Political Theology and the Pentecostal Principle

Tillich's conception of the Protestant principle is linked to the possibility of an interruptive (irruptive) sovereign power. The Protestant principle is the dynamic that irrupts in the normal state of affairs to reintroduce the figure of sovereign power from an unspoilable realm of the world. But the essential character of the pentecostal principle lies as the actualization of potentialities *emergently given* within the infinite fabric of "en-spirited" life.[55]

By way of political theology, how do we interpret this dimension of the Protestant principle? The interruptive sovereignty that steps in comes as a kind of *katechon* (arresting force) to control lawlessness, consequences of demonic behavior, and chaos from below. The idea of an interruptive principle is ever concerned with power, risk, sinfulness, or idolatry from people.

And against the backcloth of the doctrine of justification by faith, the irruptive divine sovereignty marks forgiveness in that special Arendtian sense: here the consequences of action go no further.[56] To the contrary, the pentecostal principle is about promises (still in the Arendtian sense). It represents or points to the island of possibilities in the ocean of uncertainty. Life is always threatened by nonbeing (hence anxiety), by irruptive state (sovereign) power making exceptional decision or by potentiality that wants to remain im-potentiality, but there is always hope (courage) for emergent creativity, for inherent dynamism toward concretion of possibilities. The pentecostal principle is a miracle of realizing promises, the expectation of the new, or the realization of the "ontological prophecy" that every existent demands its own proper possibilities[57] or drives beyond itself.

It is all about openness to the unfinishedness of life and the emergence of new alternatives. In the next chapter, we will explore nature's emergence to aid our thinking on politics and to rethink today's management orientation of politics. The discussion pushes the management orientation of pol-

55. This paragraph develops from reading Ruth Marshall, "The Sovereignty of Miracles: Pentecostal Political Theology in Nigeria," *Constellations* 17, no. 2 (2010): 213-14. I thank her for drawing my attention to this aspect of her work.

56. Hannah Arendt, *The Human Condition* (Chicago: University of Chicago Press, 1958), pp. 220-47.

57. Giorgio Agamben, *The Time That Remains: A Commentary on the Letter to the Romans*, trans. Patricia Dailey (Stanford: Stanford University Press, 2005), p. 39.

itics to incorporate the management of novelty and calls for a new ethics that is in line with the pentecostal principle. This is an ethics where central focus is not on code; rather its accent is placed on the processes of actualization of potentialities. The goal of politics is the creation of possibilities for all citizens to participate in the *polis* and to realize their potentialities and in so doing enable the community to realize its potentialities for the common good and for human flourishing. The accomplishment of this "miracle" is placed within the context of the prophetic spirit (and later in chapter 4 within the broader context of the pentecostal spirit). The prophetic spirit as a way of being, as an *orientation* to social existence is the context of possibility in which this miracle may be experienced.

2 Emergence and Ethics

The Ethos of Pneumatological Methodology

In this chapter I wish to engage the pentecostal principle with the science of emergence. To do so I will connect it to four methodological "moments" that can serve as guides for ethical thinking in a new spirit. The first of these moments entails an analysis of the biology of emergence as an explanatory model to help us think about social relations and how the process of actualizing potentialities works in human societies. Here, our principal task is to convert the key insights of the paradigm into ethical arguments, in order to show that social systems and practices are experimental, reversible, contingent, and provisional, rather than necessary or permanent. The second moment is an analysis of the orientation that promotes an ethical stance toward dealing with the unclosed and undisclosed becoming of all systems and the obstacles that may prevent them from serving higher levels of human flourishing. We call this orientation the prophetic spirit; it works by analyzing and contesting the logics of power, injustice, and domination — by laying bare the concrete and complex ways persons are excluded from living according to the best of themselves, and by working for the realization of improved possibilities of existence. These two moments I will treat in the section of this chapter titled "Emergence."

The third moment involves an analysis and recognition of the limits of the actualization process as it plays out in concrete life against the wall of human dignity. These limits constitute the structural basis of the actualization process, negating, preserving, and transforming the mode of operation of the pentecostal principle in human socialities. The deployment of emergence as an ethical paradigm also brings ethical thought to the limits

71

of regnant epistemological theories since Kant. I consider this moment in the section called "The Limit of Ethics." The final moment, explored below as "Ethics as an Unended Mode of Action", is a call for a playful relation to ethical codes as a way of counteracting their effect on freedom, the capacity to initiate something new, that is, play that deactivates and renders the codes inoperative, not by negating and annihilating them, but by fulfilling and recapitulating them in the figure of love.[1] What are our ethical possibilities if codes become (are treated as) "pure means" rather than means to an end? How can ethics as pure means help us to reclaim a sphere of action that is authentic — that is, begun without predetermined ends in mind — without destroying the normative as such?

As a pure means, emergence is an "unended" action or process. It creates a space for something to happen, without predetermining what that will be. Appropriating the language of Giorgio Agamben, it is a means without finality, to render visible a means as such, mediating nothing but its own mediality. Or, we might argue that it has "purposiveness without purpose," or is an end in itself like the arts. Yet this way of putting it still leaves emergence in the realm of ends, not pure means. Many theologians and philosophers, unlike most scientists, find it difficult to think of emergence as a pure means, pure mediality, pure medium, noninstrumental means, means without an end. Is there a co-promising position between these two groups? One possibility, a Benjaminian solution, would involve not locating the means with the end in the same process, but rather locating purpose in a higher realm (the region of the unknowable, the zone of *invisible* ends) so that it appears as means without ends to ordinary observers.[2] Yet this only takes us to an aporia: because emergence's ends are invisible it is impossible to ethically analyze them within the theological-ethical framework that is based on a system of ends, and it is this framework that leads its adherents to deny the pure mediality of emergence in the first place.

When writing this book, I initially thought that the preceding paragraph would obviate the need to plunge into the theological language of

---

1. Here I am alluding to Agamben's description of how Paul under the messianic power deactivated the laws of Judaism and fulfilled them as Christian love. See Giorgio Agamben, *The Time That Remains: A Commentary on the Letter to the Romans,* trans. Patricia Dailey (Stanford: Stanford University Press, 2005), pp. 97, 108.

2. Walter Benjamin, "Critique of Violence," in *Selected Writings,* vol. 1, ed. Marcus Bullock and Michael Jennings, trans. Edmund Jephcott (Cambridge, MA: Harvard University Press, 1996).

teleology. But in the thinking process, the dialogue between me and my-self, one part (let us call it *thinking ego*) advised that I state the "teleological character" of the pentecostal principle. It asked: What is the teleological character of emergence and its possible implications for the pentecostal principle? Another part *(writing ego)* responded: How can I engage the language of teleology without betraying emergence as a pure means?

Let me attempt to respond to these questions by stating that emergence is an intelligible facticity. To emerge is to mean, and if the world or existence is a whole, then this or that emergent form is its part and all parts have their meanings in relation to that whole. As each part accrues meaning the initial sense of the whole is also transformed. Facticity and intelligibility (sense) form a pair. There is a gap between the two. As finite human beings our knowledge of this gap is *intuitus derivatus* (as knowledge is only knowledge of something), and thus in thinking of the telos of emergence we easily reach the limit of knowledge. We are confounded by the fact of emergence. What overall purpose can it possibly serve, if any? We wonder at the phenomenon of emergence. Since it is not reducible to its earlier parts, emergence in a very crude sense has the ring of the enigma of *creatio ex nihilo*. This wonder is related to the gap. But for God for whom knowing and being coincide, whose mode of knowing is *intuitus originarius*, there is no such gap; no gap between what is thought and what is — for knowing requires no object beyond the self. God gives meaning and is the limit of meaning.[3] We are going to argue that the divine is the limit of emergence and emergence is purposeful in the experience of this limit as it opens up new forms of relations.

What emergence creates is relation, the groundless ground of exis-tence of being ex-posed, of being with others. And the meaning or ques-tion of teleology has become the question of the limit of being-with and being together. For emergence as a pure means, meaning begins where purpose at best is not even pure purpose but where purpose comes apart as it asymptotically approaches its infinite limit (divine depths, milieu). To understand the telos of emergence we have to think of telos differently. Purpose is not the limit (telos, end) of emergence, but the limit of emer-gence is divine. In other words, emergence is purposeful in the experience of its limits. Emergence is a specific experience of the void, the nothing-ness which opened from the moments of creation and pro-creation. Emer-

---

3. This presentation is inspired by Anne O'Byrne, *Natality and Finitude* (Bloomington: Indiana University Press, 2010), pp. 119-23.

gence is not *creatio ex nihilo,* for the *ex* happens exactly in the void. The natal activity of emergence is posited by nothing. This is the nothing, the indetermination that is between every existent and the other, which passes into every relation and makes way for the new. This nothing is the fount of possibility.

What this means is that the question of telos is ultimately a question of priority of possibility. And D. Lyle Dabney has argued that a focus on "priority of possibility" is an orientation to the work of the Holy Spirit and is the starting point for theology. The theology of the third article is about the Spirit of God that harbors and undergirds the *possibility* that brings the real into emergent being.[4] With such a focus on possibility resources for addressing the theological-ethical issues of today are sought not in comprehensive, totalizing conceptualities but rather in "'emergent' processes and realities — novel, unexpected and unforeseeable events and developments which represent new possibilities of understanding and creating continuity within the profoundly fragmented and fragmenting world in which we find ourselves."[5]

Now let us link these insights to a quite different perspective on how to reason about the issue at hand. The experience of emergence as a specific experience of the void is inseparable from the coinherence of the quality, facticity, and the very tendency (creativity) of emergence. Following the path of Charles Sanders Peirce puts us on a different trajectory toward deciphering the telos of emergence, having to hold that it is to be empirically discerned and fallibilistically constructed. More importantly, it puts us on a theological trajectory of thought toward the teleology of emergence.

What certain qualities, facts, and laws (tendencies, generalities) does emergence convey to the Christian believer? Or, put differently, what would the *pneumatological imagination*[6] alert us to with regard to emergence? With the pneumatological imagination, the believer does not just engage with emergence as a biological event but also as means of relating to a deeper world of meaning and significance. This concession means that

4. D. Lyle Dabney, "The Nature of the Spirit: Creation as a Premonition of God," in *Starting with the Spirit: The Task of Theology Today,* ed. Stephen Pickard and Gordon Preece (Hindmarsh: Australian Theological Forum, 2001), p. 101.

5. D. Lyle Dabney, "Starting with the Spirit: Why the Last Should Be the First," in *Starting with the Spirit,* p. 10.

6. Amos Yong, *Spirit-Word-Community: Theological Hermeneutics in Trinitarian Perspective* (Eugene, OR: Wipf and Stock, 2002), pp. 200-217.

the telos is best sought semiotically (epistemologically) rather than metaphysically-ontologically. When fully pressed into service, the pneumatological imagination reaches further to theological evaluation (theological semiotic) of the telos of emergence. The question that arises now is this: how does emergence as a sign mediate the human encounter with (and knowledge of) God? It simultaneously conceals and discloses the work of God. It is in the nature of theological semiotics to be both cataphatic and apophatic — hence all talks about telos, end, finality is open-ended, fallibilistic, and radically provisional.

Thus, teleology (if we are still pressed to identify it) will not refer to any final cause or fixed essence. The laws of nature are regarded as habitual, dynamic, and general in Peirce's sense of them. This perspective allows us to perceive them as possibilities and tendencies opened to interactions between creaturely freedom and the messianic now (eschatological presence of God, if you like) through the dynamic relations of reality that is the Holy Spirit.[7] Alternatively, the perspective allows us to concur with Simon Conway Morris that some form of order ("convergence") is possible in the developmental process, some limited and channeled way of developing certain properties. Morris's idea of contingency does not undermine our own emphasis on contingency as his idea does not deny huge diversity and inevitability of contingency.[8]

The thinking ego also asked about the implications of the teleological character of emergence for the pentecostal principle. The understanding of the teleology presented in the preceding paragraphs requires us to keep all ethical judgments and theological interpretations of scientific phenomena aware of their limitations and their fallibility. This idea of teleology may provoke a concern that emergence-derived ethics is not bound by any order or directionality as usually necessitated by the safe and reliable grammar of traditional and *traditioning* theological discourse. The avoidance of the language of fixed essence or purpose should not be construed to mean that there would be arbitrariness in the application of the pentecostal principle to ethical methodology or issues. The emphasis of pentecostals on *orthopathos* (à la Samuel Solivan[9]) — that is, the focus on the

7. Amos Yong, *Spirit of Creation: Modern Science and Divine Action in the Pentecostal-Charismatic Imagination* (Grand Rapids: Eerdmans, 2011).

8. Simon Conway Morris, *Life's Solution: Inevitable Humans in a Lonely Universe* (Cambridge: Cambridge University Press, 2003), pp. 13-14.

9. Samuel Solivan, *The Spirit, Pathos, and Liberation: Toward an Hispanic Pentecostal Theology* (Sheffield: Sheffield Academic Press, 1998).

holiness of God, the eschatological orientation of divine-human relationship, the "liberating passion" of the Holy Spirit toward transformation of all suffering into a joyful play with God — upholds the inclination of the pentecostal principle toward human flourishing.

Rather than entailing arbitrariness in the application of the pentecostal principle, what the austere notion of "teleology" entails is the pneumatological imagination that can interpret "living in the Spirit" as the divine-human relationship that is "open to the ongoing encounter with novelty and surprise — no a priori limitations can or should be imposed on what life in the Spirit might bring about."[10] From a methodological perspective, the intersection of the pentecostal principle and the "teleology" of emergence can be described as imagination at play. Emergence as pure means directs our attention away from submitting the ideal of the pentecostal principle to the routinization of performance, purpose, order, and meaning that is intrinsic to the *given world*. The pneumatological imagination calls for transfer of all reality into the play of the Holy Spirit who is manifesting in the concrete, personal, and particular contexts and moments of human existence. This is a play that transforms and assimilates the particular purposes of the current situations, the given performative trajectory of our current world into freely evolving potentialities.

Emergence

When I use the term "emergence" in this chapter, I will be referring to novel properties, traits arising from a given set of matter in the right sort of organized complexity. Such properties are novel not only because they cannot be found at lower levels of complexity, but also because they cannot be predicted from the interactions between preexisting elements or parts. Emergence names the process whereby the "underivable"[11] can be birthed amid many derivable conditions. As a proposition of science, it also expresses an ethos, an orientation to existential relationships and the existentially meaningful in the here and now.

A philosophy of emergence in social consciousness may lead to radical

---

10. Yong, *Spirit-Word-Community*, p. 160.

11. Emergence as I understand it reminds me of Paul Tillich's concept of the kairos and "the underivable." See his *Systematic Theology,* Volume 3: *Life and the Spirit; History and the Kingdom of God* (Chicago: University of Chicago Press, 1963), p. 324.

changes in human sociality and social ethics. Emergentist philosophy calls forth a world that is open to novelty, uncertainty, disruption, and chance more than ever before. It promises to move morality further along the path of inclusiveness and universalism — and also to move it toward fundamentalism, exclusion, and parochialism. Successful dealing with the emergentist world may require a struggle of the institutions of governance against their own tendency to circumscribe the possibilities open to the governed, or to cover up the knowledge of their own temporality. Likewise, the response or governance patterns of emergence are diverse, and full of ambiguities and tensions. One response pattern we might call the draconian or belligerent type. In such a pattern, a society faced with perceived threats in an uncertain environment seeks to buy time to respond to these threats by calling for large-scale sacrifice and the implementation of draconian measures. It may also try to restore vigor and harmony through the removal of agents deemed to be sapping the strength of the society.[12] It may deem it necessary to purify the country of the pollution of some internal elements. The hope is that by taking these measures the imagined destructions will pass overhead and be visited on other societies. Alternatively, systems that feel threatened by the forces of the present and future may choose to nibble on the pleasures of their past adaptations and successes. These systems retry the old ways of damming the flood of changes, possibly blaming the "usual suspects" or turning against some segments of society, the enemies within.

In this section relating to the first and second methodological moments we will examine two aspects of the connection between emergence and ethics. My goal is to give an ethical account of these connections and gesture toward them as a complex site for diverse ethicists' engagements with the biological and philosophical interpretations of emergence. We will explore how to convert the biological paradigm of emergence into a series of ethical arguments. The conversion will enable us to describe in social-scientific language the social world which emergence suggests to us. Then we will outline a form of social ethics that is necessary for citizens to cope with the character of such a social world. My first task in conceptualizing or constructing the connections between emergence and ethics is to imaginatively construct a "model" of an emergentist social world. This is a community that is conscious of and open to novelty, op-

---

12. Richard Fenn, *The End of Time: Religion, Ritual, and the Forging of the Soul* (Cleveland: Pilgrim Press, 1997), pp. 1-9.

portunity, uncertainty, disruption, and chance that the pentecostal principle demands of all forms of sociality. For I believe such a "model" can help us to rigorously investigate the interplay between the pentecostal principle and ethics.

A Model of an Emergentist Social World

An emergentist world is at its core a world of contingency plus possibilities.[13] The phenomenon of emergence presents us with pure possibilities — the *novum* is always becoming. Emergence carries with it the notion that in every combination of elements there is a *not-yet* which names "both a surplus and a remainder over what-has-become."[14] This promise of becoming comes at the cost of contingency. The animating power or thrust of emergence "dwells in the region of the not-yet, a place where entrance and, above all, final content are marked by an enduring indeterminacy."[15] The sheer fact that some thing or process not originally present in the constituting parts of a system can surface means that matter or any system contains "an immanent reference to a not-yet beyond" and this obliges us to think of human interactions in a new way. It means that nothing is necessary or inevitable or foreordained.[16] When no one knows the full range of possibilities that exists in any social setting there is no way to know ahead of time what is inevitable, foreordained, or even necessary. Any possibility that emerges might not have emerged. Ethics in this scenario is a game of contingency. According to Niklas Luhmann, "this concept results from excluding necessity and impossibility. Something is contingent insofar as it is neither necessary nor impossible; it is just what it is

13. For a discussion of the interplay of contingency and possibility, see J. Wentzel van Huyssteen, *Alone in the World? Human Consciousness in Science and Theology* (Grand Rapids: Eerdmans, 2006), pp. 54-56.

14. Ben Anderson, "'Transcending without Transcendence': Utopianism and an Ethos of Hope," *Antipode* 38, no. 4 (2006): 696.

15. Ernst Bloch, *Literary Essays*, trans. Andrew Joron (Stanford: Stanford University Press, 1998), p. 69.

16. We must be careful to note Simon Conway Morris's concern and argument for convergence here. He argues, contra Stephen Jay Gould, that some form of order is possible in the developmental process, some limited and channeled ways of developing certain properties. The idea of convergence does not undermine our emphasis on contingency as Morris's idea does not deny huge diversity and inevitability of contingency. See Morris, *Life's Solution*, pp. 13-14.

(or was or will be), though it could be otherwise."[17] Ethics, like life, is in "phase space." According to J. Wentzel van Huyssteen,

> Phase space is an image for the fact that every event that does happen is surrounded by a ghostly halo of nearby events that did not happen but could have. Phase spaces are large, since they comprehend a wide range of all possibilities.[18]

This openness leaves open the prospect of ethics either moving toward embrace of the other and inclusiveness, or toward fear that fuels exclusion, draconian measures, and the removal of all possible limits to the administration of terror. As sociologist of religion Richard Fenn puts it, "There is an understandable terror that comes from knowing that one is operating in a field of possibilities that is open; no one knows what the sum of these possibilities may be, let alone which of them might be chosen by the other players in the game."[19] With so many possibilities, complexity, and an intensely competitive environment, the person or system is always at the margins of a breakout of new worlds and a breakthrough into a new world. And at the margins time is always running out. No system is in a position of sufficient power over events to have time on its side. At the margins creativity is also straining to burst forth in the form of emergent qualities.

The emergentist philosophy represents a sensitivity to matter as being and becoming. Its orientation is utopological, not in the sense of discovering a blueprint for an elsewhere or elsewhen, but as a dynamic, open "utopia" of *else-be*. This is utopia in the sense of an acknowledgement of unfinishedness of every state, being, or totality. It is an expression of abundance. This dynamic, open-ended conception of utopia rejects transcendence and immanence. Its systems are self-made and self-referential. It rejects immanence not from the point of view that there is no immanent reference to the not-yet, but in the sense that there is immanent force or vitality in the pre-existing components or subsystems of a system to lead to the higher level. Though this form is always present, it is not easy to predict when a new, emergent form will arise. Emergent form comes into being when it comes into being, that is, when its parts com-

---

17. Niklas Luhmann, *Social Systems* (Stanford: Stanford University Press, 1995), p. 106.

18. Van Huyssteen, *Alone in the World?* p. 56, citing Ian Stewart, *Life's Other Secret: The New Mathematics of the Living World* (New York: Wiley, 1998).

19. Richard Fenn, *Time Exposure: The Personal Experience of Time in Secular Societies* (Oxford: Oxford University Press, 2001), p. 18.

bine in the right sort of complexity. Emergence stands at the edge of every togetherness or at the possibility of combinations of systems.

In the lights of the philosophy of emergence the world is experimental, unfinished; it is in process and is a process. Emergence is a phenomenon that takes place in process when elements and components come together. The fact that complexity can arise from simple elements simply calls our attention to this: every set of relations or systems is a being that is not yet "given," only a *transcendere*. Bloch explains it this way:

> This Not-Yet is of course not such that, for example, in the atom or in the sub-atomic 'differentials' of matter everything which comes out later or will come out later already existed according to its 'disposition' in reduced form, as if *encapsulated*. Such a backward interpretation of the Not-Yet would suppress or fail to understand precisely the dialectical leap into the New. Just as self-evidently, there is in the dialectical tendency-latency, open to the Novum, of material process no *preordered*, i.e., likewise finally posited purpose in the style of the old teleology, let alone a teleology mythologically guided from above.[20]

Here lies the hope, or rather the ethos of hope, in the philosophy of emergence. Keep in mind that emergence by definition carries the promise that if elements are synchronous in time and space there could be transition to a higher stage of complexity or consciousness, new modes of and levels of operations, functions, and behavior. This is a continuous process. As van Huyssteen puts it,

> The emergence of new phenomena at different levels of scale and organizational complexity in nature necessarily entails the emergence of new processes and laws at these levels. . . . New products and processes constantly develop from earlier modes of organization, bringing new orders of structure into being.[21]

The fundament of the process means that every combination or sychronicity cannot be completed; yet we as humans must strive to complete it by rearranging the elements or parts. It is hope in movement. Humans can and do actually use their self-aware minds to creatively explore

---

20. Ernst Bloch, *The Principle of Hope*, vol. 3 (Cambridge, MA: MIT Press, 1986), p. 1373.
21. Van Huyssteen, *Alone in the World?* pp. 48-49.

the phase spaces of their ethical landscape and home in on the regions of the phase spaces where better forms of inclusion and equity could happen. To have this hope that every arrangement can transition to a novelty that creates hitherto nonexistent properties as well as robust space for cooperation is to have an ethical practice. This is so because emergence "provides the measure to judge life [social systems] in the name of what exceeds life [social systems]."[22] Thus, if properly handled, emergence can serve as framework to expose the ambiguities which are present in the sociological character of society and to show all that is driving it away from transcending itself. The theological ethicist in a transversal dialogue with the sciences may use it as "prophetic" move to bring social system under the unambiguous life of the Spirit by answering the questions implied in the ambiguities through justice demanded in the name of God.[23] To ask for justice in the name of emergence is not a call to impose one kind of scientific-philosophical worldview on the rest of society. It is, rather, an expression for the expectation of the new, the not-yet. This expectation translates into two ideas: a conception and realization of society and humanity in which hindrances to venturing beyond the given have been removed. Second, it is to criticize the current socioeconomic arrangement not by the standards of present actuality or some social ideal, but according to justice which is inspired by emergence and which lies beyond all forms.[24]

It appears we are already in the emergentist world. "Empire" as described by Michael Hardt and Antonio Negri[25] does not present us with a final authority to judge and control the decisions of all players in the system. It presents us with a radical openness. No nation-state is sure that what it knows about the players in the global system at any given moment represents the full range of possibilities in its interaction with them. In the face of this uncertainty and with no foreordained principles of selection of actions, a nation-state may find itself acting with a great deal of anxiety. The nation-state may only be acting to reduce the range of possibilities, to limit its exposure to the uncertainties presented by infinite possibilities. We can see an example of this anxiety in the rhetoric of former U.S. President George W. Bush. For Bush, the openness of the globalizing process brought terrorism to America's doorstep, resulting in a perceived need to

22. Anderson, "'Transcending without Transcendence,'" p. 702.

23. Paul Tillich, *Political Expectation* (New York: Harper and Row, 1971).

24. Tillich, *Political Expectation*, pp. 10-39.

25. Michael Hardt and Antonio Negri, *Empire* (Cambridge, MA: Harvard University Press, 2000).

conduct a wide-ranging "War on Terror" lest terrorists strike within the United States again. Such fear-based attempts to control or limit possibility are not necessarily the best responses, either for nations or for individuals. A better alternative in the face of radical contingency is the capability to boldly imagine and rigorously critique new theories. The world of emergence "requires a social character that is correspondingly open to high levels of ambiguity, existential tension"[26] and enhancement of personal responsibility to create open spaces for challenging forms of bondage to old authorities and for imagining other possibilities.

The philosophy and the implied ethics of emergence in the sense we have laid out are well suited to express both continuity with other social ethics and a new paradigm in ethical reasoning. There is something familiar about it when it is associated with other philosophies and paradigms that address the complexity and indeterminacy in life and self-referential systems. Yet there is also something novel about it. Emergence is a process of transfiguration that offers us a new way to think about the relation between complex wholes and their parts. Thus for every ethical ordering that may stand before us either in ignominy or glory the notion of emergence attunes us to anticipate new possibilities. A crucial task of ethics in light of this notion of emergence becomes that of raising the specter of prophetic spirit amidst the citizenry to enable it to deal with the unclosed and undisclosed becoming of all systems and combinations that may confront it in the future.[27]

In the next section I will attempt to show how to convert emergence as a biological paradigm or explanatory model into a series of ethical arguments. Then we will address the contingency portion of emergence (as contingency plus possibilities) in a *transversal* dialogue. It is germane to mention, as van Huyssteen has argued, that there is no clear philosophical blueprint or timeless recipe for doing transversal dialogue. We can only argue from a specific disciplinary tradition while at the same time pursuing overlapping concerns in other disciplines. He states that "because of the multidimensional, transversal nature of human rationality, we are enabled to enter the pluralist, interdisciplinary conversations with our full personal convictions intact; at the same time, we are theoretically empowered to

---

26. Fenn, *Time Exposure*, pp. 4-5.

27. "Prophetic spirit is a way of being that is always at work broadening and deepening the horizon of our lives and, in the process, giving rise to ever new awareness of breadth and depth in our understanding of being." See Mark L. Taylor, *Religion, Politics, and the Christian Right: Post 9/11 Powers and American Empire* (Minneapolis: Fortress, 2005), p. 97.

step beyond the limitations and boundaries of our contexts, traditions, and disciplines."[28]

Emergence: From Biological Paradigm to Ethical Framework

Emergence, as I have suggested, is a mode of relation with a complex, indeterminate unclosed world where potentialities and possibilities always exceed the what-has-become.[29] Once viewed as a mode of relation rather than just an analytical framework for explanatory-diagnostic exercise it appears to point individuals to ways in which they could learn to "affect and be affected by the 'surplus-giving relations and the qualitative excess of liveliness overspilling every determinate expression.'"[30] This is the perspective that informs how we are going to segue from the amoral, scientific concept of emergence into the social-ethical milieu which enacts moral obligations. How should we then approach, philosophize, or theologize about ethics given what we now know about emergence? In general, theologians who have worked on emergence have approached it as an explanatory framework against the physicalism-dualism dichotomy in interpreting the world. But emergence can offer us a paradigm to think about social relations if it is turned into a series of ethical arguments. Emergence is a paradigm uniquely suited to address the uncertainties of modern social life in an open, globalizing world and to inform an ethical theory on adaptation to complexity.

The starting point for turning the philosophy of emergence into a series of ethical arguments is to note the aspects of the philosophical position of emergence that could inform ethical theories. First, the philosophical position of emergence posits that systems are hugely *unpredictable*. In fact, at the core of one of the leading emergentist philosopher's definition of the subject matter is unpredictability. Philip Clayton maintains that "emergence is the view that new and unpredictable phenomena are naturally produced by interactions in nature; that these new structures, organisms, and ideas are not reducible to the subsystems on which they depend, and that the newly evolved realities in turn exercise a causal influence on the parts out of which they arose."[31]

28. Van Huyssteen, *Alone in the World?* p. 41.
29. Anderson, "'Transcending without Transcendence,'" p. 704.
30. Anderson, "'Transcending without Transcendence,'" p. 706.
31. Philip Clayton, *Mind and Emergence: From Quantum to Consciousness* (Oxford: Oxford University Press, 2004), p. vi.

Second, emergence, understood as a philosophical position, questions the whole method of explaining events or phenomena in terms of initial conditions, constituent parts, and underlying laws. The import of this is that emergence holds a crucial key to understanding creativity and the adaptive process of social systems and to the wide variety of qualities and capabilities that are producible. One possible ethical focus is precisely this *openness* of social systems or relations, their emergent freedom, their lack of specific predetermination, which may produce selective pressure toward inclusiveness and universalism in ethics. The philosophical position of emergence forces on us the consideration that our social relations are made for and constituted by this emergent freedom. And if we follow Mark Heim in his arguments, we would even state that our human nature or the image of God is an emergent dynamic.[32] In this brave new world of emergence, ethics may not go well with predetermined prescriptive codes but must function like open-source software development, whose only requirements are sensitivity to feedback from all agents in any given environment and the capacity to recognize immediately useful patterns. These patterns often have short life spans because the feedback from all agents causes the system to behave differently, making it possible for the whole nature of the system to become different very quickly.

What is the implication of this for social systems? What is at stake when the development of social systems mimics that of open source software? It means that there is no leader to follow, no authority to save us from the ravages of the passage of time. We are all exposed to uncertainty and burdens of the passage of time without the benefits of institutions that can claim some transcendent or teleological role. Like the swarm of "nano-particles" Michael Crichton describes in his 2002 novel *Prey*,[33] we have to build our ethical castles without an apparent leader, without a central control agency. Life in an emergent world may well be nasty, brutish, and short — yet it may also be sweet and liberating. It is sweet and liberating because as Luhmann describes it, in a contingent world's social system "no preordained value consensus is needed . . . and when no value consensus exists, no one can thereby invent it."[34]

Third, if nothing is given or necessary because there is no transcen-

---

32. Mark Heim, "A Cross-Section of Sin: The Mimetic Character of Human Nature in Biological and Theological Perspective," in *Evolution and Ethics: Human Morality in Biological and Religious Perspective*, ed. Philip Clayton (Grand Rapids: Eerdmans, 2004), pp. 255-72.

33. Michael Crichton, *Prey* (New York: Avon Books, 2002).

34. Luhmann, *Social Systems*, p. 105.

dental force outside the system of interactions, because it is a series of relationships in which it is yet to be seen what new possibilities could come out, then emergentism is existentialist in orientation. Fourth, although an emergent form in its current state may appear to be a completion of some latent process, the past never prefigures the present and the emergent form is not the result of a prior part or element in the system at work. It is born by a self-referential and self-organizing process and as such should not be seen as completing the work of any development. It is true that the constituent parts are historical, but it is truer to say they have no historical preference in the sense of every new event being pre-coded in the activities of the past or being an ingredient of predetermined plan. This understanding puts the idea of *novum* at the center of the theory of emergence.

Fifth, an emergent form is not a mirror of any one of its individual parts. By definition, no one part can be magnified to the collective function or reality represented by the emergent form. Thus no part in a system, no single viewpoint, position, or way of life in a collection can be privileged or placed at an advantage over all others. An emergent form is not reducible to the constituent parts on which it supervenes. It privileges all at the same time.

Sixth, if the future is unpredictable yet full of possibilities and there is no collective destination for all in the system, and there is no allegiance or attachment to the past, then there could be "tense expectation" for a "propitious moment" in the here and now. The ancient Greek god of opportunity, Kairos, is at play here and is forever searching for "the genius of the decisive moment."[35] All this suggests that emergentist ethics may have to respond to present-oriented utopianism in large-scale social systems.

Economists deal with uncertainty by collapsing the future into the present through the discounted cashflow valuation technique. As one economist has put it, "If the future can be collapsed into the present so effortlessly by reducing uncertainty to risk, long-term issues and 'anxieties' of regeneration, conservation and stability are possibly avoided."[36] As I suggested above, in their quest for control over the future, governments and politicians may attempt self-debilitating draconian measures and warfare to quickly rein in the range of possibilities. Ethicists have no such re-

---

35. Karl Mannheim, *Ideology and Utopia* (London: Routledge & Kegan Paul, 1936), pp. 195, 198, quoted in Jocelyn Pixley, *Emotions in Finance: Distrust and Uncertainty in Global Markets* (Cambridge: Cambridge University Press, 2004), p. 170.

36. Pixley, *Emotions in Finance*, p. 171.

course, since emotions and possibilities are (or should be) viewed as endogenous in the highly future-oriented emergent world.[37] Rather, their option is to exploit the openness that emergence entails and engenders in order to enable catholic inclusiveness and to question the dominant and domineering structures of power that oppose freedom and justice. The power of emergence may be considered a transformative force that transgresses all boundaries as it intensifies and complexifies organic (social) life and connections.

If our interpretation of emergentist world philosophy as creativity that is ever straining toward openness, the realm of new possibilities, and tipping over to touch the "front" or "horizon" is essentially correct, then it means that social ethics must aim to prepare citizens to deal with a world of increasing complexity, openness, possibilities, and uncertainty. The fundaments of the organization of society should lead to intensification of possibilities and potentialities at all levels as we deal with uncertainty while holding on to the expectation of new emergent qualities at any moment. This requires a new ethos that embodies hope and a prophetic expectation. On one hand, such a commitment to an emergentist worldview requires "an ethos that embodies an inventive, but evaluative, relation with the world that trusts that potentialities or possibilities exceed what has become"[38] in the organization of society, the distribution of its rewards, and its response to crises. On the other, such commitment obliges us to embrace the prophetic spirit. We need a citizenry that can sense the unprecedented, can identify opportunities and threats, and craft the appropriate responses rooted in their creative and prophetic power.[39] We need to fashion an ethics that will enable individuals to cope with emergence, to rely on the spirit rather than on rules, archaic traditions, and predetermined ethical codes for navigating what is and what must be a bewildering world.

The ethical task is to formulate norms that will not stifle the impulses of cooperation while resisting the exclusionary tendencies that are built into it. Against such exclusionary tendencies, we need to develop and nurture what Mark Lewis Taylor calls the prophetic spirit, "a way of being that

37. An ethics of caution is the one way of coping with the uncertain future. As Pixley puts it, "as caution is inherently an emotion of a long-term view, it leans to ethical justice. . . . [C]aution and humble acknowledgement of organizational (human) frailties is desirable and not impossible, however unpredictable." See Pixley, *Emotions in Finance*, p. 189.

38. Anderson, "'Transcending without Transcendence,'" p. 704.

39. As Hardt and Negri ask, "Don't the necessary weapons reside precisely within the creative and prophetic power of the multitude?" See *Empire*, p. 65.

broadens and deepens relationality"[40] and can "stir up in us the courage to care and empower us to change our lives and our historical circumstances."[41] This spirit lives and operates in communities of social practice that embody the viewpoints and values of justice.

Yet is it contradictory to introduce the notion of a prophetic spirit into a discourse on emergence? There are four possible responses to this challenge. The obvious one is that I am a Christian ethicist and not a scientist and it should be expected that I will make the necessary move to inject one of the subject matters of my discipline into the discourse in order to enrich our understanding of it. Second, it is not actually correct to say that emergence rejects spiritual phenomena. The spiritual dimension of existence, according to emergentist philosophers and many anthropologists, can be considered as an emergent quality of human development. Third, spirit may represent guided freedom rather than predetermined ethical codes necessary in dealing with uncertainty in constructing proper political ethics. Fourth, Paul Tillich's concepts of kairos and the underivable are veritable bridges to link the prophetic spirit as a way of being to the emergentist way of thinking.

Indeed, it is hard not to recognize the family resemblance between emergence and Tillich's concept of kairos. As Taylor interprets it,

> The notion of a gift that surprises and exceeds expectations points to a tension that was at the heart of all Tillich's thought, the *kairos*. Tillich's thought — whether about ethics, philosophy, politics or theology — was done out of a sense of something emerging, something the structure and character of which *could* be partially anticipated, but which was also uncontrollable and unknown. *Kairos* was both crisis and opportunity, both resonant with lived historical time, yet full of the surprising and unanticipated.[42]

For Tillich, the underivable is not bound or reducible to the substances or parts on which it supervenes. The underivable which is a higher-level occurrence constrains and affects the character of the original elements in play. Tillich writes,

40. Taylor, *Religion, Politics, and the Christian Right*, p. 97.

41. Cornel West, *Democracy Matters: Winning the Fight against Imperialism* (New York: Penguin, 2004), p. 115, quoted in Taylor, *Religion, Politics, and the Christian Right*, p. 97.

42. Mark L. Taylor, "Tillich's Ethics: Between Politics and Ontology," in *The Cambridge Companion to Paul Tillich*, ed. Russell Re Manning (Cambridge: Cambridge University Press, 2009), p. 198.

The new which results from causation qua quantitative transformation is different from the new which results from causation qua qualitative transformation within an individual substance, and both kinds of newness are different from that newness which is the result of causation through the creative act of man's (sic) spirit. In the first two cases, determination is predominant over the freedom of positing the new. In the case of the spirit, freedom prevails over determination, and *the underivably new* is created. In the creation of *Hamlet* by Shakespeare the material, particular form, personal presuppositions, occasional factors, and so on, are *derivable*. All these elements are effective in the artistic process which created *Hamlet;* but the result is new in the sense of the underivable. . . .

> *The new is not bound to the individual substance, but arises out of the substance and has effects on the character of the substances. The individual substance becomes spirit-determined. . . .*[43]

All this has almost set the stage for us to engage Taylor's concept of the prophetic spirit. There remains one bridge to construct to span the thought of both theologians, namely, Tillich's understanding of the spirit, which influences Taylor's concept of the prophetic spirit. The spirit, or spiritual presence, is not some transcendental phenomenon, perched on some supernatural plane as against the world of moral-cultural situations. It is not opposed to finite historicity. It is immanent to all finite life and inseparable from it. At the same time, though, the spirit as emergent or underivably new is beyond and more than the mere physical; it is with and within (and not above) the structures and dynamics of complex nature and culture. It is a directional dimension of the folding and unfolding of these structures and dynamics. It directs them to experience their own unlimited potentialities. Accordingly, Taylor argues that Tillich "would thus be at home with Grace Jantzen's reminder that immanence and transcendence are not opposites, that one could write of a 'sensible transcendental,' where the 'transcendental' refers not to something external to sensibility but to 'the projected horizon of our (embodied) being.'"[44]

According to Taylor, the "prophetic spirit is a way of being that is always at work broadening and deepening the horizon of our lives and, in the process, giving rise to ever new awareness of breadth and depth in our

43. Tillich, *Systematic Theology,* vol. 3, p. 324. Emphasis added.
44. Taylor, "Tillich's Ethics: Between Politics and Ontology," p. 199.

understanding of being."[45] With respect to an ethics of emergence, this prophetic spirit is particularly useful for gaining insights into institutions and power structures that may exclude persons from living according to the best of themselves. It arises when individuals and societies deliberately discern inequalities, injustice, misery, exclusion, and hindrances to flourishing in their midst, and it stirs up the courage to expose and change them. In this sense, the prophetic spirit connects being and resistance to engender becoming or to cut an opening in the oppressive lattices of any system so that human life can flourish anew.

Note that I have used the phrase "deliberately discern" in the transformation of consciousness into prophetic spirit. For Taylor, the prophetic spirit is not an alien or heteronomous imposition on social life. Rather, it is a profoundly human dimension of the cultural and historical practices constituting social life. By framing it this way, Taylor hopes to revive a "notion of the spirit that is not opposite to matter but intrinsic to it — an animating vitality of sensuous earth, a dynamic at work in the biological, historical, cultural, and social powers of earth."[46] This spirit becomes prophetic when it chooses to strain to touch the real, which is "crucial for human freedom as a kind of flourishing related to the occurrence of the new."[47] The prophetic spirit is consciousness leaning anxiously over the opening of new being and putting pressures on the border of the possible, engaging rather than succumbing to the pressures exerted by uncertainty and historicality. If emergence can be imagined as possibility-plus-contingency (or uncertainty), the prophetic spirit focuses on possibility, on an ethos of hope in the midst of an open-eyed struggle to change historical circumstances. This ethos is an embodiment of the pentecostal principle, an orientation to real, rather than so-called "objective," possibilities.

The reality from which objective possibilities are discerned is not expected to produce the startlingly new. Such a reality is encircled by the cycle of what has already been and is deeply conditioned by present circumstances, which are taken as given. When this mindset thinks about the future, its focus is not on latent possibilities, but on palpable ones that are carefully conceived, calibrated, and calculated. By contrast, the reality from which real possibilities are discerned is one marked by processive openness which looks to the future with vibrant hope. This hope is not passive or re-

---

45. Taylor, *Religion, Politics, and the Christian Right*, p. 97.
46. Taylor, *Religion, Politics, and the Christian Right*, pp. 105-6.
47. Taylor, *Religion, Politics, and the Christian Right*, pp. 105-6.

signed, and it does not look beyond history; rather, it is open to the future of new creation in history. Do-nothing, expect-nothing hope is mummified hope. The hope that derives from an orientation to the real possible is a living hope that must be expected and sought. It is an adversarial,[48] provocative hope whose driving logic is the logic of new creation and whose purpose is to keep the person of hope always unreconciled to the demonic, destructive tendencies of modern social systems or today's limiting circumstances.[49] It is *ek-static* — it pulsates with overflowing impulses for straining and stretching toward new horizons of expectation, and it draws us onward into building communal structures of relationships and embrace to counter domination, injustice, and sufferings.

The Limit of Ethics

Emergence and the prophetic spirit have informed us about how nature, society, and individuals "construct" a path (a *methodos*) toward actualization. In so doing, they have revealed something about the pentecostal principle. Ironically, actualization itself points us to the absence of a road, an aporia, to any solid ethical stance. Thus, actualization is not only the modus operandi that unlocks the pentecostal principle, it also reveals the principle's limit. By this I do not mean its completion, end, or final determination, but rather an indetermination of or at its limits.

To explore this indetermination I will focus on two aspects of actualization: its fulfillment and its processual nature.

I have already indicated that every fulfillment of potentialities is at best asymptotic because there is no certain givenness to the possibilities, and actualization is always incomplete and incompletable. To know that any actualization is perfect and complete we have to stand outside the process and command an external view, which is an impossibility. In the lan-

---

48. Needless to say that hope is by nature adversarial. Hope is based on promise. Promise is a contradiction of the present reality as we know it. If a potential bridegroom promises his future wife, "I am going to marry you," he is in fact saying, "Your present reality will change. What you are today will not be what you will be tomorrow." Her hope is the anticipation of a new and different condition or reality. Their joint hope includes a willingness to engage with ideologies and structures that negate the realization of the anticipated future. There is always an aspect of hope that is a "negation of negative."

49. See Jürgen Moltmann, *Theology of Hope: On the Ground and Implications of a Christian Eschatology* (Minneapolis: Fortress, 1996), pp. 289-90, 330-33, 334-35, 337.

guage of Gödel's incompleteness theorem, we can say that the totality of actualization cannot be used to prove a statement that exceeds it. Simply put, there are fundamental limits to certainty and to what human beings can ever know.

This brings us to the second point: the processual nature of all actualization. There is a limit to the speed at which we can acquire knowledge to effect change or increase human flourishing. There are sources of systematic unpredictability in social life, and these relate to what Alasdair MacIntyre calls the "game-theoretic character of life, pure contingency, decisions that are contemplated but not yet made, and radical conceptual innovation."[50] He continues: "Any invention, any discovery, which consists essentially in the elaboration of a radically new concept cannot be predicted, for a necessary part of the prediction is the present elaboration of the very concept whose discovery or invention was to take place only in the future. The notion of prediction of radical conceptual innovation is itself conceptually incoherent."[51]

There is a limit to knowledge or predictability in all areas of life. Einstein's theory of relativity shows there is a limit to how fast we can travel, the speed of light has a finite limit; biologists tell us that our eyes "peak in their perception of yellow, which is the wave band the sun peaks at";[52] quantum mechanics points us to the fundamental uncertainty of physical reality at the subatomic level, and meteorology points out the "butterfly effect," in which small disturbances produce large consequences. All this points to the fact that the expansion of knowledge, which is key to understanding how the pentecostal principle unfolds in the world, is more like an improvisation than a fixed score. Not only is the outcome not clear and certain, it has limits. We do not know where they are, but they are and we accept our limits and keep pushing ahead. What is important about the systematic unpredictability of the advance of knowledge is of course the consequent unpredictability of the pentecostal principle, yet it is this future we need to know if we are to know about the future of our society. We cannot know the end from the beginning. We know in part and we can only act in part.

This fundamental, permanent unpredictability of human life is the

50. Alasdair MacIntyre, *After Virtue: A Study in Moral Theory* (Notre Dame, IN: University of Notre Dame Press, 1984), pp. 93-100.

51. MacIntyre, *After Virtue*, p. 93.

52. Krista Tippett, *Einstein's God: Conversations about Science and the Human Spirit* (New York: Penguin, 2010), p. 156.

state of exception that "founds" basic human freedom and it is a rebuttal of all bureaucratic approaches to and conventional thinking on ethics. This is what is generally called the sovereignty of Fortuna. Of course, in a certain sense it contests the sovereignty of state power (law, nomos, control) by asserting its own state of exception meant to found a different connection between power and law, to conceal the violence of the law, and to establish supreme control over all forms of human life in a given domain. But the contingency in all of existence ultimately stands against all biopolitical efforts to master the life of the citizens.

In the midst of these two powers claiming a state of exception in social life, the pentecostal principle introduces a third sovereignty with its own claim of exception. Ruth Marshall argues that pentecostalism's reliance on the working of divine power in the "messianic now," its antinomian tendencies, and its belief in miraculous exception, sketch another figure of sovereignty. This third sovereignty, unlike various forms of state sovereignty, cannot be used to found a unified community and identity over which a sovereign can preside. It deterritorializes community and identity. As Marshall explains:

> In particular, the determination at the heart of the figures of the miraculous and the modes of veridiction it deploys, means that while it restages the theological-promises of justice and emancipation in a powerful new form, it fails to initiate or institutionalize the connection between power and (religious) law, between authority and obedience. Pentecostal practices of faith do not lead to the creation of a unified community or identity, and thus undermine any theocratic political project.[53]

I concur with Marshall, yet I think there is a more interesting aporia that pertains to sovereignty, predictability, and human life. None of these can "suppose" a community or an identity. Unpredictability or uncontrollability is in no way "added onto" the dimensions of sovereignty, predictability, or human life itself; rather, it is co-originary and coextensive with them. It is their common mode of exposition. According to Jean-Luc Nancy, "to be exposed" means to be "posed" in exteriority, according to an exteriority, having to do with an outside in the very intimacy of an in-

---

53. Ruth Marshall, "The Sovereignty of Miracles: Pentecostal Political Theology in Nigeria," *Constellations* 17, no. 2 (2010): 201.

side.[54] Nancy is also useful in opening an alternative interpretation of why Marshall's "pentecostal practices of faith do not lead to the creation of a unified community or identity." It is not merely attributable to failure to initiate or institutionalize a connection between power and law, between authority and obedience. He argues,

> Exposition, precisely, is not a "being" that one can "sup-pose" (like a sub-stance) to be in community. Community is presuppositionless: that is why it is haunted by such ambiguous ideas as foundation and sovereignty, which are at once ideas of what would be completely suppositionless and ideas of what would always be presupposed. But community cannot be presupposed. It is only exposed. This undoubtedly is not easy to think.[55]

ℵ Indeterminacy and Democratic Openness

It is essential to mention here that understanding and respecting the nature of social existence as ultimately indeterminate and at best something that can only offer us security-in-danger is not a call to resign ourselves to fate, but a call for social and political contestation in the heart of community, not at the margins; a call to depoliticize governance (sovereignty) and subject it to democratic openness. Marieke de Goede quotes Sanjay Reddy:

> Recognition of the limits of human capacity to predict and control the future enables in Sanjay Reddy's words "enlarged room for social and political contestation [of] . . . the indeterminate future. It enables the indeterminate future to be transformed into an open political domain, rather than existing as an undemocratically and scientifically defined and mapped out horizon of alternatives."[56]

I have so far dealt with the limits of ethics only with regard to the aporias pertaining to the actualization process. But the structural basis for the rest-

---

54. Jean-Luc Nancy, *The Inoperative Community*, trans. Peter Connor, Lisa Garbus, Michael Holland, and Simona Sawhney (Minneapolis: University of Minnesota Press, 1991), pp. xxxvii.

55. Nancy, *Inoperative Community*, p. xxxix.

56. Marieke de Goede, *Virtue, Fortune, and Faith: A Genealogy of Finance* (Minneapolis: University of Minnesota Press, 2005), p. 175. For the Sanjay Reddy reference see his "Claims to Expert Knowledge and the Subversion of Democracy: The Triumph of Risk over Uncertainty," *Economy and Society* 25, no. 2 (1996): 228.

lessness of actualization itself, the infinite longing for self-realization, the movedness of emergence of any human sociality, also meets its limit in the basic encounter of one person with another in concrete existential context. This drive, whether in a person or a sociality, can never possess the "other self." Tillich makes this point clear when he argues, "One can destroy it as a self, but one cannot assimilate it as a content of one's own centeredness. The attempt to do so by totalitarian rules has never succeeded. Nobody can deprive a person of his claim to be a person and to be dealt with as a person."[57]

At the foundation of the moral life is the encounter of one human being with another, two independent beings with individual desires. A person's sense of personhood is shaped within the context of relations to others and by definition they become moral beings in a communal setting.[58] It is through the personal encounter we recognize the binding force of the moral imperative; as Tillich puts it, "'oughtness' is basically experienced in the ego-thou relation."[59]

Each person discovers him- or herself through the resistance offered by the other, who retains his or her subject-quality in the encounter. "In the resistance of the other person the person is born. Therefore, there is no person without an encounter with other persons."[60] In this encounter each person retains his or her intrinsic moral dignity, which is the source of the resistance that struggles against being treated as an object.[61] If the other is conquered then he or she is destroyed as a person.[62] The other self always represents the "unconditional limit to the desire to assimilate one's world, and the experience of this limit is the experience of the ought to be, the moral imperative."[63] Tillich explains further:

57. Tillich, *Systematic Theology,* vol. 1, p. 40.
58. Tillich, *Systematic Theology,* vol. 1, p. 176.
59. Tillich, *Systematic Theology,* vol. 3, p. 40.
60. Tillich, *Systematic Theology,* vol. 1, p. 177.
61. "Man [sic] becomes man in personal encounters. Only by meeting a 'thou' does man realize that he is an 'ego.' No natural object within the whole universe can do this for him. Man can transcend himself in all directions in knowledge and control. He can use everything for his purposes. . . . But there is a limit for man which is definite and which he always encounters, the other man. The other one, the 'thou' is like a wall which cannot be removed or penetrated or used. He who tries to do so destroys himself. The 'thou' demands by his very existence to be acknowledged as a 'thou' for an 'ego' and an 'ego' for himself. This is the claim which is implied in his being." See Paul Tillich, *Love, Power, and Justice: Ontological Analyses and Ethical Applications* (London: Oxford University Press, 1954), p. 78.
62. Tillich, *Systematic Theology,* vol. 1, p. 177.
63. Tillich, *Systematic Theology,* vol. 3, p. 40.

> Man, facing his world, has the whole universe as the potential content of his centered self. Certainly, there are actual limits because of the finitude of every being, but the world is definitely open to man; everything can become a content of the self. . . . But there is one limit to man's attempt to draw all content into himself — the other self.[64]

Having now examined the limits to actualization as posed by some of the fundamental issues in social ethics, we can now ask whether there is a way to think about the limits that does not foreclose thought or threaten to completely undermine emergence as a methodological pillar of the pentecostal principle. There is, and we can accomplish it by pushing the limits to their own limits and considering the results. This we do by investigating two theses. The first of these is the assertion that all we can ever know about actualization are emergent phenomena; the second is that emergence as such is eternal. This latter thesis implies the hypostasis of the emergent process; thus we are no longer dealing with emergence in a strict sense, but with a metaphysics that eternalizes and externalizes the dynamic of existence, coexistence (the power of novelty), turning it into a substance existing in and of itself. It becomes an entity that must be, and not one that might or might not exist. Thus, the hypostatization contradicts the very principle of contingency (the possibility that something can be, not be, be other than it is; persist or perish, the possibility of it being and not-being), which is the heart of emergence. This thought, aimed at delivering us from any charge of hypostatization, has to be quickly qualified. It follows that in the appropriation of emergence to ethical thought we should avoid falling into the trap that it works independently of its incarnation in human beings or human socialities. It is not possible for us to step outside of our coexistence to know if a disincarnation of emergence might be true.

None of this should be construed to mean that emergence as a natural phenomenon cannot be an event or process that is *anterior* to any human form of the relation to the world or to the appearance of humans on earth. Put differently, I am not saying, in the terminology of French philosopher Quentin Meillassoux,[65] that it cannot be an "ancestral" event, a fact whose existence is indifferent to thought or human existence. Now

---

64. Tillich, *Systematic Theology,* vol. 3, p. 40.

65. Though his thought is not friendly to religion and theology, his ideas on contingency are relevant to our conversion here. See Quentin Meillassoux, *After Finitude: An Essay on the Necessity of Contingency,* trans. Ray Brassier (London: Continuum, 2008).

this is where our journey into the limits of ethics gets very interesting. If emergence is a process that is unconnected to a relation-to-the-world, then, following Meillassoux, ethicists may do well to turn to a new understanding of "absolutes"[66] at the epistemological basis of any theory of ethics. The recourse to emergence to aid ethical thinking may well have brought us to the limits of ethical thought as they are founded on the regnant epistemological theories since Kant. The ancestrality of natural events and scientists' "witness" of it compel a rethinking of the "status of becoming." As Meillassoux argues,

> To think ancestrality is to think without thought — a world without the givenness of the world. It is therefore incumbent upon us to break with the ontological requisite of the moderns, according to which *to be is to be a correlate.* Our task, by way of contrast, consists in trying to understand how thought is able to access the uncorrelated, which is to say, a world capable of subsisting without being given. But to say this is just to say that we must grasp how thought is able to access an *absolute,* i.e. a being whose *severance* (the original meaning of *absolutus*) and whose separateness from thought is such that it presents itself to us as non-relative to us, and hence is capable of existing whether we exist or not. But this entails a rather remarkable consequence: to think ancestrality requires that we take up once more the thought of the absolute; yet through ancestrality, it is a discourse of empirical science as such that we are attempting to understand and legitimate. Consequently, it becomes necessary to insist that, far from commanding us — as the various forms of positivism would wish — *to renounce the quest for absolute, it is science itself that enjoins us to discover the source of its own absoluteness.* For if I cannot think anything that is absolute, I cannot make sense of ancestrality, and consequently I cannot make sense of the science that allows me to know ancestrality.[67]

The implication of Meillassoux's argument for social ethics is that ethicists "must think an absolute necessity without thinking anything that *is* absolute necessary,"[68] that is, they must focus on the absolute necessity of social laws that are contingent, to think the nature of contrary modali-

---

66. Meillassoux, *After Finitude,* pp. 28, 63-66, 121-28.
67. Meillassoux, *After Finitude,* p. 28. Italics in original.
68. Meillassoux, *After Finitude,* p. 34.

ties. So the turn to absolutes is also the turn to contingency,[69] which is at the heart of emergence; and we have arrived here without falling into the trap of hypostatization.

This rethinking of the limit in new register does not really relieve us of the burden of the aporia that we started with. The focus on the ethical as the novelty, the underivably new, or as emergence suggests that events are incalculable and unpredictable and points to our increasing inability to reduce something that happens to a pre-register of possibilities. The ethics that is about the pursuit of novelty, or a religion like pentecostalism that pursues miracles or is oriented to surprises, is pushing itself to the point where there is no enclosure of possibilities which in itself threatens the enclosures *(ēthos)* that provide for stability and security of social life. If the possible as such is necessarily un-totalizable,[70] it may mean that we are living in a permanent state of exception sustained not by state power in this case, but by the inherent "violence" of the contingency underlying all social existence, a state of exception that does not necessarily suspend the normative order as such but makes it radically open to the novelty and surprises.

Ethics as an Unended Mode of Action

To counteract this "violence" we need to think of ethics as a play that is capable of neutralizing the impact of the impasse between means and ends that contingency inscribes into morality. The most fitting response to the ravages of contingency is ethics as "the sphere of pure means."

The major problem of contingency is that it ruptures the nexus between means and end in a thousand ways that paralyze morality. It does this by dissolving every end in the acid of untotalizable possibilities. Owing to the fluidity and instability of events, production *(poiēsis)* can never be a means to an end in sight, for the destination may move before the journey is completed. Ends are irreparably set astray. Ends are removed from the sphere of mediation, which presents to moral agents the aberration of finality without means. Action *(praxis)* that aims to do what is right is similarly affected. Contingency exacerbates the traditional tension be-

69. For ethicists, contingency does not mean a process necessarily underwritten by the principle of unreason.

70. Meillassoux, *After Finitude*, p. 127.

tween ends and means, heightening the power of "the false alternative between ends and means that paralyzes morality."[71] It denies every consequence of any action its redemption, since there is no kind of destination
and because every end is always "beside itself, in an empty space"[72] where
beginning unfolds. Every end is only a paradigm *(para-deigma)* for new
beginning; "it is the unraveling, the indetermination of a limit."[73]

To cope with (the extreme case of) contingency demands "a kind of
mediation that is pure and devoid of any end . . . ," that is, means that are
"removed from the sphere of mediation without thereby becoming
ends."[74] We need to reconceptualize ethics as an experience of "pure
mediality," playful relation to codes and structure, in order to reclaim or
initiate authentic ethico-political action. "What characterizes [play] is that
there is neither production nor enactment, but undertaking and supporting. In other words, [play] opens up the sphere of *ethos* as the most fitting
sphere of the human."[75] Undertaking and supporting here mean assuming
full responsibility for acting and doing that promotes the ethos of freedom. Varro succinctly clarifies it when he writes:

> A person can make [*facere*] something and not enact [agree] it, as a poet
> makes a play, but does not act it (*agree* in the sense of playing a part); on
> the other hand the actor acts the play, but does not make it. So the play
> is made [fit] by the poet, but not acted [*agitur*] by him; it is acted by the
> actor, but not made by him. Whereas the *imperator* (the magistrate in
> whom supreme power is invested) of whom the expression *res gerere* is
> used (to carry something out, in the sense of taking it upon oneself, as-
> suming total responsibility for it), neither makes nor acts, but takes
> charge, in other words carries the burden of it *(sustinet).*[76]

71. Giorgio Agamben, *Infancy and History: On the Destruction of Experience* (London:
Verso, 2007), p. 155.

72. Giorgio Agamben, *The Coming Community,* trans. Michael Hardt (Minneapolis:
University of Minnesota Press, 1993), p. 9.

73. Agamben, *The Coming Community,* pp. 9, 100.

74. For the quotes see Agamben, *Infancy and History,* p. 155.

75. Agamben, *Infancy and History,* p. 154.

76. Varro, *De Lingua Latina,* VI, 77, quoted in Agamben, *Infancy and History,* p. 154.
Brackets in original.

א Pentecostal Playful Worship

There is a certain playfulness in pentecostal-charismatic worship services compared to those of the mainline Protestant and Catholic churches. According to Jean-Jacques Suurmond, "the essential contribution of Pentecostal spirituality lies in its playful character. This is evident above all from the charismatic celebration which is not characterized by either order or chaos but by the dynamics of play."[77] Suurmond also emphasizes the uselessness of play: "It serves no purpose, but it is an end in itself [what I have called a pure means]. The attitude of play seems to be the only right attitude to God, our fellow human beings and to creation. God does not serve any purpose, since God is an end in himself. However laudable our striving may be, as soon as God is used to achieve one purpose or another, we reduce the divine to an instrument. Then God is no longer God."[78]

Pentecostals are relatively less "ritualistic" and formal than other Christian denominations. Worship services[79] in pentecostal-charismatic churches are more a series of events, marked more by openness to the realization of potentialities of God's plan than by liturgical structuring. It creates a context in which people are oriented to the extraordinary as mundane and in which miracles can be experienced.

The services are playful not only because of their lightheartedness and joviality, but also in the sense that we see (liturgical) structures being converted into events — just as Claude Lévi-Strauss characterized play (games) in *The Savage Mind.*[80] This

---

77. Jean-Jacques Suurmond, *Word and Spirit at Play* (Grand Rapids: Eerdmans, 1994), p. 220.

78. Suurmond, *Word and Spirit,* p. 29.

79. Romano Guardini once wrote that worship is "a kind of holy play in which the soul, with utter abandonment, learns to waste time for the sake of God." See Romano Guardini, *The Church and the Catholic and the Spirit of the Liturgy* (New York: Sheed and Ward, 1935), p. 179, quoted in David L. Miller, *Gods and Games: Toward a Theology of Play* (New York: Word, 1970), p. 158.

80. Claude Lévi-Strauss, *The Savage Mind* (Chicago: University of Chicago Press, 1966), pp. 30-33. As it will become increasingly clear to the reader, this book's notion of play is different in many respects from that of Suurmond and even that of Wolfgang Vondey. In his recent book, *Beyond Pentecostalism,* Vondey treats play as an unended action and in this I agree with him, but our conceptualizations of the term differ a great deal. There are five key aspects to the notion of play in this book and they are systematically theorized in chapter 4 and especially in chapter 5:

    (a) The primary focus here is not on play as a counterpoint to work, the problem of leisure, or seriousness (although these are not denied), but as a *deactivation* of law and radicalization of saving grace.

    (b) This study conceptualizes play as a *pure means,* purposelessness. It regards play as having the structure of aesthetic judgment — an unended action.

    (c) Play as *profanatory* behavior.

    (d) Play exhibits non-zero-sum dynamics, which is key to understanding the inher-

character of pentecostal worship sheds light on its practice of "recapitulation of the past," passing summary judgment on it, and without totally rejecting it. This is what I have in mind. If ritual transforms events into structures and adjusts all contradictions between the past and the present into the encompassing whole, the synchronic structure and diachronic eventalities into continuous, synchronic temporality, "play, on the other hand, furnishes a symmetrically opposed operation: it tends to break the connection between past and present, and to break down and crumble the whole structure into events."[81]

Perhaps it is also germane to direct our attention to a certain theological playfulness with grace (or rather the boundary of grace and work) in pentecostal-charismatic worship. The worship is always trying to effect a tiny displacement of that rigid line between grace and work — as if straining to add "something" of work (surplus, *superaddi*) to grace in order to get some desired results. It is seeking nothing essential or substantial to the perfect working of grace, only an accidental supplement at its edges to make it more forthcoming for whatever task is at hand — to make it "glow" some more, to make it vibrate with the pressing concerns of the mundane. Here the reader will notice that I am alluding to Aquinas, who writes that a "halo" can be added to beatitude to make it more brilliant, an inessential supplement to the *status perfectionis*.[82]

Thus we can think of the pentecostal-charismatic worship service as "a zone in which possibility and reality, potentiality and actuality, become indistinguishable. The [person, the act, the career, and so on] that has reached its end, that has consumed all its possibilities, thus receives as a gift a supplemental possibility. . . . This imperceptible trembling of the finite that makes its limits indeterminate . . . is the tiny displacement that every thing must accomplish in the messianic world."[83]

Having a playful relation to the codes and norms means rethinking ethics as the sphere of pure means. Pure mediality restores pure potentiality (unconstrained by vocation and identity) as exposition of human beings as *argōs*-being and its mobilization against contingency. Before we proceed is it important to explain what I mean by *argōs*-being because it holds a key to comprehending the meaning of ethics as a sphere of pure mediality. Aristotle wonders if nature left man without a function, work

---

      ent dynamism of relationality of human socialities and growth of social complexity.

    (e) Play as freely evolving potentialities. It is the eros toward open future, the to-come as the quest for potentials. Play is the mode of being of potentiality itself.

81. Agamben, *Infancy and History,* p. 83.
82. Agamben, *The Coming Community,* pp. 53-55.
83. Agamben, *The Coming Community,* p. 55.

(ergon) that is proper to human beings, or if they are essentially workless *(inoperoso)*, functionless *(argōs)*.

> For just as the goodness and performance of a flute player, a sculptor, or any kind of expert, and generally of anyone who fulfills some function or performs some action, are thought to reside in his proper function [*ergon*], so the goodness and performance of man would seem to reside in whatever is his proper function. Is it then possible that while a carpenter and a shoemaker have their own proper function and spheres of action, man as man has none, but is left by nature a good-for-nothing without a function [*argōs*]?[84]

Aristotle quickly retreated from this thought and supplied the answer: "activity of the soul in accordance with virtue." This is the essence of human beings, at least and insofar as she is in the *polis* and it is the end she pursues. Today, we are no longer quick to identify what is the proper timeless function of human beings. And we regard community as *inoperative* as it is only the experience of *compearance* (as Jean-Luc Nancy has taught us). So, and rightly, Agamben argues that human action cannot be regarded as a means that makes sense only with respect to an end.[85] Thus, he would want us to understand politics not with regard to a particular end, but a sphere that corresponds to the *argōs*-standing of human beings. He writes:

> Politics is that which corresponds to the essential inoperability . . . of humankind, to the radical being-without-work of human communities. There is politics because human beings are *argōs*-beings that cannot be defined by any proper operation [function] — that is, beings of pure potentiality that no identity or vocation can possibly exhaust.[86]

Let us now come back to our point that pure mediality restores pure potentiality (unconstrained by vocation and identity) as exposition of human beings as *argōs*-being and its mobilization against contingency. This restoration breaks the dialectic of the proper and improper — dialectic in which (improper) contingency extends its rule everywhere and ethicalism

---

84. Aristotle, *Nicomachean Ethics*, 1097b 25-30. The translation is that of Martin Oswald (Indianapolis: Liberal Arts Press, 1962).

85. Giorgio Agamben, *Means without End: Notes on Politics*, trans. Vincenzo Binetti and Cesare Casarino (Minneapolis: University of Minnesota Press, 2000), pp. 115-16.

86. Agamben, *Means without End*, p. 140.

demands its exclusion as it cannot think the thought of seeing contingency and pentecostalism as the same thing and how to mobilize humankind's inoperability against contingency. Pure means puts our actions into that common zone of indiscernibility between proper and improper, where there is "neither appropriation [the expansionism of contingency] nor expropriation [the exclusionism of ethicalism], but as appropriation of an expropriation."[87] When ethics corresponds to the sphere of pure mediality what is seized and delivered from contingency is the "essential potentiality and inoperability" of humankind, or in other words, their infinite longing for excellence.

We have so far examined ethics as a sphere of pure means. We made the move to interpret what this means, but the movement itself is based on having playful relation with ethical codes. Having a playful relation to codes sounds revolutionary or even too pentecostal to some; but in reality "play" is one of the two tendencies, the diachronic and the synchronic, operating in every society. As we have already noted, according to Lévi-Strauss, rituals (working as synchronic power — in the language of this book, nomos or necessity) transform events into structures and adjust all contradictions between the past and the present into the encompassing whole. On the other hand, play (operating as the diachronic force — in the language of this book, kairotic possibility or contingency) transforms structure into events. These two forces represent opposing forms of temporal orientation of social systems. One is oriented toward the long-term, the other toward the short-term.

In the hands of two other anthropologists, Jonathan Parry and Maurice Bloch, these dual forces become two cycles of exchange. Parry and Bloch argue that there are two forms of exchange in any given society: the cycle of short-term exchange is concerned with transience and the cycle of the long-term is concerned with the reproduction of the social and cosmic order. It is pertinent to state that the two cycles are essential to each other. The long-term restorative cycle depends on and must negate the short-term transactional cycle that is concerned with individualistic transactions and not with timeless order.[88]

---

87. Agamben, *Means without End*, p. 116.

88. Jonathan Parry and Maurice Bloch, eds., *Money and the Morality of Exchange* (Cambridge: Cambridge University Press, 1989), p. 29; Maurice Bloch, *Ritual, History, and Power: Selected Papers in Anthropology* (New York: Berg, 1989); and Maurice Bloch and Jonathan Parry, eds., *Death and Regeneration of Life* (Cambridge: Cambridge University Press, 1982).

Agamben goes further, to say that ritual and play, in their struggles in which one cannot permanently win, always maintain a differential margin between them. This margin he calls "history" or "human time."[89] According to him, "every historical event represents a differential margin between diachrony and synchrony, instituting a signifying relation between them."[90] It is only play that is operative in this human time: "In play, man frees himself from sacred time and 'forgets' it in human time."[91] Play, Agamben argues, is a participation in a form of rituals (the realm of sacred, the synchrony) where the meaning has been forgotten; thus, it mediates between the sacred and the secular. "Playland is a country whose inhabitants are busy celebrating rituals, and manipulating objects and sacred words, whose sense and purpose they have, however, forgotten."[92] The forms of the sacred are maintained while forgetting their meaning. "This ritual with a forgotten purpose articulates a means without an end in so far as the end has been forgotten."[93] So play overturns the sacred, makes it inoperative, without destroying it. According to Agamben in his 2005 book, *The Time That Remains,* this is just what Paul does with the Old Testament law as he proclaims the *messianic now.*

The real question is how the two sides can be reconciled. It is not enough to emphasize either one of the sides: play or rituals. One of the best ways of accomplishing this is the pure means. For in pure means, "the making visible of a means as such," "potential and action [facts and events], contingency and necessity, becomes indiscernible." "It makes apparent the human state of being-in-a-medium and thereby opens up the ethical dimension for human beings."[94] Pure means gives the mode of operation of or the ethos fitting with the inoperative community and the *argōs*-being, a state of mediation that does not transcend to or become subordinated to a higher end. This role that pure means plays is always best understood within play itself. In playfulness, ethical codes are rendered inoperative, deactivated — not annihilated. They are fulfilled and recapitulated in the figure of love as Paul says it should be in the messianic now.

89. Agamben, *Infancy and History,* pp. 82-84.

90. Agamben, *Infancy and History,* p. 85.

91. Agamben, *Infancy and History,* p. 79.

92. Agamben, *Infancy and History,* p. 79.

93. Benjamin Morgan, "Undoing Legal Violence: Walter Benjamin's and Giorgio Agamben's Aesthetics of Pure Means," *Journal of Law and Society* 34, no. 1 (March 2007): 61.

94. Agamben, *Infancy and History,* pp. 152, 155.

ℵ Same Origin

The pentecostal principle (life's energy and creative impulse) and contingency (the necessary endless end) share the same origin. They are names for the "power to not not-be," the unbounded Yes and Amen to the world of being. To strip means of purpose is one way of deliberately attuning our being to contingency that is necessary and by definition lacks purpose and sense-fullness. Unended action is made to traverse contingency and in traversing it transforms it into the great opportunity for the advent of the underivable new, or to enjoy it as the most intense, shadowless messianic now in which the difference between this true world and the world to come is "just a little."

Concluding Remarks

The most important conclusion to draw from the philosophy of emergence and the limits of ethics as exposed by contingency is that we do not have complete information, complete ethical codes, or a comprehensive system of values and calculations to guide the operations of the pentecostal principle. We can only nurture kairos. This sounds paradoxical, you may say. How can we nurture something spontaneous and unexpected, something whose arrival is new? At least one way of doing this is not to deliberately decide on the consequences of rules or engineer them to produce concrete, predictable results. According to Friedrich A. Hayek, this means maintaining an environment conducive to the rise or in-breaking of kairos:

> [E]nforcement of rules of conduct must therefore always aim at results in the long run, in contrast to the rules of organization [human-designed system] serving known particular purposes which must essentially aim at predictable short run results. . . . A concentration on particular results necessarily leads to a short run view, since only in the short run will the particular results be foreseeable, and raises in consequence conflicts between particular interests that can be decided only by an authoritative decision in favour of one or the other.[95]

There is no complete ethical code, and the implicit search for it is antithetical to freedom and inimical to the kind of pluralism countries need to

95. Friedrich A. Hayek, *Law, Legislation, and Liberty,* Volume 2: *The Mirage of Social Justice* (Chicago: University of Chicago Press, 1976), p. 29.

maintain peace and justice. No one of us is so omniscient that we can formulate a common ethical code comprehensive enough to direct the actualization of the potentialities of all persons in any given society. There is no single supreme value to which all individuals' purposes and actions must be subjected. If we were to choose one such social goal, whose would it be?

Besides, a kairos-oriented ordering of society demands at the minimum that we do not determine once and for all the social goal, common purpose, or direction a society must follow. It is impossible to create complete morality and plan for the needs of a whole society in any complex economy with dispersed knowledge. We must be open to the unexpected and be willing to transcend what the interests of any class or ethnic or political group determine for society. This is one good reason to infuse pluralism into national political and economic thinking. Once again Hayek is useful in clarifying the issue:

> The welfare and happiness of millions cannot be measured on a single scale of less and more. The welfare of a people, like the happiness of a man, depends on a great many things that can be provided in an infinite variety of combinations. It cannot be adequately expressed as a single end, but only as a hierarchy of ends, a comprehensive scale of values in which every need of every person is given its place. To direct all our activities according to a single plan presupposes that every one of our needs is given its rank in an order of values which must be complete enough to make it possible to decide among all the different courses which the planner has to choose. It presupposes, in short, the existence of a complete ethical code in which all the different human values are allotted their due place.[96]

The lack of complete ethical code, the absence of a definitive essence in the inoperative community, and the dispersal of knowledge in a complex society demand that we need to be on the side of economic and political pluralism. The public space captured by narrow interests may well represent the greatest obstacle to equity, justice, peace, pure means, and the biggest hindrance to kairos-ordering of economies, converting structures into events, and producing new temporalities (human times).

In the next chapter, we will investigate the process of making ethical

---

96. Friedrich A. Hayek, *The Road to Serfdom* (Chicago: University of Chicago Press, 1944), p. 57.

arguments for public policies in pluralistic societies like the United States. We will develop an explicit procedural method of ethical analysis relevant to public policy decision-making. The chapter will propose an ethical methodology as a form of public discourse, a meta-ethical model showing how themes, concerns, and insights of public theology can be systematically organized into practical policy arguments. It will provide a robust "mechanics" to aid public theologians to prepare ethical analyses for public policies. The methodology of the chapter as set forth flows from a conception of ethics and ethical analysis that is rooted in the pentecostal principle and the "many tongues" of the Day of Pentecost.

3 Many Tongues of Pentecost

Ethical Methodology as a Paradigm of Pluralism

Scholars today agree that there is a plurality of pentecostalisms. The pentecostal principle admits such diversity, as we have seen and will continue to see. We can therefore state the thesis that pentecostal ethics invites not one but many perspectives regarding issues of public policy. It admits an ethical methodology that can enter into debates on public issues and proceeds in ways that can draw from the best of current knowledge without undermining the centrality of scripture in its position. What could be the theological reasons for such an approach to ethics? The Lukan account of the Day of Pentecost (Acts 2) shows that many languages and experiences ("many tongues") are necessary to give account of common matter or the works of God. "The strong and perhaps unmistakable inference to be drawn is that the preservation of the many tongues of the Day of Pentecost is an indication that God values not only linguistic diversity but also cultural plurality."[1]

The event of multiple languages or many tongues that characterized the Day of Pentecost prioritizes a pneumatological approach to pluralism that invites us to honor multiple voices in discerning and solving the problems of common social existence. This event cannot be interpreted simply as diversity of tongues. Insofar as the 120 disciples engaged in translation and communication (those observing them were no longer mere observers, but active participants in what was going on) there was an "energetic engagement with diversity." It was this kind of engagement that created the

---

1. Amos Yong, *In the Days of Caesar: Pentecostalism and Political Theology* (Grand Rapids: Eerdmans, 2010), p. 93.

first church, "the common society from all that plurality." Luke does not just mention tongues, he takes time to name the cultures that produced the tongues; I interpret this to mean that their identity, their differences, and angularities were worth noting and maintaining as they came into a common society not based on one essence but on each gift. The ethical implication for this is that at a minimum the participation of citizens in the public sphere should not entail the shirking of their religious and other commitments, but movement from there to context of plurality and active engagement with the diversity of other voices (including those of science) in bridge-building dialogue for the sake of common flourishing. In this chapter, we will develop both a theological rationale for ethical methodological pluralism and a precise framework to enable pentecostal ethicists to be "comfortable with the cacophony of the many tongues"[2] in the public square which has lost its sacred canopy.

The area of modern academic theology known as public theology is most seriously focused on developing framework, procedures, and protocols for navigating and appreciating the diversity of voices, perspectives, experiences, and kinds of knowledge that stake claims in the public square. Yet based on the philosophical-theological perspective being developed in this book, we cannot simply assert that the regnant approach of public theology is adequate for pentecostal ethical methodology. Current models of public theology, regardless of their political orientation, seem to focus on how to move from the particular to the universal or vice versa. Yet whatever their strategies for doing so, these models remain captive to the logic of dichotomous opposition between the universal and the particular, and enthralled in articulating together the universal and the particular. And the best of them only succeed in transforming the dichotomous logic into a higher synthesis.[3]

An alternative approach will be to move from the particular to the particular by way of analogy rather than logic. The pentecostal principle, as we have seen, is not about the alternative "A or B," neither "A nor B," but about proposing an analogical third. This third is irreducible to any one of two terms, yet makes intelligible a new ensemble and a new context and stands in for all of them in its singularity. This third is a paradigm that entails a movement from the particular to the particular.

---

2. Yong, *Days of Caesar*, p. 94.

3. This introductory section (this paragraph and the next four) was inspired and is informed by Giorgio Agamben's notion of paradigm. See his *The Signature of All Things: On Method* (New York: Zone Books, 2009), pp. 9-32.

In the light of this perspective, the task of making a public policy argument in a pluralistic society is not about the particular-general binary, with all resistance relating to the movement from one end to the other. It is rather about making a paradigmatic case for one's position, whose role will be to constitute and make intelligible the very problematic pluralistic context of the public space, public debate, and public engagement. As Aristotle explains, "the paradigm does not function as a part with respect to the whole, nor as a whole with respect to the part, but a part with respect to the part, if both are under the same but one is better known than the other."[4] Before him, Plato maintains that "a paradigm is generated when an entity, which is founded in something other and separated in another entity, is judged correctly and recognized as the same, and having been reconnected together generates a true and unique opinion concerning each other."[5] Giorgio Agamben adds that a paradigm entails a movement from the particular to the particular and, without ever leaving the particular, "transform[s] every particular case into an *exemplar* of a general rule that can never be stated a priori."[6]

This is a chapter on ethical methodology for public policy debate that takes seriously the paradigmatic perspective of pluralism for political theology. The methodology serves as a paradigm (model, example, exemplar, *exemplum*) in the Platonic, Aristotelian, and Agambenian senses for making a positive or negative case against a public policy.

As it will become clear to the reader, the paradigmatic pluralism occurs in the public engagement not because one who is not already in motion (i.e., standing) decides to move forward, but from recognition that in the very motion, the revelation of one's preference in the debate, one is already implicated in the pluralistic project. In this methodology pluralism is not added on to one's argument (stance), but the very nature and intelligibility of the movement of thoughts in one's argument generate and produce pluralism. Such pluralism does not merely occur between multiple religious-ideological commitments or between (any of) them and a general rule (such as tolerance, civility, benevolence, "Abrahamic re-union," and so on); "it occurs instead between a singularity (which thus becomes a paradigm) and its exposition (its intelligibility)."[7]

---

4. Aristotle, *Prior Analytics*, 69a13-15, quoted in Agamben, *Signature of All Things*, p. 19.
5. Plato, *The Statesman*, 278c, quoted in Agamben, *Signature of All Things*, p. 23.
6. Agamben, *Signature of All Things*, p. 22.
7. Agamben, *Signature of All Things*, p. 23.

This chapter has two major parts. In the first part I will attempt to relate the Lukan narrative of the Day of Pentecost to the necessity of pluralistic methodology of ethical analysis. Then I will explain the mechanics of ethical analysis for public policies in a pluralistic society. The chapter ends with concluding remarks which briefly reinstate the theological rationale for a pluralistic ethical methodology and also help the reader to transition to chapter 4.

The Day of Pentecost and the Mechanics of Ethical Methodology

The paradigmatic perspective of pluralism, as I have stated above, has not yet been widely embraced by pentecostal scholars.[8] Take, for instance, the recent work of Amos Yong, *In the Days of Caesar*.[9] This is a very impressive systematic pentecostal-theological intervention into political theology; on the whole, Yong's pluralistic political theology opens up a space for pentecostals to have the kind of conversation about public policy that will be much more nuanced, flexible, and contextually sensitive, and informed by theological rather than just pragmatic considerations. And yet it is silent on public theology, the matter of the modality of engaging in the actual work of public policymaking in a contested public square. How can a particular pentecostal identity or viewpoint on social issues that play out in the common enter into the public square and become publicly (universally) accepted for policy in a civil society which includes Christians, Muslims, atheists, and others? How will pentecostal scholars and students go about producing arguments or policy frameworks without discarding their own particular identities? Yong's book is explicitly concerned with navigating multiple voices and pluralism in pentecostal political theology, but it avoids those voices that may be in antagonistic contest (not necessarily bitter) for formulating public policies and sustaining the common good.[10] How can a

8. Samuel Solivan comes close to this perspective when he states that "The Pentecost event recorded in Acts 2 provides some leads concerning a possible starting-point in doing theology from a Pentecostal perspective. The first lead is the affirmation of language and culture [pluralism]. The second lead is using particularity as a starting-point, as opposed to universality." See Solivan, *The Spirit, Pathos, and Liberation: Toward an Hispanic Pentecostal Theology* (Sheffield: Sheffield Academic Press, 1998), p. 114.

9. Yong, *Days of Caesar.*

10. Yong, *Days of Caesar,* pp. 38, 91-95, 112, 255-57, 335-36, 364.

harmony of multiple voices be produced, so that pentecostals need not retreat into gated spiritual communities (ghettos)?

Two of the challenges of concretizing the paradigmatic pluralism in today's multifaith society are how to think about public policy theologically, and how to translate the vision of the Day of Pentecost into frames of policy, as a re-source of the *common*. In this chapter I will lay out the mechanics of this translation process.

These mechanics, I believe, are core parts of the pentecostal principle, and they are essential in the process of building relationships between the many voices in a pluralistic society. And the language of relationship, of evolving potentialities in encounters, and of the common is what Steven G. Smith calls the language of spirit. The mechanics offers us a passport or the skills to go into a pluralistic world, remaining true to our identity and embracing our particularity, to positively influence public policy in the common. After all, every opportunity we have to address major ethical questions in our time will necessarily take place within the context of a conversation where multiple visions are present. We need to be brave enough to learn the ropes of stating the truths of the pentecostal principle in a deep, mutually enriching context of engaged dialogue with others.

The context of irreducible pluralism and dialogue is our problematic concrete — a set of troublesome and risky relationships — that will not go away. "What we have to do, then, is find an argument that is, as philosophy [and theology], maximally explanatory, but that establishes the principles argued for through conceptual sensitivity and rectitude instead of coercion."[11] For as Smith writes,

> I find that I am not in a position to comprehend . . . apart from the determination of another program, another element in my situation that calls for the response of this rather elaborate enactment in words. I face others — the host of other beings with places of their own in the world, and . . . preeminently the others who are intenders. This first act of my life has two dimensions, that the others are there and that I am not at liberty to ignore them . . . I am in the first place the one whom actual others have not left alone. My existence is qualified from the ground up as existence-toward them. I am not free not to be this, but at the same time I am only free to propose and argue, to say what is and what should

---

11. Steven G. Smith, *The Concept of the Spiritual: An Essay in First Philosophy* (Philadelphia: Temple University Press, 1988), p. 79.

be, because I am this. Philosophy [theology, spirituality] as I practice it cannot swallow the others into any other program than being with them, because its own truth is that it springs (not just historically and logically) from being with them.[12]

Thus, this chapter puts forth a method that is committed to this alternative way of understanding pluralistic engagement. For the sake of graduate students and others who are training in social ethics, this commitment is extracted, seized, and delivered as concrete mechanics, "techniques," and procedure for public analysis of policies and projects in the common where we are already ex-posed, every identity exposed from the inside. The development of such explicit techniques of public ethical analysis, which not only reflects the current state of ethical thinking, but is also a display and an example of pluralism in itself, is critically lacking in public theologians' engagement with public policy debates.

That public theology is relevant to public policy debates and formulation should be self-evident. After all, public theologians aspire to develop ethical frameworks and discourses about how we should live together in plural civil societies. Public theology is offered as a form of discourse.[13] Unfortunately, contemporary public theologians have largely failed to develop models for ethical analysis directly appropriate for public discourse and relevant to public policy decision-making. While they have developed methods and theologies for understanding and interpreting the nature and dynamics of civil society, including the emerging global civil society, they have not explicitly provided a procedural method of ethical analysis that is informed by public theology.

In this chapter, I propose an ethical methodology as a form of public discourse, a model that incorporates the insights of public theology. Public

---

12. Smith, *Concept of the Spiritual,* pp. 77-78.

13. As Max Stackhouse puts it, "[P]ublic theology intends to selectively put modernizing developments on a more secure basis by exposing, and where appropriate correcting, the submerged theological assumptions that are internal to them and sustaining them. Such an intent entails the belief that theology as a critical and constructive discipline is, properly, a *mode of public discourse* that both interprets the key areas of the common life in ways indispensable to the historical and social sciences, by pointing out the religious and ethical presuppositions that are operating in a given ethos, and simultaneously offers normative ethical guidance for the reformation and sustenance of a viable civil society, the basis of civilization." See Stackhouse, *God and Globalization,* Volume 4: *Globalization and Grace* (New York: Continuum, 2007), p. 85. Emphasis added. See also pp. 91-99, 112.

theology has rejected theology as a discourse that withdraws into a spiritual gated community of sectarian isolation. It has similarly rejected ways of speaking about the reality of God and God's will that are not valid in the contested common that is the modern civil society. It has instead proposed an understanding of ethics that speaks socially and theologically to the developments and issues of our times, and has taken the position that theology is capable of investigating — "according to the highest standards of truth and justice that are known and debated in reasonable discourse" — the relative validity of various religious claims about how civil society should operate.[14] It has also taken on the responsibility of clarifying the religious and ethological foundations of policies and ideas that shape civil society.

In the model of ethical analysis that I am proposing I show how public theologians can come into an informed judgment on public policies in the light of how people ought to live in civil society. It provides a robust "mechanics," which is ideationally rooted in public theology and deliberately crafted, to aid both experienced theologians and doctoral students to prepare ethical analyses for public discourse in a pluralistic society like the United States.

As a teacher in one of America's oldest seminaries I have to parse together from various works a discernible pattern or method of analysis to train my students in public theological-ethical analyses. When teaching public theology, I am interested in not only leading students through the history, themes, and debates in the field, but also in training them to be good ethical analysts in the public sphere. I have encountered students who wanted to work for public policy institutes, where they hoped to be in positions to influence public policy debates from informed theological standpoints. Similarly, there have been students who wanted to serve traditional parish pulpits but also desired to acquire the competence to analyze public policies from a public theology perspective. There has not been a handy and readily available model to guide such beginners in the practice. With this chapter I hope to fill the gap, to creatively advance the development of public theology.

My desire to fill the gap is not just about giving (would-be) ethicists another instrument in their toolbox. Rather, it is to convey to them the no-

---

14. Max Stackhouse, "Introduction: Foundations and Purposes," in *On Moral Business: Classical and Contemporary Resources for Ethics and Economic Life,* ed. Max Stackhouse, Dennis P. McCann, and Shirley J. Roels, with Preston N. Williams (Grand Rapids: Eerdmans, 1995), pp. 10-34.

tion that ethics is a methodical form of reason and speech. This is fundamental to understanding public theology as a form of discourse and discerning from what philosophical position it sallies forth into the public
arena. It is important to note right away that ethics as reason and speech is
not about an ethicist's process of reasoning through a problem and then
voicing his or her thought about the moral fabric of society. What I have in
mind is much more fundamental. I am here thinking of ethics as a process
that unlocks the power of truth, justice, and harmony embodied in any
form of human sociality. This process of unlocking truth, justice, and harmony is not aimed at providing the means or wisdom for perfecting the
bureaucratic management of any current social order or sociality — although this is an aspect of reason we will call technical reason. But there is
also ontological reason, which is really about the determination of the
proper ends, or *teloi,* of any form of human sociality.[15] Ethics points us to
ends beyond the existing forms of human sociality. It insists that an existing order can find those ends beyond itself only when its agents rise beyond themselves.

Reason is principally about the determination of the ends of human
sociality. These are ends that should point us beyond the existing forms of
human sociality, to move our gaze further beyond ourselves. Reason is the
source of meaning; it is the search for fulfillment, representing an inescap-
able moral call on humanity to deepen and widen being. Ontological reason is the precondition for technical reason. Ontological reason is the process in which technical reason reaches beyond itself and its world.
Ontological reason is the movement of technical reason toward ultimate
meaning and significance. Technical reason is the presupposition of ontological reason, and ontological reason is the fulfillment of technical reason.
The two concepts of reason are in means-end relationship. Technical reason deals with the discovery of the means of actualization of human potentials. Ontological reason is the longing for the source of all meaning,
the driving force toward the good itself.[16]

---

15. Practical reasoning (wisdom) as the ability to exercise sound judgment and discern
the best means to attain goals is part of the deliberative process that goes into technical reasoning, which is about finding the means (wisdom) and technical mastery for attaining and
advancing an end or goal. Ontological reasoning is about the determination of proper ends
and the ultimate vision that should guide society.

16. Paul Tillich, *Systematic Theology,* Volume 1: *Reason and Revelation, Being, and God*
(Chicago: University of Chicago Press, 1951), pp. 72-77. Given our arguments about unended
action, technical reason appears to be best suited to the public space in a pluralistic society.

In this quest for fulfillment our brains, voices, and bodies are all involved in both resisting existing orders that absolutize themselves, and in forging and straining toward a new window of "else-where" and "else-when." This image of a window points us toward both what is present and what is absent in an extant order. In ethics we are trying to paint a portrait of our community and/or the subject of our focus. The portrait becomes a space through which the community or the subject is seen. But it also provides a lens and a perspective to see what is absent in the community. Like all windows, an ethical window marks the boundary between what is currently obtained (what is inside the house) and what is outside, what we can strive for in the open, unconfined space. Through this window we are trying to see what is outside ourselves, outside our current existing order, but the window is not always totally transparent; we see through an inherited (though continually reworked) mental representation. We are trying to see the world, the cosmos outside, through our particular *thrownness* (situatedness or existence) into the world.

Theological-ethical reasoning is thus in large part an attempt to provide a window on creativity and an avenue to show how the creative principles at work in human coexistence and the larger cosmos can be harnessed for human flourishing (*eudaimonia* in the Aristotelian sense). It is an ordered speech that attempts to link forms of human sociality to the perceived[17] inner thrust of God's liberatory activity in the world. In other words, ethics attempts to relate the inner life of social institutions to the invisible rhythms and creative force that sustain and move the universe. I have here in mind Paul Tillich's notion of theonomous ethics.

Mechanics of Ethical Methodology

Let me now state how the second part of this chapter will unfold. It is divided into three sections; the first lays out a philosophy of ethical analysis.

---

17. I carefully choose the word "perceived" to indicate that human perception of God's activities in the world is always a particular decision. "We *must* make decisions about where God is at work so we can join in the fight against evil. But there is no perfect guide for discerning God's movement in the world. Contrary to what many conservatives would say, the Bible is not a blueprint on this matter. It is a valuable symbol for pointing to God's revelation in Jesus, but it is not self-interpreting. We are thus placed in an existential situation of freedom in which the burden is on us to make decisions without a guaranteed ethical guide." James H. Cone, *A Black Theology of Liberation* (Maryknoll, NY: Orbis, 1986), p. 7. Emphasis in original.

It develops some insights about ethical analysis that serve as gangway connecting the notion of ethics in the above introductory remarks and the practical, nitty-gritty task of constructing a meta-ethical model. Based on the philosophy developed, I describe in the second section the appropriate methodology for doing theological-ethical analyses of social problems. It is important to mention that the methodical steps spread out in this section are not like a cookbook recipe. In preparing food, attention to the recipe has an end other than itself, but the methodology adumbrated here does not; good and effective methodology in itself is an end. Cooking is an activity of producing something beyond the cooking act itself. In contrast, ethical methodology as understood by this author is the activity of doing ethics well as such. Methodology is not fundamentally the production of goods external to the ethical reasoning, but the excellence or perfection of internal goods, goods constituting the internal aims of the social practice of public theology. Third, I offer some final remarks aimed at uncovering the deep theological-social theoretical assumptions that are internal to the model.

A Philosophy of Ethical Analysis

The first thing we need to know in the task of analysis is the answer to this important question: What is ethical analysis? In my understanding, ethical analysis is a tripartite process that involves (a) identifying a problem that threatens the moral fabric and stability of society; (b) showing how the particular problem has moved society away from that which underlies its existence and expresses itself in it as the ultimate concern; and (c) indicating that by solving the problem the society will be brought in close responsiveness to its ultimate concern.

Every society or tradition has certain categories, concepts, and images from which to draw and in which to root its analysis when executing (b) and (c) above. It makes eminent sense to examine — even if only preliminarily — moral problems through them, in order to show how the various dimensions of the problem and the community that bears its burden are illuminated when understood in relation to the moral and spiritual constructs of the community. The ultimate concern for most societies is usually understood as God; but in some societies it may be understood as a philosophical absolute (such as eudaimonia, rational order, will to power). In any case it is that which is most important and taken seriously as the deepest and most fundamental reality. If this ultimate concern is envisioned as God or a doctrine of God, then we are doing theological-ethical analysis. If, on the other hand, a philosophical construct or absolute is considered to be ultimate, then we are doing social-ethical analysis.[18]

In either case, ethical analysis is both a critical and a constructive investigation of a social problem in the light of a community's ultimate point of reference for all life as well as for its immediate concerns. And public ethical analysis is about identifying obstacles to the realization of the promises at the heart of a society's ultimate reality and showing ways to remove or overcome them. In faith — that is, in terms of believing and showing concern about that which is considered ultimate — the ethical analyst works to remove all obstacles to the vision of the good life or the common good. She is constantly and deliberately searching for obstacles to be overcome in the hope of realizing the good life, eudaimonia, the kingdom of God, or the common good. Does she ever reach the end of this process? By no means! This is so because, as Paul Tillich puts it, faith is concern about the ultimate. We never grasp this reality; it is always beyond our reach. So we will never rest content with the quality of humanization and humanness in a given human sociality. Faith invites us to test all our human creations to see and judge whether there is something greater or better on the horizon and to always press on to it.

In a certain sense, ethical analysis is faith seeking resistance. Every genuine ethical analysis aims to overcome resistance to the common good in the name of the ultimate principle. The ethicist is driven to her task by an urge to overcome — which is not necessarily the same thing as an urge to dominate or control. She thirsts to confront and overcome the resistance she encounters in ideas, problems, groups, and institutions that threaten the moral fabric of society and hinder the fulfillment of society's ultimate good. This urge never rests because its object can never be fully attained. The ethicist never comes to the point or state of affairs in which all resis-

---

18. Some readers may find the distinction between theological-ethical and social-ethical analysis questionable because the difference between them is only attributed to whether an ethical analysis refers to God (gods) or a philosophical construct as the ultimate concern of society. The distinction is further muddled by the fact that there are philosophical constructs of God. I have made this crude distinction only to gesture to the idea that in a pluralistic society there are some who may believe in God (whether that deity is personal, anthropomorphic, biblical or not) and others who do not believe in God or are agnostic and thus prefer to erect a non-God, non-divine philosophical ideal as the ultimate point of reference for orientation to life. It is only in this sense that I want the distinction to be interpreted.

tance has been overcome because the ideal in the name of which she struggles is always in the future. An ethicist's work is never done. Hers is an activity in pursuit of an else-where and else-when of "pure delight," an ultimate human good. The ethicist struggles against all that stands in the way of the common good. In other words, she strives until the paramount goal or end of her community is attained — but nay, it can only ever be asymptotically approached. In reality, she never adjudges her society as having reached that level of human flourishing where all strivings for truth, justice, and harmony may stop.

In conclusion, let me state that every genuine ethical analysis in any society is set in motion by four conditions. First, there is an ultimate concern that serves as a telos for that society. Ethics is a search for God and how God is revealed in humanity and in the struggles for human flourishing. Essentially, then, to undertake theological ethics is to search for God in the midst of history and to relate a community's understanding of the nature of ultimate reality and its derived truth to the logic and dynamics of human sociality. The truth we are talking about here is an anthropocentric, earthly one. Yet at the same time it is a truth sourced from an understanding of the ultimate; is pre-formed, formed, and in-formed and is appropriated through an encounter with a concrete humanity, the reality of a people at a specific historical juncture.

This power of truth "touches ground," as my former teacher, Dr. Peter Paris would say, when it is on the side of human freedom and affirms human flourishing in its broadest meaning. Thus the search for God is, in a certain sense, a search for human freedom and flourishing in the name of an "ought-to-be." In terms of the prophetic tradition of the Israelite prophets of the Bible, the ought-to-be is a demand for justice in the name of Yahweh, in the name of the principle that implies ultimacy and universality. The God in whose name the ought-to-be is given and sustained is "the God of justice, who because he represents justice for everybody and every nation, is called the universal God, the God of the universe."[19] The "ought to be" stands as a critique of the present situation and drives it beyond to a utopological-progressive state of communion between human beings and between God and humans.

The second condition that sets ethical analysis in motion is this: there are (perceived) obstacles and resistance to the realization of the ought-to-be. Third, there is a desire to overcome such resistance by the power of

19. Paul Tillich, *Dynamics of Faith* (New York: HarperCollins, 2001), p. 3.

one's analysis, which can induce political will and social action to alter the prevailing situation. An ethical analysis is not a completely dispassionate exercise. It involves a vision or desire to change certain social circumstances, the *eros* to aid a given society to reach a higher level of human flourishing. Finally, the ethical analyst must be willing to oppose her proffered solutions because no solution or institution is timeless. They must all be subjected to the demands of the incoming future. Every generation must be allowed to be creative on its own terms. Every age must seek for its "permanent" laws and institutions, which must be washed away like sand castles at the beach, if need be, by the crashing waves of the incoming future. Ethical analysis is an activity of creative destruction. The ethicist who is unwilling to surpass that which she has created or inherited in the name of that which encompasses and transcends her "heirloom" has not fully grasped the notion of ethics as the science of harnessing the creative principles at work in existential conditions for human flourishing or the common good.

The Methodology of Ethical Analysis

[A]n inquiry in social ethics should begin with some actual, concrete problems arising among human beings in their public actions. That is to say, such an investigation should begin with some conflicting views about the good that humans can and should do. . . . The result of such an investigation should be some resolution of the problem or a restatement of the problem in order to liberate the agents and their activities and to establish thereby the conditions for more creative enterprise.[20]

It is now time to sketch the network of analyses that constitutes ethical analysis and give determinate content to the philosophical position I have just sketched out.[21] For the sake of convenience, I will divide the process of ethical analysis into three major segments or stages: first, social or ethos analysis; second, resources for reflecting on the problem; and third, ethical solution and payoff. At the end of the presentation of the three segments, I

20. Peter J. Paris, *Black Religious Leaders* (Louisville: Westminster John Knox, 1991), pp. 31-32.

21. I would like to thank Professors Max Stackhouse and Mark Taylor of Princeton Theological Seminary for their comments on an earlier version of this section in 2007.

will provide a flowchart that summarizes the contents of the stages and how they are articulated.

It is germane to mention at this juncture that the task of ethical analysis is not only about public issues and pursuit of social justice. Ethics includes personal conduct, individual fairness, and our actions and behaviors in the private spheres. It is only for our limited purposes here that the ethical is limited to the social, the common, spheres of human coexistence. Furthermore, ethics is also concerned with corporate behaviors which are in the public sphere. This chapter has not explicitly addressed business ethics. Nonetheless, it contains insights and ideas for business ethics. The focus of the chapter is on ethical methodology for public policy (or public policy debates), which covers economic ethics and the economy. Economic ethics and economy encompass business (corporate) ethics and businesses.

If a public policy is going to be enacted to cover businesses — an important segment of the public — then the methodology as explained here applies to such a process. And if a corporation is thinking of jumping into a public debate in a pluralistic society like ours it can follow the methodology of this chapter to craft its argument. It may not use God as the ultimate concern, but it can formulate another supreme good. The chapter makes provision for alternative views of ultimate concern, supreme good, or philosophical construct. On the other hand, the methodology of this chapter will not be of much use to the analyst who thinks of business ethics in the narrow sense of "legal ethics," that is, the covering of bases to avoid liabilities and injury to public reputation of corporations, and staying out of obvious legal troubles.

Social Analysis

Every ethical analysis starts by defining or describing a problem or ethical concern that an ethicist believes to be threatening the moral fabric and stability of a particular society or community. In doing so, the ethicist needs to state clearly and precisely why the issue identified constitutes such a problem, and why citizens need to focus on eliminating or ameliorating it.

The problem having been adequately identified, the ethicist next undertakes a close investigation of it, grounded in the social sciences but drawing as well on the humanities, hard sciences, and other disciplines. Here it is often helpful to provide her target audience with empirical analyses backed by historical and contemporary data.

In this part of the analysis she aims to take into consideration the multiple forces or propensities that structure a society and its problems.

Her next step is to examine the ethos — the web of values, norms, organizing principles, and so forth — of the society and how it relates to the problem under analysis, here again relying on the work of specialists in related fields. This step is important because if an ethicist hopes to change something, she must understand the presuppositions undergirding it. She must wrestle with the values implicit in the culture, comprehend what makes particular actions and behaviors legitimate, good, right. There are resources in every community to draw from in analyzing an ethical problem. There are traditions, constitutions, laws, and exemplars of moral excellence to bring to bear on the problem and its possible solution. This brings us to the next segment of the methodological process of ethical analysis.

Resources for Reflecting on the Problem

Moving into the next phase of the analysis, the ethicist must discuss the theological, biblical (or other textual), and philosophical resources she will bring to bear on the problem. She must do so with an eye toward grounding and funding a potential solution or response, for her overall aim here is to formulate her theological (or philosophical) presuppositions about human beings and their place in the world vis-à-vis God or the ultimate. Of course, she may need to develop a fresh theology in light of the issue before her. Either way, the important thing is to articulate as clearly as possible the vision or concept of ultimate reality that will legitimize the proposed solution, whether it is appropriated from an existing paradigm or constructed afresh.

In doing this the ethicist ought not to rely on theology alone. She should undertake a rigorous ethological analysis of the operating norms in the applicable society, to make sure the solution is appropriate for the problem. Such appropriateness may be evaluated from two angles: that of the right and that of the good, that is, deontologically and teleologically.[22] In deontological terms, the ethicist needs to know if the operating norms are in accord with the best knowledge available theologically by common grace — that is, to see whether they are in accord with the laws of God. Te-

---

22. Stackhouse, "Introduction," pp. 12-14.

leologically, the question is whether they are in accord with the best theological vision of the purposes of God we can know. Of course, the ethicist working outside a theistic paradigm can do the deontological and teleological investigations by using other constructs, such as Kant's categorical imperative or Aristotle's eudaimonia (flourishing life, happiness). In all this, the ethicist is inquiring as to what resources in the ethos can contribute to a solution or better solution. More importantly, she wants to find out "whether what is going on ought to go on. . . . Are the functioning principles and governing goals valid?"[23] On this note, the second major segment of the methodological flowchart (see stage 2 below) comes to a close — and we shall now proceed to the next and final segment.

Solution and Payoff

In this last and largely prescriptive segment of the process, we encounter six doorways. These offer, as Max Stackhouse puts it, "guidance about how we might, insofar as it is possible, form a more valid ethos and develop those attitudes, institutions, habits, policies, and programs that are in accord with a more ethically viable ethos, rightly legitimated by a valid theological view of ultimate reality."[24]

At this point, the ethicist has clearly identified the social problem, its impact on the moral fabric of the community, and the theological and philosophical resources she hopes can offer valuable insights in the search for solution. Now she is ready to suggest a solution. This is the first of the six doorways she has to traverse. The background question that drives her discourse at this stage is, What is the ethical solution (response, idea, paradigm, or intuition) that flows from my theological analysis (discourse) that bears upon the problem? Her task here must remain incomplete until she shows how her vaunted solution either strengthens the community or ameliorates (resolves, reframes) the identified problem.

Second, the presentation of the proposed solution should be informed by a dialogue with important thinkers in the field. Ethicists are not gods who pronounce solutions from Olympian heights. Thus, an ethicist must show how her preferred solution is better than those offered by other scholars or how it improves on existing practices of the community.

23. Stackhouse, "Introduction," p. 11.
24. Stackhouse, "Introduction," p. 16.

Third, once the solution is well defined and defended, the ethicist must show how it fits into the ethos of the community. She must tell her audience why her solution should be considered a fitting response by the community at the given historical juncture in which it finds itself. Asking how the proposed solution fits or does not easily fit into the ethos may require confrontation or transformation of the ethos in that respect.

Fourth, the ethicist needs to ask herself whether to propose new institutions or organizations to effect the necessary changes or support the realization of the proposed solution. If her answer is yes, she must determine the cost-benefit impact of establishing the new institution in the community. She goes to this length because she needs to convince decision-makers that her solutions will benefit society.

Fifth, many societies in the world are now pluralistic, and thus a public ethical analysis needs to adapt to this reality if it is to be taken seriously. The postmodern world that we live in today, with its characteristic lack of a common sacred canopy over the public square, demands that an analyst must make a case for her values and solutions to perceived problems in the public domain. The ethical analysis is incomplete until the author addresses herself to these pertinent questions: How will my solution be perceived in a pluralistic civil society with multiple religions and worldviews? Will it pass muster with social-scientific and academic viewpoints? What are some of the deontological, ethological, and teleological aspects of my proposed solution or response that can serve to build or uphold common morality (common good) in an open civil society?

Finally, what are the possible payoffs to the community if the proposed solution or response is accepted and adopted? In working out the payoffs, it is important for the ethicist to bear in mind that benefits and costs are not always expressible in calculable, short-run economic terms. She may need to find other ways of illustrating the costs and benefits.

I have presented the steps for ethical analysis, but ethics is not only about analysis. It is also about social action. So it is important to situate our methodology within the context of social action informed by social or ethical principles. The ethical methodology we have just developed enables the ethicist or activist to do two things: first, to clearly see, understand, and judge (based on her theological or philosophical principles) the state of the problem; and second, to identify the most fitting solutions which can address the problem in the light of one's theology or social principles, and pluralism. These should lead to the final stage of action, praxis. The real purpose of analysis is to recognize the ways in which to act in order to change the circumstances that threaten the common good. Pope John XXIII puts it well in his May 15, 1961, encyclical letter, *Mater et Magistra,* when he states,

> There are three stages which should normally be followed in the reduction of social principles into practice. First, one reviews the concrete situation; secondly, one forms a judgment on it in the light of these same principles; thirdly, one decides what in the circumstances can and should be done to implement these principles. These are the three stages that are usually expressed in the three terms: look, judge, act.[25]

Flowchart of Ethical Analysis

In the preceding pages I set out the mechanics for executing an ethical analysis. I also briefly located the analysis in the context of an overarching purpose of social action. It bears noting that the methodology that has been presented is an ideal format. Most ethicists do not religiously follow this step-by-step approach. They often use a network approach, looping in and out of these stages in a non-sequential manner. The important thing is that the various elements, segments, or stages we have laid out are discernible in their works. A good and rigorous ethical analysis will always define or state the problem it intends to address, give a sense of the theological (philosophical or ethological) resources it is using to shape the discourse, and fund the offering of a solution to the problem. Of course, not every analysis will endeavor to present each of these three dimensions in the manifold richness of a unified and coherent discourse as I have endeavored to present in this chapter. I have explicitly presented an ideal that is implicit in the majority of good ethical analyses.[26] The purpose is to enable students to clearly

25. Pope John XXIII, *Mater et Magistra* (1961), no. 236. Available online at www.vatican .va. It is tempting at this point to consider the major social encyclicals that tackle issues of social justice and public theology that are indicated in this chapter. To do this will take us too far afield as this chapter is only concerned with developing an ethical methodology for public theology, not with the concrete and specific analysis of any social issue. It will also be interesting to see how the ethical methodology of the major social encyclicals fits or does not fit with the method developed in this chapter. This is yet another task that we must let pass for now.

26. For examples of the use of this methodology in ethical analysis see Nimi Wariboko, *The Depth and Destiny of Work: An African Theological Interpretation* (Trenton: Africa World

follow the pedagogy of ethical analysis. I now offer a summary of the methodology in a "flowchart" format for quick reference.

Stage 1: Social Analysis (Ethos Analysis)
a. What is the problem or concern? Why is it a problem? This is the issue considered to be threatening the moral fabric and stability of the society or community.
b. Examination of the problem. Draw from social sciences, humanities, sciences, and other disciplines to help others understand the problem in its crucial dimensions. It helps to provide some empirical analyses backed by historical and contemporary data. This is one way of taking into account the multiple forces that structure a society.
c. Examination of the ethos (values, norms, etc.) of the society and how it relates to the problem. Changing anything involves understanding the presuppositions that underlie it.

Stage 2: Resources for Reflecting on the Problem
a. Identify theological, textual, and philosophical resources that will be brought to bear on the problem and also ground and fund a possible ethical solution, paradigm, response.
b. Analyze the operating norms in the ethos (discovered by ethology) to see if they are basically right (deontologically, that is, in accord with the best knowledge available theologically by common grace or in accord with the "laws of God"). And see if they are also actually good (teleologically, that is, in accord with the best theological vision of the purposes of God we can know).

Stage 3: Ethical Solution and Payoff
a. What is the ethical solution (response, idea, paradigm, intuition) that flows from the theological analysis/discourse that bears upon the problem? Show how it can either strengthen the community or reduce (remove, reframe, solve) the identified problem.

Press, 2008); Nimi Wariboko, *God and Money: A Theology of Money in a Globalizing World* (Lanham, MD: Lexington, 2008); Mark Lewis Taylor, *The Executed Gods: The Way of the Cross in Lockdown America* (Minneapolis: Fortress Press, 2001); Miroslav Volf, *Exclusion and Embrace: A Theological Exploration of Identity, Otherness, and Reconciliation* (Nashville: Abingdon, 1996); and Amos Yong, *Theology and Down Syndrome: Reimagining Disability in Late Modernity* (Waco: Baylor University Press, 2007).

b. This solution should be framed by dialogue with important thinkers in the field.

c. Once the solution is well defined, show how it fits into the ethos of the community identified in Stage 1 above. Explain why the solution should be considered a fitting response by the community that is at a given historical juncture. Asking how the proposed solution fits or does not easily fit into the ethos may require confrontation or transformation of the ethos in that respect. Inquire also as to what resources in the ethos could contribute to a better solution.

d. Determine whether a new institution or organization needs to be proposed in order to effect the necessary changes. If so, what is the cost-benefit impact of this new institution on the community?

e. Discern how the proposed solution will be perceived in a pluralistic civil society with multiple religions and worldviews. Will it also pass muster in academic circles? What are some of the deontological, ethological, and teleological aspects of the proposed solution that can serve to build or uphold common morality (common good) in an open civil society?

f. What are the possible overall payoffs to the community if the solution or response is accepted and adopted? Remember, benefits are not always expressible in calculable short-run economic terms.

Concluding Remarks

This chapter has shown how ethicists committed to the particularity of pentecostalism can develop a public theology argument that moves not only toward the wider theological academy, but also toward the multiple constituencies that make up the postmodern, highly diversified public square. The deep structure beneath the ethical model it presented is the centrality of the Pentecost narrative and the place of the "many tongues" in pentecostal theological imagination. The perspective of the many tongues invites us to think about public policy debates not from one normative paradigm "but a multiplicity of . . . models and modes of exchanges, each potentially making a distinct contribution to the kind of [polity] of shalom that our world needs."[27]

There are other dimensions to the deep structure worth revealing at

27. Yong, *Days of Caesar*, p. 257.

this juncture. What I have submitted as a model is a discourse that attempts to relate ultimate ends, theological presuppositions, to social reality, social sciences, ethos, and pluralism. It is rooted in a Troeltschian discourse of how to relate the formal spirit of the church to the material realities that constitute the civil society, to the goods and purposes of the inner-worldly life. One of Ernst Troeltsch's contributions to Christian ethics is to show how the church is able to bring together in unity the transcendent goals of Christianity and cultural values as it engages its public. The ethical methodology of this chapter has shown how the theologian can navigate the problematic relation between Christianity and culture, can mediate the tension between (religious) Christian moral purposes and humane ethical motivation without retreating behind sectarian walls. As Brent W. Sockness argues:

> The modern religious crisis is an ethical and cultural one not to be solved by writing new dogmatic treatises. The question is how to mediate and hold together the tense polarity between religious and humane morality, or, to borrow Troeltsch's illustration, how to square the piety of Luther and Bach, on the one hand, with the humanity of Goethe and the statesmanship of Bismarck, on the other hand. . . . For Troeltsch, the exploration of the "fundamental problems of ethics" is largely a matter of developing a conceptual scheme or set of categories capable of doing justice to the nature of moral reality as we find it historically and actually experience it.[28]

The model has shown us a simple way to make Christian ideas relevant to social issues even when they infinitely transcend the social and ultimately pull it toward God's purposes. Put differently, it reveals how theological ethics or public theology can move away from conceptual analyses to engage with concrete policy discourse on social problems. This engagement with policies and with contemporary history is necessary to make public theology practical. The rigors of a deliberate and well thought out ethical analysis can offer practical guidance to decision-makers as they deal with the urgent issues of our time.

There is another aspect of the deep structure of the model worth

---

28. Brent W. Sockness, "Looking Behind the Social Teachings: Troeltsch's Methodological Reflections in 'Fundamental Problems of Ethics' (1902)," *The Annual, Society of Christian Ethics* (1995): 243-44.

pointing out in order to further expose the submerged theological-social theoretical assumptions that are internal to it and also sustain it. The ethical analysis I have developed in this paper does not only attempt to grasp the social analysis and empirical reality of problems, but also strives to plumb the depths of the presuppositions about human nature and community's understanding of God in its discourse. The thinking is that without the analyst understanding the deep presuppositions, the deepest and broadest ethos of forms of human sociality, she might miss the vital non-material motivating factors for/against a public policy, ethical reforms within the economy and society, or the pursuit of the common good. As Stackhouse, one of America's eminent ethicists, has argued, public theologians enter into debates about political and economic policies based on the conviction that the political economy — and indeed all civilizations — are deeply influenced by religion, worldview, and ethical presuppositions.[29] Stackhouse is, of course, drawing from what Max Weber taught us long ago. Weber argued that religion is an independent factor that substantively shapes culture, and economic systems in particular are influenced by religious factors that are in constant interaction with material interests.[30]

Having said all this, I would like to state that neither public theology nor the ethical methodology described in this chapter is about giving direction to governmental policy. Both of them — at least as I understand them — are aimed at recognizing the religious dynamics that influence social life. Whether we are talking about public theology in its thematic-discursive format or in its analytical-methodological format as presented in this chapter, the attention is on the need to develop capabilities that address and guide the basic ordering of the common life in non-particularistic theological terms. The overarching intention is to present arguments that promote greater inclusiveness, greater justice, and higher levels of human flourishing that spur on men and women to transformative praxis.

THE MAIN theological impulse of this chapter as driven by the "many tongues" motif in pentecostal theological imagination is not only to intervene in debates relating to the public policy, but also to help in crafting the "public forum in which all creatures will bear witness in the particularity

---

29. Stackhouse, *Globalization and Grace.*

30. Max Weber, *Economy and Society: An Outline of Interpretative Sociology* (Berkeley: University of California Press, 1978). See also his *Protestant Ethic and the Spirit of Capitalism,* trans. T. Parsons (London: Allen & Unwin, 1930).

and peculiarity of their own tongues, to the goodness, truth, and beauty of their Creator."[31]

In particular, the preceding discourse of ethical methodology is meant to enable pentecostals to engender a reflexive and reflective response to the necessity and crisis of pluralism interior to the historico-cultural situatedness of the twenty-first-century world. The beginning of a critical engagement with the publics of this world from the standpoint of the Pentecostal principle and its ethics is the awareness of the pentecostal spirit, that is to say, a knowing of the moral self-interpretation of a historical community of persons who are (or think they are) the bearers of the principle. The engagement must be appropriately grounded in the specificity of their spirit, "which acts as the normative sieve that strains, sifts, and negotiates [their] orientation to the future."[32] Now here we may ask — indeed must ask: What is pentecostal spirit? The response to this pertinent question is what will preoccupy us in the next chapter.

---

31. Yong, *Days of Caesar*, p. 364.

32. Tsenay Serequeberhan, *The Hermeneutics of African Philosophy: Horizon and Discourse* (New York: Routledge, 1994), p. 28.

4 The Pentecostal Spirit

Way of Being for the Pentecostal Principle

Here I want to attempt to apprehend the spirit of pentecostalism as a social movement based on our understanding of the pentecostal principle and also recognizing the fact that pentecostals are not necessarily the (exclusive) bearers of the pentecostal principle. This involves discerning how a social group captures the essence of the principle and translates it into concrete practices that constitute social life. It also involves identifying a particular mindfulness, sensibility, or a display of character, and commitment of personal and social lives that we can define as the reality for the pentecostal principle. A more direct ethical approach to this task is to think of it as a group's way of being as reflected in its self-interpretation of its moral life.

The pentecostal spirit is a way of being that is radically open to divine surprises, always at work resisting obstacles to human flourishing, and committed to creating, broadening, and deepening new possibilities for life. The word "spirit" here means the totality of a group's creative self-interpretation of itself or its moral life. In any temporal orientation we see that the unity of the "is" and the "ought" of a people and history is the site for the relationality of the triad of nomos-ethos-kairos. The human spirit of an age is the ethical ideal that arises from the tension between the symbol of the "is" (what is already) and the "ought" (what ought to be realized) in the directedness of communal structures (meaning-fulfilling, existential relationships) toward better future alternatives, toward freedom.[1]

---

1. By freedom I mean not *free will* but the belief (demand) that something new could be realized through acting agents.

This tension or struggle is "the dialectic stimulus of history, never allowing history to come to a rest."[2] Put another way, spirit refers to the principle of self-consciousness or subjectivity.

A critique of and resistance to all forms of absolutism is the mode of thought and orienting vision inherent in the culture (spatial-temporal phase) that Tillich identified as the Protestant Era. This particular expression of the human spirit is different from what is emerging in the Pentecostal Era. The current era is about creativity that goes beyond critique and deconstruction to weaving and reweaving the infinite fabric of life with the life-affirming, liberating, and non-engineered threads of its ultimate source of existence. Put another way, it is creativity that justly and appropriately responds to divine ontological creativity.

The rest of this chapter unfolds as follows: first, I will describe the expressions of human spirit under Protestanism and pentecostalism. A major dimension of the pentecostal spirit and the global pentecostal movement itself is the consciousness of natality (new birth). There are five forms of birth or beginning that are philosophical thematics in pentecostal spirituality. Descriptions and analyses of the forms of natality in pentecostalism constitute the second part of this chapter. The consciousness of natality involves intentional acts of rupture, which lift the crust of tradition and habitude off the common world, offering what we might call a new "time gap of existence."[3] This act of world (re)making, this act of bringing the world into greater actuality through human inventiveness, is among other considerations, an attempt to cultivate the self. The analysis of the technology of self-cultivation, identity, and subjectivity forms the third part of the chapter.

The fourth part investigates the playful character of the pentecostal spirit. Pentecostalism "profanes" the sacred without abolishing the sphere of the sacred. It deactivates the aura that attends to the rites and stories (myths) of the sacred sphere. The analysis of the deactivation of the sacred leads to a discussion of what I will call a "deactivation of grace" under pentecostalism. Pentecostalism opens up grace into new possible uses: deactivating the apparatuses of grace as power of salvation and bringing them into common use. The chapter ends with an examination of the various

---

2. Paul Tillich, *The System of the Sciences According to Objects and Methods,* trans. Paul Wiebe (East Brunswick, NJ: Associated University Press, 1982 [1923]), p. 204.

3. See Nimi Wariboko, *Ethics and Time: Ethos of Temporal Orientation in Politics and Religion of the Niger Delta* (Lanham, MD: Lexington, 2010).

ways the pentecostal spirit can inform pentecostal ethical methodology. The understanding of the pentecostal spirit revealed in this chapter enables us to suggest new directions for ethical methodology in the light of the pentecostal principle.

The Expression of Human Spirit:
From Protestantism to Pentecostalism

It is germane to note here that the expressions of the human spirit in both the Protestant Era and Pentecostal Era are undergirded by a similar drive: to give every individual regardless of class, race, or any other social predicate the full opportunity to fulfill his or her potentialities, and to create and renew given social relations and finite moral worlds. The difference between the two lies in how this moral imperative is cognized, interpreted, inscribed, and supported in the culture. One focuses on resisting obstacles to the emergence of the new; the other focuses on the capacity to initiate the new. In reality or praxis, the two can be distinguished but can never be separated. They are two edges of the same blade — and right now the cutting edge, the face that is sparkling in the shadowless noonday sun, is the pentecostal side.

The current state of pentecostalism in the world may not properly reflect this spirit; nonetheless, it captures the inner meaning of the Christian principle of self-consciousness (the moral imperative) more than Protestantism does. If one was free before the Reformation, and some became free after the revolt, all are free under pentecostalism. This is the moral interpretation of the pentecostal core belief that all can prophesy, all can lead, all can initiate the new, and all can equally be carriers of the Spirit.[4]

This assent to freedom, to the realization of potentialities, points to another significant area of difference between the pentecostal spirit and the Protestant one. The difference lies in the fact (understanding, perception) that for pentecostals the moral imperative is one and the same thing as a creative imperative. For pentecostals the *imago Dei* (which is related to the first divine moral command) is not so much about reason or

---

4. For an interesting perspective on the church as a community of prophethood of believers see Roger Stronstad, *The Prophethood of All Believers: A Study in Luke's Charismatic Theology* (Cleveland, TN: CPT Press, 2010). For a quick glance at the argument of the book, see pp. 1-3, 66-70, 111-22.

relationality as it is about the creative powers God has put in human be-ings. Being created in the image of God means having the power to trans-form adverse personal and social conditions in order to abet human flour-ishing. In order to elucidate the theology behind this practical insight, let us turn to the thought of John Wall, a non-pentecostal theologian who has brilliantly theologized the *imago Dei* as the power of imitative creativity.[5] According to Wall, "moral life involves a capability for the *imitatio creatoris,* that is, humanity's deeper self-humanization by imitating the di-vine act of creation in the ongoing creation of our finite moral worlds."[6] In Wall's thinking, the first set of moral commands from God to human be-ings cannot be separated from and is best interpreted in the light of the *imago Dei.*

Wall gives an interesting interpretation of Genesis 1:26 and 28, espe-cially as these verses relate to humans being created in the image of God and God's very first biblical command to humanity to be fruitful and mul-tiply. To be created in the image of God (bearers of *imago Dei)* means God has affirmed the goodness of human capability to create, in imitation of God, for themselves. Humanity has been affirmed to create their own soci-eties and relations, to share in the fruitful creation of their relational, so-cial, historical, and moral worlds. As God has made God's self fruitful and multiplicative in the plurality and diversity of creation and in the replica-tion of God's image in humankind, humans are to analogously create their own image for themselves. To create their own image is to imitate what is deepest within themselves, the image of God.

According to Wall, imitating God, or rather the activity of creation it-self, involves understanding the salient moral lessons of the story of Gene-sis 1. The Genesis creation narrative is about bringing forth, about the poetics of the new. Thus bearing the image of God, for Wall, means hu-manity has a fundamental and original capability to "create social rela-tions that are new and hitherto unimagined."[7] The command to human-kind to multiply goes beyond biological procreation and points to broader social generative creativity.[8] As Wall puts it,

---

5. John Wall, "*Imitatio Creatoris:* The Hermeneutical Primordiality of Creativity in Moral Life," *The Journal of Religion* 87, no. 1 (January 2007): 21-42; Wall, *Moral Creativity: Paul Ricoeur and the Poetics of Possibility* (New York: Oxford University Press, 2005).

6. Wall, "*Imitatio Creatoris,*" p. 22.

7. Wall, "*Imitatio Creatoris,*" p. 36.

8. Given the diversity of God's creation, imitating the Creator calls human beings to cre-ate a historical moral world that is radically inclusive. See Wall, "*Imitatio Creatoris,*" p. 39. As

[The] command to imitate God's fruitfulness and multiplication is at least in part a command for humankind in turn to create and renew given society. Male and female are symbols of the primordial moral ability for the kind of (re)productive tension or stretching that may engender new forms of community on the basis of difference.[9]

No one should be surprised by the differences between the pentecostal spirit and the Protestant spirit and the close connection between the moral imperative and the creative imperative that we have uncovered. One thing that has long been clear about the pentecostal movement is its consciousness of natality. "New birth," "born again," "born of water and spirit," "new creation" — all these are terminologies that emphasize new beginnings, the renewing of the mind for a new phase of life, and then initiation of something new. They are pointers to new beginnings that mark not only eruptions in the common world where the self dwells, but also they are speaking forth and taking shape in the core of the self, remaking subjectivity.

Natality and Pentecostalism

The notion of pentecostal subjectivity is rooted in and grows out of its understanding of natality.[10] I stated above that there are five forms of birth or beginning as a philosophical thematic in pentecostal spiritual practice: spiritual natality, factual natality, political natality, friendship natality, and temporal natality. Pentecostals trace the first of these, spiritual natality, to the first giving of their life to Jesus Christ, considering it an event of novelty and unprecedented potentiality for the new. The birth signifies the opening of new horizons for the future: the potentiality of the world for capacity for beginning afresh to improve the self and its unfinished world, the shared common existence. In the early days of pente-

---

soon as God created God's image, it is named as multiple or plural: male and female. "Whatever kind of fruitfulness and multiplication may be commanded, it is to take place within human relations' difference and otherness. The cosmological creation of humankind is also ethical in the sense that it mythologizes ultimate possibilities for otherwise broken or alienated human relations" (p. 37).

9. Wall, *"Imitatio Creatoris,"* p. 38.

10. My understanding of natality is deeply informed by Hannah Arendt's political philosophy.

costalism, when the argument about speaking in tongues as evidence of Holy Spirit baptism raged on, the thinking was that this first birth was also a birth into tongues-speech (language). Birth and language coincided — both births happened at once. The moment of the person's thrownness into the born-again world was always already accompanied by linguistic natality. This inseparability itself points to the new believer's capacity to begin something new. The new language he or she speaks may be conditioned, but it is not entirely determined by preexisting human languages; its grammar, rules, and contents are not an imitation of preexisting languages. By this innovation, the new believer is an actor in the Arendtian sense of the word.

The factual natality is the daily spiritual discipline, the "crucifixion" of the body, the tearing of the subject (self) from the self and from the familiar circumstances in order to conform to a relevant image of a faithful disciple of Christ. It also involves the seeking of experience and ecstasy of miraculous exception that serve to affirm one's unabated citizenry in the world one entered at new birth. The subject continuously works on him or herself, undergoing necessary transformations, in order to grasp the full promises of the initial birth. This is the daily renewal (necessity, purgatory) of the initial birth. This process is never complete; it is circular. New illumination of the truth and the self only fuels a new ensemble of techniques, technologies, and desires for further actualization and transformation of the "inner man" or woman.

The political natality is the actualization of gifts (spiritual and non-spiritual), which makes a space for individuals in the shared common existence as distinguished carriers of the Holy Spirit and creative transformers of culture in the name of Christ. The world has to be prepared for the second coming of the Messiah. The spiritual form of natality represents the beginning of somebody with the capacity to initiate the new; the factual natality represents fidelity to that event, but the political natality has something more to it. It is not only the beginning of some*body,* but also the beginning of some*thing.* By virtue of political natality the pentecostal man or woman inserts him or herself into the pluralistic world where he or she aspires to act as an "apostle of the Messiah" charged with transforming the world. This insertion, this phase of ongoing rebirth, may be stimulated by what is happening in the culture at large, but it is never conditioned by it; its impulse springs from the spiritual and factual beginnings to which the pentecostal is responding by beginning something new, the transformation of culture. (It is important to mention that this form of political natality takes different shape in different societies and the Western notion of the politics is not always useful in discerning it.)[11]

Another form of natality is friendship natality, or *philos*-natality. It has long been known in Christian history that the birth into the Spirit is a birth into friendship with God and fellow believers on a universal level. Joachim of Fiore in the twelfth century called the Age of the Spirit, that is, the charismatic form of life, "friendship," and named it the highest stage of freedom. Friendship with Jesus is a particular messianic claim early Pentecostals made — as their successors do today — in line with Jesus' saying in John 15:15: "I do not call you servants any longer, because the servant does not know what the master is doing; but I have called you friends, because I have made known to you everything that I have heard from my Father."

Departing from Joachim's modalistic interpretation of history and resorting to a trinitarian pattern, Jürgen Moltmann deepens our understanding of this form of natality. He considers it to be a transition, a qualitative step, and not a quantitative leap, in the relationship with God. It is not an evolution from servant to friend, as Joachim and many a pentecostal in a triumphalist mapping out of superior identity would have us believe. He argues that

> By virtue of the indwelling of the Holy Spirit, people enter into this new 'direct' relationship with God. The freedom of God's friends does not evolve out of the freedom of God's children. It only becomes possible when people know themselves in God and God in them. That is the light of the Holy Spirit.[12]

This knowing of oneself in God, this knowing of the light of the Holy Spirit, is what pentecostals regard as a special quality of their walk with God. Friendship with God finds expressions in friendship with fellow believers, in personal and intimate relationships with one another. We read how color and class lines were erased at the Azusa Street revival. (Of course, this friendship is in constant struggle with many particularities of historical existence.) What binds pentecostals together in friendship is not common social position (as servants), not "consanguinity" (as brothers

11. For an example of pentecostals' understanding of politics, see Ogbu Kalu, *African Pentecostalism: An Introduction* (Oxford: Oxford University Press, 2008), pp. 200-216.

12. Jürgen Moltmann, *The Trinity and the Kingdom,* trans. Margaret Kohl (Minneapolis: Fortress, 1993), p. 220.

and sisters), but the intimacy they share through the indwelling Spirit and the joy they find in direct relationship with God and with one another.

A proper understanding of this fourth form of natality may throw light on the ontological basis of political natality and also the fellowship-community that arises in Acts 2 in the wake of the Pentecost. It will show us the potential political significance of the born-again experience and the fundamental healing of being that is possible with a deepening of pentecostal spirituality. Those who are familiar with the work of Aristotle will agree that in the preceding two sentences I have not asserted anything new in philosophical thought. One of the great insights of Aristotle's discussion of friendship (in *Nicomachean Ethics*, 1170a28-11b35) is that friendship is co-sharing of the same existence, the co-sharing of the sensation of being.[13]

---

13. Instead of reproducing Aristotle's particularly difficult and dense passage in the body of the chapter, I present it in the notes for those who want to consult it. I will be quoting from Aristotle, *Nicomachean Ethics*, trans. Terence Irwin (Indianapolis: Hackett, 1999), 1170a28-1171b35:

Life itself, then, is good and pleasant, as it would seem, at any rate, from the fact that everyone desires it, and decent and blessed people desire it more than others do — for their life is most choiceworthy for them, and their living is most blessed.

Now someone who sees perceives [senses] that he sees; one who hears perceives that he hears; one who walks perceives that he walks; and similarly in the other cases also there is some [element] that perceives that we are active; so that if we are perceiving, we perceive that we are perceiving, and if we are understanding, we perceive that we are understanding. Now perceiving that we are perceiving or understanding is the same as perceiving that we are, since we agreed that being is perceiving [sensing] or understanding [thinking].

Perceiving that we are alive is pleasant [sweet] in itself. For life is by nature a good, and it is pleasant to perceive that something good is present in us. Living is also choiceworthy, for a good person most of all, since being is good and pleasant for him; for he is pleased to perceive something good in itself together [with his own being].

The excellent [good] person is related to his friend in the same way as he is related to himself, since a friend is another himself. Therefore, just as his own being is choiceworthy [desirable] for him, his friend's being is choiceworthy for him in the same or similar way. We agreed that someone's own being is choiceworthy because he perceives that he is good, and this sort of perception is pleasant in itself. He must, then, perceive his friend's being together [with his own. ("One must also con-sent that his friend exists")], and he will do this when they live together and share conversation and thought. For in the case of human beings what seems to count as living together is this sharing of conversation and thought, not sharing the same pasture, as in the case of grazing animals. . . .

For friendship is community, and we are related to our friend as we are related to ourselves. Hence, since the perception of our being [the sensation of existing] is choiceworthy [desirable], so is the perception of our friend's being.

Giorgio Agamben summarizes this "extraordinarily dense" passage from Aristotle like this:

> Within [the] sensation of existing [the sensation of pure being that all human beings have] there is another sensation, specifically a human one, that takes the form of a joint sensation, or a con-sent *(synaisthanesthai)* with the existence of the friend. *Friendship is the instance of this "con-sentiment" of the existence of the friend within the sentiment of the existence itself.* But this means friendship has an ontological and political status. The sensation of being is, in fact, always already divided and "con-divided [*con-divisa, shared*], and friendship is the name of this "con-division." This sharing has nothing whatsoever to do with the modern chimera of intersubjectivity, the relationship between subjects. Rather, being itself is divided here, it is nonidentical to itself, and so the I and the friend are the two faces, or the two poles of this con-division or sharing.[14]

What this means is that the intensity of awareness of one's being as one engages with the Holy Spirit in particular encounters or contexts can trigger eros toward the other. The point at which I sense this intensity of my being (when, for example, I taste that the Lord is good and my existence is sweet) is the point of my participation in the Holy Spirit; and because the other and I are indwelled by the same Spirit and we are both in the same Spirit, my sensation of being can more than ever before "go through a con-senting which dislocates me and deports me toward the friend, toward the other self."[15] Life in the Spirit is divided, it is not identical to itself, such that I and others are multiple sites of this co-sharing or con-division. Put differently, I and others are the temple (not temples) of the Holy Spirit, and otherness is immanent in this temple, even in this my own tent (life) that houses being (existence). Formally, then, friendship natality can be defined as the birth of awareness of con-sentiment of being with the other as we are birthed in and bathing in the experience of the Holy Spirit. It is the birth of the network of being, living, friendship, and expansive fellow feeling that produces a new subject and guides the emergence of a subjectivity toward the good.

Before proceeding to the final form of natality, I would like to link this discussion of friendship natality to our discussion in the introductory chapter about of the fellowship and community that emerged from the

---

14. Giorgio Agamben, *What Is an Apparatus?* trans. David Kishik and Stefan Pedatella (Stanford: Stanford University Press, 2009), p. 34. Emphasis in original.

15. Agamben, *What Is an Apparatus?* p. 35.

Acts Pentecost event. There I argued, drawing from the philosophy of Jean-Luc Nancy, that the Pentecost event was a form of *partagé*, divided and sharing. I maintained that the fellowship is "an exposition in common and to the in-common." I also asserted that the meaning of the political is "the site where being in common is at stake" or, in the language of Agamben, "sensation of being is at stake." Aristotle's philosophical analysis of friendship, which clearly links it with *being* (existence) and *living* (life), has also revealed both its ontological status and its political significance. What is political is primarily (or is constituted by) this co-sharing, consenting which has no object, except the experience of being, being-together. Thus the political is fundamentally a *pure means*.

All this charges friendship natality with political potentiality and possibilities for "healing" of relationships (which as we have learned from Aristotle and Steven G. Smith are ontological and foundational for philosophical and theological thought). If the pentecostal who considers the other as her political and religious other can "con-sent" that the other (her friend in the Spirit) exists, that they are both partaking in the same being, we can make some progress toward creating a common space for dialogue. For Hannah Arendt friendship is about the creation of this space (*inter-est*, in-between) for dialogue and disputation about the meanings of events in the world. It is this space — which both links and separates — that can sustain friendship among persons who together comprise the world. We have already argued in chapter 3 that Christians, and especially pentecostals, need to learn to enter the disputations in this world without destroying the interspace that is the very condition of plurality and emergence of publicly accepted truth. As Arendt puts it:

> Every truth [truth of world events] outside this area, no matter whether it brings men good or ill, is inhuman in the literal sense of the word; but not because it might rouse men against one another and separate them. Quite the contrary, it is because it might have the result that all men would suddenly unite in a single opinion, so that out of many opinions one would emerge, as though not men in their infinite plurality but man in the singular, one species and its exemplars, were to inhabit the earth. Should that happen, the world which can form only in the interspaces between men in all their variety, would vanish altogether.[16]

16. Hannah Arendt, *Men in Dark Times* (San Diego: Harcourt Brace & Company, 1968), p. 31.

Finally, there is temporal natality, the deliberate staging of natality with respect to the rhythm of existence. Existence by itself is shapeless, without any structure, an inarticulate substratum of spirituality that can be subjected to desired forms. When the born-again experience is added to it, existence acquires rhythm, structure. Structure here is not just a simple aggregation of the facts of life into an ensemble of meaning, creating a whole that has more meaning than the sum of the parts. Similarly, structure is not the "something else" that is added to an ensemble of life's facts and interpretations that makes the whole more than the sum of the parts and coagulates them into a unity. Thus, the thinking here about structure is not about a search for either "that which causes something to be what it is" or that ultimate, minimum irreducible element of the new life. It is about form that maintains existence in presence, puts it in its "proper station in presence."[17]

But what grants existence its proper place? Existence is an ongoing flow of activities, a pure flow in an infinite space-time continuum (or fabric, if you like). Social existence, in particular, appears as a perpetual movement of instants, the inexorable course of daily mortal life, running toward ruin, destruction, and death. Interrupting or interfering with this flow creates rhythm, introducing a split and stop in its relentless march. "Thus in a musical piece, although it is somehow in time, we perceive rhythm as something that escapes the incessant flight of instants and appears almost as the presence of an atemporal dimension of time."[18] In the same way, when the born-again has put herself in the ecstatic and mundane transformational context, panel-beating the self into a relevantly shaped vehicle of the Holy Spirit, a particular type of moral subject, she perceives a stop in time, "as though she is suddenly thrown into a more original time. There is a stop, an interruption in the incessant flow of instants that, coming from the future, sinks into the past, and this interruption, this stop, is precisely what gives and reveals the particular status,"[19] the mode of presence proper to her existence. The born-again experience appears to have broken the automatism, the inexorability of social existence, and let her find her present space between past and future.

This split is enacted in the midst of a flow: in the flow of time, in the flow of social existence. While born-againness reveals the proper place of exis-

---

17. Giorgio Agamben, *The Man without Content,* trans. Georgia Albert (Stanford: Stanford University Press, 1999), p. 98. Pages 94-103 of this book inspire this section on temporal natality.

18. Agamben, *Man without Content,* p. 99.

19. Agamben, *Man without Content,* p. 99.

tence, locates her in the presence proper to her as a work of God's hand, the flight of life's instants — which do not reveal their meaning and place fully as they move on — continues apace. The split is thus an inside that is "also a being-outside, an *ek-stasis* in the more original dimension."[20] The experience of being born-again gives her the sense of her proper place (an ecstatic dwelling in it), but still retains her in the quotidian draw of existence.

So now we understand structure as rhythm, as what determines the proper ("original") place of existence. By opening to the pentecostal her perceived authentic spatial and temporal dimension of existence, the born-again experience (encounter) also "opens for him [her] the space of belonging to the world, only within which he [she] can take the original measure of his dwelling on the earth and find again his [her] present truth in the unstoppable flow of linear time [and inexorable daily course to destruction and death]."[21] It is in this authentic space in time or in the world that the pentecostal sallies forth to re-create the self and the world, is able to put her being and the past and future at stake in order to achieve the transformation of her subjectivity and access the full promises of the born-again experience. This is why the born-again experience is called "beginning," and is architectonic in the archaic sense of production of origin.[22]

In sum, born-againness can be considered as a form of production of temporality, a new temporality to fashion relevant subjectivity for the kingdom of God, and as a route to transcendence. The reborn mindfulness, this consciousness that breaks the automatism of ongoing social processes, that interrupts the normal patterns of sights and rhythms of sounds of social existence to create the space for human existence, a space of appearance, renews (re-creates) the believer's sense of reality. The consciousness of natality involves intentional acts of rupture, which lift off the crust of tradition and habitude over the common world, to offer a new time gap of existence.

Cultivating the Pentecostal Self

This act of world-(re)making, this act of bringing the world into greater actuality through human inventiveness, is, among other considerations, an attempt to cultivate the self. It is a way of instructing the self in continuous attunement to unfolding potentialities, to miracles, and to the spiritual

20. Agamben, *Man without Content*, p. 99.
21. Agamben, *Man without Content*, p. 101.
22. Agamben, *Man without Content*, p. 101.

depths of existence. It is a way of instructing the self to hear, feel, and imagine the world differently. It is to attune and place the self at the points of crossing between expected ordinariness of existence and the elemental, miraculous depths of extraordinariness so as to transform almost all phenomenal perceptions into caesural moments. Lest we forget, the whole point of the cultivation of the self is to make the outcomes of all these instructions into a sustained way of life and thought, to mold the self into a particular identity.

But pentecostal identity is a specter that cannot be pinned down, something difficult to name, create, or summon. It is a process of ontological proportions: in its drama attempts are continuously made to produce a new terrain of humanity, to fashion and refashion being. When a person becomes born again she becomes a new creation, her old identity has passed away. How can this be? The effaced, primordial identity, which has been rendered inoperative but not abolished, is absently present as a palimpsest. This suppressed identity and its transfigurations are the "ghostly matter" upon which all the undoing and rethinking of subjectivation do their dance and which in turn haunts clean subjectivity. In pentecostalism identity is *chora* of subjectivity.

The identity of the pentecostal spirit is fluid, rhizomatic, improvising its form and dynamics both in melodic harmony with its cultural milieu and in rejection of it. Identity is the taking-place of subjectivity. This is to say at once three things: the exposure of the innermost properness of a subject, the face or exteriority of the pliable limits of subjectivity, and the typonym of the multidirectional passageway from common (potentiality) to proper (act). It is in this movement of subjectivity, as the subject subjects herself to her context, of which she is both a subject and the same time subject over, that she is able to grasp and determine her proper taking-place in the time gap and thus express her fluid identity.[23]

This identity is fluid not because of what is expressed, that the limits are blurred, disorderly, or flow together as a stream. It is so only because every form that emerges quickly vanishes, with a new form springing up and also disappearing immediately. Identity is a virtual. Identity is the generic potentiality of subjectivity.

All this should not be surprising to us because of "the unsystematic nature of the born-again identity" and the ways it renders inoperative "old

---

23. This paragraph is inspired by Giorgio Agamben, *The Coming Community*, trans. Michael Hardt (Minneapolis: University of Minnesota Press, 1993), pp. 12-19.

distinctions and hierarchies and replaces them with new ones."[24] Ruth Marshall makes this comment in her analysis of the identity of pentecostals in Nigeria. But we can deepen her analysis a little. The Nigerian pentecostals are always dividing the thin lines of identity to show themselves manifest as the remnants of Christ working in anticipation of his second coming. They are continuously and strenuously engaged in what Agamben calls "the cut of Apelles,"[25] dividing the division already traced out by Christianity and African traditional religion, modernity and premodernity, and local and foreign/global influences. The subset of African Christians is divided into African Christians who reject African traditional religion and culture (and yet their whole outlook is still not detached from the traditional worldview) and those who do not. There are "non-African African Christians" and "African Christians." This latter group is further divided into Christians according to the flesh (those not considered born-again believers) and Christians according to the Spirit (Spirit-filled). The born-agains believe that they are unlike the Christians in the old denominational, missionary-instituted churches. By this cut they differentiate themselves from the mainline, "orthodox," "dead" Christians. They are now "non-Christian Christians." The same cut applies to Christians and non-Christians, or members of white-garment churches (like Aladura) and the born-agains. One even finds members of the Deeper Life Bible Church partitioning themselves off from members of Pastor Enoch Adeboye's Redeemed Christian Church of God and Bishop David Oyedepo's Winners Chapel. And all of this is not to talk about those with "anointing" and those without it in any one congregation. There is always a remnant for another Apelles' cut.

All this suggests that we cannot conceive of identity as the production of sameness and the submerging of differences in a field of alterities. What the "identity politics" of pentecostalism shows is the impossibility of any identity coinciding with itself, or any believer (African or otherwise) coinciding with herself, and the impossibility of identifying any universal sameness. Under the cut of Apelles, pentecostalism renders all distinctions, divisional markings, and classes inoperative without abolishing them and "without ever reaching any final ground," engendering a tension within every identity itself, "without ever providing it with some other identity." "In

---

24. Ruth Marshall, *Political Spiritualities: The Pentecostal Revolution in Nigeria* (Chicago: University of Chicago Press, 2009), pp. 140, 144.

25. Giorgio Agamben, *The Time That Remains: A Commentary on the Letter to the Romans*, trans. Patricia Dailey (Stanford: Stanford University, 2005), pp. 49-53.

this sense, there is neither beginning nor end . . . , only Apelles' cut, the division of division, and then a remnant."[26]

א Apelles' Cut and the Pentecostal Spirit

The tendency toward endless fragmentation reflects the problematic of pentecostalism as a historical movement, a tendency to perpetuate ecclesial disunity. But in the light of the pentecostal principle, this problematic is ambiguous, challenging us to reflect theologically or normatively on it as both a problem and a possibility. The Apelles' cut reveals something fundamental about the pentecostal spirit.

Viewed from a philosophical perspective, the cut of Apelles is not necessarily a bane of the movement. It points to the fact that no division among any group of people is always clear and exhaustive. The two sides of any binary division (A/non-A) are constitutively "not all." There is always a remnant on either side.[27] This remnant is an acknowledgment of the unfinishedness of every state, being, totality, or classification. It is an expression of abundance. In this dynamic, open-ended conception it admits of a third term (non non-A) in any binary system.

There are potentially four other ways to examine how the problematic of the Apelles' cut reveals something about the pentecostal principle or the pentecostal spirit. First, what is significant in this "division of divisions"? As Agamben puts it: "It forces us to think about the question of the universal and the particular in a completely new way, not only in logic, but also in ontology and politics."[28] The universal is not the production of the sameness, the abolition of differences, or an affirmation of shared commonness beyond which no difference can be conceived. The universal is the endless operation that renders any classification, configuration, or division inoperative. Any stasis, configuration, or being is infinitely missing its station in its becoming and is already advancing forward against itself.

Second, the Apelles' cut is above any extant cuts and divisions, negating the idea of ultimate limit. "In this sense, there is neither beginning nor end . . . only Apelles' cut, the division of division, and then a remnant"[29] which can itself be further divided. This idea of no beginning and no end, as we have seen earlier, is at the heart of the pentecostal principle.

Following Agamben, I will argue that the Apelles' cut also reveals something about the subjectivity of the bearers of the pentecostal principle or the potential political subjectivity of today's pentecostals as a people. "The people is neither the all nor the part, neither the majority nor the minority. Instead, it is that which can

---

26. Agamben, *Time That Remains*, pp. 52-53.
27. Agamben, *Time That Remains*, pp. 50-51.
28. Agamben, *Time That Remains*, p. 51.
29. Agamben, *Time That Remains*, p. 53.

never coincide with itself, as all or as part, that which infinitely remains or resists in each division. . . . This remnant is the figure, or the substantiality assumed by a people in a decisive movement, and as such is the only real political subject."[30]

Finally, the cut of Apelles may simply reflect the fluid nature of historical human relations. It points out that the world the pentecostal perspective assumes is always dynamic, protean, incomplete, and contingent. In a certain sense the incompleteness and fluidity reflected in each "cut" points to ongoing possibilities for the redemption of the world and for the emergence of novum.

We might also think about the problematic of pentecostal identity by way of the mathematical set theory, particularly the idea of the "extensional set." I have argued that pentecostal identity cannot be understood in terms of a single, defining concept or characteristic. Rather, it is marked by an open conception of being-with. This means that pentecostal identity cannot be defined by the intensional principle of selection, but instead by extensionality. It is "a set determined solely by its members." There are no clear criteria for belonging and no well-defined principles of construction. They may be grouped in one way or in some other. Peter Hallward describes extensional sets in this way:

> Sets are determined solely by their elements. Just how these elements are brought together, in the extensional conception of set, is a perfectly open question: the possibilities, as well as purely haphazard selections made without reference to any concept at all. The extensional selection may conform to a property or may be determined by a completely random choice.[31]

From another perspective, pentecostalism has no center and most of its parts operate as autonomous wholes, making it a prime example of deterritorialization. It is amorphous, constituted in a limitless place. The worldwide pentecostal movement is not a coherent social totality and as such it resists any tag of essentialism and homogeneity of identities. It is always a partial and hybrid formation and in each milieu (which is always "unhomely") it sets differences to play across religious and cultural boundaries. It is plural and multiple — an extensional set of singularities.

---

30. Agamben, *Time That Remains*, p. 57.

31. Peter Hallward, *Badiou: A Subject to Truth* (Minneapolis: University of Minnesota Press, 2003), p. 86.

To borrow the words of Michael Hardt and Antonio Negri from another context, pentecostalism "is an internally different, multiple social subject whose constitution and action is based not on identity or unity (or, much less, indifference) but on what it has in common."[32]

ℵ Apelles' Cut and Identity:
The Pentecostal Ethnic and the Spirit of Capitalism

Let me push our discussion of the problematic of the "identity politics" of Nigerian pentecostalism a bit further by situating it within post-Enlightenment modernity's displacement of the basis of identity from biology onto the realm of culture. In the words of Etienne Balibar, "biological or genetic naturalism is not the only means of naturalizing human behavior and social affinities. . . . *Culture can also function as a nature,* and it can in particular function as a way of locking individuals and groups a priori into a genealogy, into a determination that is immutable and intangible in origin."[33] The result, according to Rey Chow, is that "it is the insurmountability of cultural identity, or cultural difference, that has become the justification for . . . discriminatory conduct."[34]

The basis of identity that flows from Apelles' cut in Nigerian pentecostalism is the claim of exclusive, superior religious identity or difference. Differentialist religiosity has joined ethnic naturalism (biological heredity) and class distinction as a means of naturalizing social affinities and for justifying discriminatory conduct and stigmatization. History has repeatedly shown that discriminatory behavior often leads to group loathing. As Fredric Jameson writes, "group loathing . . . mobilizes the classic syndromes of purity and danger, and acts out of a kind of defense of the boundaries of the primary group against this threat perceived to be inherent in the Other's very existence."[35]

This turn to culture, as in the general case of racism which Balibar, Jameson, and Chow focus on, always creates (new) fundamental divisions. In the Nigerian case the division (between true and false believers) separates those who must die (the second death) and those who must live (inherit eternal life). It separates those

32. Michael Hardt and Antonio Negri, *Multitude: War and Democracy in the Age of Empire* (New York: Penguin, 2004), p. 100.

33. Etienne Balibar, "Is There a 'Neo-Racism'?" trans. Chris Turner, in *Race, Nation, Class: Ambiguous Identities,* ed. Etienne Balibar and Immanuel Wallerstein (New York: Verso, 1991), pp. 21-22. Emphasis in original. Quoted in Rey Chow, *The Protestant Ethnic and the Spirit of Capitalism* (New York: Columbia University Press, 2002), pp. 13-14.

34. Chow, *The Protestant Ethnic,* p. 13.

35. Fredric Jameson, "On Cultural Studies," in *The Identity in Question,* ed. James Rajchman (New York: Routledge, 1995), p. 274. Quoted in Chow, *The Protestant Ethnic,* p. 56.

who believe they have the real possibility for betterment of their conditions in the here and now and those who they think are held prisoners and condemned to toil in Satan's vineyard. The discursive framework that has been generated to keep this differentialist social relationship going "fragments the biological field, it establishes a break *(césure)* inside the biological continuum of human beings defining a hierarchy of [believers], a set of subdivisions in which certain [believers] are classified as 'good,' fit, and superior."[36]

The persistent drive toward "cuts" characteristic of pentecostalism cannot simply be seen as an outcome of power struggles, doctrinal differences, or other "usual suspects," but rather it is the result of a force of internal disciplining attributable or even peculiar to pentecostal spirituality.[37] This disciplining is anchored to and feeds on the belief in "calling" (or what I have earlier called, after Roger Stronstad, the prophethood of all believers). The belief is that all believers can directly hear from the Holy Spirit, all can speak forth the word of God (prophesy), and all are endowed and empowered (Spirit-baptized) to form new groups to serve the Lord, to do good works on earth. This internal disciplining may remind some of us of Max Weber's exploration of the Protestant ethic and the spirit of capitalism. This reminder raises some disturbing questions on the connections between pentecostal ethic (ecclesiological sensibility and instability) and the spirit of capitalism. To what extent is the division (or "cut") already a dynamic built into the rationalizing process of profanatory late-phase capitalism itself? What is the nature and dynamics of the mutual adaptation between the material conditions of production and their accompanying social relations in the Nigerian postcolony and religious subjectivity?

It will take us too far afield to adequately investigate the connections between the pentecostal spirit and the spirit of capitalism. If we were to do this we would have to do it not by the cheap method of asking and responding to the question of how the pentecostal spirit resists and protests against evil capitalism or the spirit of capitalism. The more interesting and productive question to ask is how the twentieth- and twenty-first-century pentecostal spirit "come[s] about in capitalism and further enhance[s] the progress of capitalism."[38] The response may then reveal that the very pentecostal resistance and protest against evil or spirit of capitalism "is an event within, rather than without, capitalist society"[39] and reinforces its asymmetries of power, enabling capitalism to flourish. Protesting or hard work is one of the ways of answering to the system.

36. Ann Laura Stoler, *Race and the Education of Desire: Foucault's History of Sexuality and the Colonial Order of Things* (Durham: Duke University Press, 1995), p. 84, quoted in Chow, *The Protestant Ethnic*, p. 9.

37. Obviously there is more to the fissiparation than disciplining. Here is not the place to recount all the factors behind divisions and split-offs in pentecostalism.

38. This way of putting the question is inspired and borrowed from Chow, *The Protestant Ethnic*, pp. 45-46.

39. Chow, *The Protestant Ethnic*, p. 43.

So another interesting question is this: how do workers answer to the inter-pellation of capitalism? This is to ask, how did workers successfully internalize and incorporate this hailing from outside? How did they give their bodies and souls to the social apparatus that hails them? According to Weber, the interpellated work-ers responded by developing a work ethic. The powers of the system worked on them in the most intimate fashion — from within. Chow writes, "What I consider most decisive about [Weber's] theory is the effective structural collaboration he pinpoints between the power of subjective belief (in salvation) as found in mod-ern, secularized society and the capitalist economism's ways of hailing, disciplin-ing, and rewarding identities constituted by certain forms of labor."[40] What is the equivalent of work ethic in pentecostal spirituality? (Of course, we know that pen-tecostals as workers in the capitalist system are responding to the hailing as Weber predicted.) How does their interpellation actualize on the plane of spirituality? In the words of Chow, "what is the phenomenon symptomatic of a ferocious and well-rewarded productionism in contemporary" pentecostal spirituality?[41]

I argue that it is the phenomenon of the massive, proliferating, energetic spiri-tual (ecclesiastical) entrepreneurship: fast-paced growth of church infrastructure (ownership), increasing church attendance, efficient and efficacious tax tithe profit farming, and the utilitarian razzmatazz (spectacular exhibition) of anointing — all of which have avoided societal transformation like the plague. In order to be, to es-tablish oneself, to be the "authentic" pentecostal self with the valorized anointing, this saved entrepreneur must both be seen to own his profitable anointing and ex-hibit (sell, franchise, project, globalize) it repeatedly. To put it in different terms, the phenomenon is the feverish, simultaneous pursuit of salvation as an object and prosperity as an abject.[42] The capitalist-spiritual entrepreneurs are haunted and trapped within the given of abject salvation — of calling as abjection.[43]

Let me bring this aside to a close by stating that the transindividual issue of

40. Chow, *The Protestant Ethnic*, p. viii.

41. Chow, *The Protestant Ethnic*, p. 111.

42. The word is used in the sense made popular by Julia Kristeva. Chow defines it as "the often culturally tabooed condition of an excessive, rejected being that nonetheless re-mains a challenge to the body that expels it." *The Protestant Ethnic*, pp. 147-48. According to Kristeva, "the jettisoned object is radically excluded and draws me toward the place where meaning collapses. . . . It is something rejected from which one does not part, from which one does not protect oneself as from an object. Imaginary uncanniness and real threat, it beckons to us and ends up engulfing us. It is thus not lack of cleanliness or health that causes abjection but what disturbs identity, system, order. What does not respect borders, posi-tions, rules. The in-between, the ambiguous, the composite." Julia Kristeva, *Powers of Hor-ror: An Essay on Abjection*, trans. Leon S. Roudiez (New York: Columbia University Press, 1982), pp. 2, 4. Quoted in Chow, *The Protestant Ethnic*, p. 148.

43. I have adapted Chow's phraseology to my limited purpose here. See Chow, *The Protestant Ethnic*, p. 152.

Apelles' cut has become transnational with the export of Nigerian church brands and sensibilities to Europe and America. The typical product of this transplantation in the United States is a hard-working pentecostal man (woman). This man with the Bible in one hand and dollar in the other, flaming tongues and all, is trying very hard to realize the American dream; but he is neither simply part of America nor separate from it.

This charged figure that emerges — a figure in whom the Protestant work ethic and pentecostal spirituality have beautifully intertwined — is a problem of social liminality in the United States. He dwells on the uneasy boundary between the universalisms of capitalism and pentecostalism on one hand, and the actual, lived particular experience of marginalization as an immigrant and an ethnic minority on the other. His ethnicity is defined by biological heredity, perceived cultural inferiority in the powerful gaze of majority whiteness, and the liminality of existing between two societies as a migrant. Besides, in the vast mainline Protestant and Catholic religious landscape that is the United States, in this land permeated with an amoral scientific worldview, he is a religious ethnic. This charged figure is no ordinary ethnic. The ethnic that results from the structural collaboration of capitalism (commodified global culture) and commoditized global spirituality is the pentecostal ethnic interpellated by the spirit of capitalism.

Play and Pentecostalism

Let us now return to the issue of playfulness as a way of reaching conclusion or as a way of uncovering the *archi*-name that we as magi (scholars, like Horatio in *Hamlet*) can use to summon and speak to the omnilateral pentecostal spirit. God willing, we shall not lack: let us go together with our fingers on our keyboards, I pray. Time is out of joint; no, rather, identity is out of joint. We are saddled with comprehending it in order to apprehend the spirit in "the virtual space of spectrality"[44] that pentecostalism has created. But enough of a joke: Exeunt!

If Protestantism suggests the spirit or image of a child,[45] pentecostal-

---

44. Jacques Derrida, *Specters of Marx: The State of the Debt, the Work of Mourning, and the New International*, trans. Peggy Kamuf (New York: Routledge, 1994), p. 11.

45. I have used the metaphor of "child" for both Reformation and pentecostalism for these reasons: Jürgen Moltmann has argued that the kingdom of God is the kingdom of the child and messianism of Christianity is the messianism of the child. See his *God in Creation: A New Theology of Creation and the Spirit of God,* trans. Margaret Kohl (Minneapolis: Fortress, 1993), p. 319; and *Spirit of Life: A Universal Affirmation* (Minneapolis: Fortress, 1992), p. 160. Paul drives this messianism of the child further down the path. The apostle Paul declares the messianic now, which makes the law inoperative, deactivating it and thus opening

ism is that of a child at play. Pentecostalism is the child at play, who wants the "magic" of the world restored; who preserves the myth (word, story) of the faith, but drops the rites. Pentecostalism is the child who wants to play with profanized sacred toys. As we have already noted in our discussion of games and rites, plays arose from the sacred (the rites) and also represent an overturning of the sacred. In the sacred sphere, rites and stories (myths) are closely connected, with rites dramatizing or staging the story being told by the myth. But as Agamben has also shown us, play breaks this unity or conjunction. "If the sacred can be defined through the consubstantial unity of the myth and rite, we can say that one has play when only half of the sacred operation is completed, translating only the myth into words or only the rite into actions."[46]

What play does is to take a sacred item from its excluded sphere, emancipate it from its connections to ends, and return it to common use without necessarily abolishing the sphere of the sacred. It "profanes" the item by ignoring its separation and the scrupulousness and attention that attend to its use; or it does so by inappropriate use. To profane in this sense means to deactivate the aura that attends to a thing as being separated and serious and bring it to common use.[47] It is through this deactivation process that play emerged, according to Agamben.

> Most of the games with which we are familiar derive from ancient sacred ceremonies, from divinatory practices and rituals that once belonged, broadly speaking, to the religious sphere. The *girotondo* was originally a marriage rite; playing with a ball reproduces the struggle of the gods for possession of the sun; games of chance derive from oracular practices; the spinning top and the chessboard are instruments of divi-

---

it up to a new, possible use in the age of grace. See Agamben, *Time That Remains*. In a certain sense, the dispensation of grace frees the child, the new faith, from the law, from the father who demands absolute obedience. Martin Luther drove this much further down the path. Reformation is also in a certain sense the child protesting against the demand and work requirements of the father in the image of the old doctrines of the Church. We should also not forget what Erik H. Erikson has taught us about Luther: his turn to grace cannot be totally divorced from Luther the son revolting against his father. Grace is what saves the child from the wrath of the father both in heaven and on earth. See his *Young Man Luther: A Study in Psychoanalysis and History* (New York: Norton, 1993).

46. Emile Benveniste, "Le jeu comme structure," *Deucalion* 2 (1947): 45, quoted in Giorgio Agamben, *Profanations*, trans. Jeff Fort (New York: Zone Books, 2007), p. 76.

47. Agamben, *Profanations*, pp. 74-75.

nation. . . . Children, who play with whatever old thing falls into their hands, make toys out of things that also belong to the spheres . . . that we are used to thinking of as serious. All of a sudden, a car, a firearm, or a legal contract becomes a toy.[48]

Pentecostalism is the child in the temple who is playing with the rituals, known standards of liturgy and decorum, calendars, styles, and so on. Pentecostalism has its "face" toward play precisely in the sense that it breaks up the unity between myth (story) and rite — the unity of the sacred act. It preserves the story of the faith but effaces the rites, frees and distracts behaviors from the sphere of the sacred, from utmost seriousness. This is not due to disbelief and indifference toward the divine, but "a behavior that is free and 'distracted' . . . released from the *religio* of norms before things and their use."[49]

Deactivation of Grace

In Matthew 18:3 Jesus says, "Truly I tell you, unless you change and become like children, you will never enter the kingdom of heaven." Pentecostalism has taken this saying to heart; indeed some might even say pentecostalism has taken this saying too far. This character of a child who is playing with items once considered sacred is in a certain sense rooted in the doctrine of grace — pushing grace, the mantra of Luther and the reformers, to its uttermost limits. What the doctrine of grace says is something like this: what saves you is not merit and effort but undeserved grace. Only the "magic" of God can do it. Eternal bliss or happiness, which the believer is not worthy to enjoy, is connected to some kind of divine magic. It is only this divine magic that will allow someone to be happy in this and in the world to come and to know that he or she is happy. Every human magic or effort will fall short. Pushed to its limit, this wisdom that salvation, happiness, bliss, the good circumstances that may befall us are never deserved means that the only way to achieve what one wants is to believe in the divine, more precisely in divine magic. Enjoyment of the earthly world lies entirely in enchantment and "the only happiness that is truly deserved is the one we could never dream of deserving."[50]

48. Agamben, *Profanations*, pp. 75-76.
49. Agamben, *Profanations*, p. 75.
50. Agamben, *Profanations*, p. 21.

Walter Benjamin writes that the child's first experience of the world is not his realization that "adults are stronger but rather that he cannot make magic."[51] The pentecostal's ongoing experience is that God is capable of magic and he or she feels capable of enjoying this magic. Thus, we can surmise that the miraculous exception or surprises that pentecostals hold dear in a certain sense deactivate the apparatuses of grace as power of salvation and bring them into common use. Put another way, pentecostals allow miraculous grace to float between the serious matter of saving the soul and ordinary, ephemeral, bodily, existential matters without ceasing to refer to the same persons whom the gospel stories have claimed. The distinctions between the two sets of matter are not abolished but are put "into a new use, to play with them."[52] This deactivation of grace ("the special divine magic") and the act of opening it up to a new possible use, emptying it of its profound sense and relieving it of its connection to ends of eternal life, while still mimicking (maintaining) the characteristic Christian activity (story) from which it has been emancipated, converts grace to a pure means, a means without end.[53]

This conversion of grace to pure means, into a play, opens up several ethical issues relating to the pentecostal spirit. Here I will consider two of them as illustrative examples. I will argue that one is good, the other is bad — but some readers may want to reverse my ethical assessment at the end of the forthcoming discourse. First, the bad news: Agamben argues in his 2007 book, *Profanations,* that late capitalism converts every object into a pure means, everything is separated from itself and is exhibited in its separation from itself; everything has become a "spectacle."[54] Late capitalism, as he puts it, is a "gigantic apparatus for [creating and] capturing pure means."[55] As insightful as this comment is, it is not really the most profound inspiration I got from reading this book. Rather, his analysis of the

51. See Walter Benjamin, "Fritz Fränkel: Protocol of the Mescaline Experiment of May 22, 1934," in *On Hashish,* ed. Howard Eiland (Cambridge, MA: Belknap, 2006), p. 87, quoted in Agamben, *Profanations,* p. 19.

52. Agamben, *Profanations,* p. 87.

53. This is how Agamben describes the activity that results from freeing an object or behavior from its genetic inscription within a given sphere: "The activity that results from this thus becomes a pure means, that is, a praxis that, while firmly maintaining its nature as a means, is emancipated from its relationship to an end; it has joyously forgotten its goal and can now show itself as such, as a means without an end." *Profanations,* p. 86.

54. Agamben, *Profanations,* pp. 81-82.

55. Agamben, *Profanations,* p. 87. See also pp. 81-82.

difference between consumption and use in the extreme phase of capitalism is most insightful and thought provoking, as it shows that what cannot be used is given over only to consumption and spectacular exhibition. Pure use, according to Agamben, exists for an instant in the act of consumption, but never as something that one could have or possess as property. "That is to say, use is always a relationship with something that cannot be appropriated; it refers to things insofar as they cannot become objects of possession."[56] Spectacle and consumption, he concludes, "are two sides of a single impossibility of using."[57]

The extreme phase of pentecostalism that deactivates grace and puts it into play in pentecostals' hunt for miracles ("divine surprises") is making believers consume "products" that they can never appropriate. The divine magic cannot be an object of possession and thus the consumption of miracles has incorporated within it an inability to be used. And as in the extreme phase of capitalism, "what cannot be used is, as such, given over to consumption or to spectacular exhibition."[58] Needless to say that in the extreme reaches of pentecostalism, with its wide array of prosperity gospel preachers, faith healers, and flamboyant televangelists, consumption and spectacle are in full force and like capitalism there is an ugly indifference toward the caesura between the sacred and the profane. There is high consumption of miracles as well as marketplace objects in the house of pentecostalism. And there is a lot of exhibition and spectacle going on in there. Everything is put in play. So much for the bad news, let us shift our remaining attention to the good news.

The pentecostal penchant for pure means has the potential to help us rethink some major aspects of ethics. The praxis of pure means is not always a bad thing, as we discerned in chapter 2. Here I want to relate the notion to the practice of pure giving, to ḥesed. Ḥesed as retrieved from ancient Jewish wisdom is about giving that has no end or goal; giving as pure means.[59] According to Jewish tradition, the world is built by ḥesed, and we can venture to say that true pentecostal ethics is founded on pure means. Just as the early apostles immediately put property, money, and social status to new use, to play with them, today's pentecostals can deactivate money and the apparatuses of money in order to transform them into

---

56. Agamben, *Profanations*, p. 83.

57. Agamben, *Profanations*, p. 82.

58. Agamben, *Profanations*, p. 82.

59. Michael Fishbane, *Sacred Attunement: A Jewish Theology* (Chicago: University of Chicago Press, 2008), pp. 152-55.

pure means, to arrest from the global monetary system the possibility of use that it has so captured and to "profane" money from its sacred service to the extreme phase of capitalism. Of course, I am not holding my breath for this; so do not hold yours either. For the house of pentecostalism has not recognized giving as a pure means, as is made evident by ravages of the trade-by-barter prosperity gospel in many of its quarters. One wonders if the spirit of pentecostalism is not the spirit of extreme phase capitalism?[60]

Pentecostal Spirit and Ethical Method

On a more positive note, the pentecostal spirit, which sees the miraculous in the mundane, the common in the celestial splendor, and the play in the sacred, has implications for ethical methods. In this regard, we recall Ralph Emerson's famous passage: "Nature is not fixed but fluid. Spirit alters, moulds, and makes it. . . . Every spirit builds itself a house; and beyond its house a world; and beyond its world, a heaven."[61] Every spirit builds itself an ethics, and beyond its ethics a finite moral world, and beyond its world, a heaven *(helan)*.

The world, the set of human relations, is not fixed but fluid. The spirit of every age, the ethics, the group's moral interpretations of every era, builds itself a moral world. And it takes the ethics of another spirit to alter, mold, and transform what is built. The world the pentecostal spirit presupposes and at the same time aspires to upbuild is fluid, dynamic, protean, incomplete, and shot through with contingency. The pentecostal perspective assumes the fixity of the world as the absence of the pentecostal spirit, the freedom of the spirit; to the pentecostals the world is volatile, it is fluid, it admits of being undone. The heaven that the pentecostal spirit builds beyond its world is within this world. Others call their beyond-world "heaven," a space; I suggest that pentecostals could call theirs "time." Jesus taught us to pray so that heaven will not be above us, but ahead of us, making it a matter of time. To revisit briefly our *Hamlet* allusions, pentecostals' heaven is out of joint.

---

60. The interested reader may even want to further explore the remarkable connections between the pentecostal principle and the spirit of capitalism as described by Karl Marx and Friedrich Engels in *The Communist Manifesto* (Harmondsworth: Penguin, 1985), pp. 83-84.

61. Ralph Waldo Emerson, *Nature: Selected Writings of Ralph Waldo Emerson*, ed. William H. Gilman (New York: New American Library, 1965), p. 222.

ℵ Heaven as Time

In Matthew 6:9-10, Jesus prays, "Our Father in heaven, hallowed be your name, Your kingdom come. Your will be done, on earth as it is in heaven." In this prayer Jesus Christ is saying that when we pray we should ask God to make our heaven to be not above us, but ahead of us. He is enjoining us to lift up our eyes and see the possibilities that are approaching on the horizon — so at least it seems to those who have a certain interpretation of heaven which I will shortly describe.

The Bible offers us numerous ways of understanding heaven. There is heaven as the sky. There is heaven as the region of the stars, the astral world. Heaven also refers to the dwelling place of God. This term appears in both the singular and the plural in the Bible, so that we have the heaven of heavens as well. But the usage of heaven also includes the sense of a place of possibilities, an image of alternatives to what life on earth is offering.[62] Heaven in this fourth sense refers to all that is beyond the limitations and frontiers of our current existence. It refers to that which can create the new.

So when Jesus tells us that we should ask for God's will to be done on earth as it is in heaven, he is telling us to let our heaven come down to earth. If the alternative possibilities to our existential angst and the hope for the *principle* of the new are to be on earth as they are in heaven, then our heaven is no longer above us in space but is ahead of us in time. Heaven becomes a matter of time, an anticipation of its manifestation on earth. We pray now, we act in the present, and the future is changed. Heaven, as a symbol of the new and the alternative, no longer belongs to the order of space but to that of time.[63]

If it is a matter of time, then it is all about the future. The prayer that is calling down a heaven is a prayer that is reconfiguring the future. This is the future that is in history, not beyond it. So every prayer is a protest against the ambiguities, distortions, and poverty of the present. In prayer, we are saying there is a better alternative; there is a heaven that can come down and no matter how glorious the present order of things there is a better option. The person in prayer is calling both self and others to be continuously creative, to create a new "us," a new "we."

The new "we" is a people anticipating something new, asking themselves, what are the alternatives? What is new for them? No one knows from where the new will come. For the new of God is that which is beyond the new of humans and their institutions. It is the kind of new that underlines the import of Revelation 1:8 when Jesus says "I am . . . who is and who was and who is to come. . . ." It is not the new that flows from the trajectory of the past and the present. It is the new that asks for, creates, and sustains the alternative possibility, the unexpected path.[64]

---

62. Moltmann, *God in Creation*, pp. 158-81.

63. Moltmann, *God in Creation*, pp. 158-81.

64. Jürgen Moltmann, *The Coming of God: Christian Eschatology,* trans. Margaret Kohl (Minneapolis: Fortress, 1996), pp. 23-28.

Pentecostals' "displacement" of heaven is not an attempt to place existence beyond history or to see life as *sub specie aeternitatis,* but to be at the beginning of new time, to express a penchant for and epistemology of the unattainable perfection "that round every circle another can be drawn; that there is no end in nature, but every end is a beginning; that there is always another dawn rise on mid-noon, and under every deep a lower deep opens."[65] To be in heaven is to be in the boundless house of time. To be in time means to be in the grip of a penchant for newness in order to bend the arc of existence toward the not-yet. In this curving exercise, space is continuously created (expanded). Like the universe it creates its own space and expands into it.

It is from this inclination for contingency and revisability, this impatience with ossified certainties, this refusal to lift paeans of praise to fixtures in nature (society) that we must discern the sensibilities and sentiments of pentecostal ethical methodology. In this regard, just as the pentecostal spirit evades and resists obstacles to human flourishing, just as it pursues experimentation and freedom, our ethical methodology must swerve from and resist interpretations that undergird and accept the given social world as it is. Ethical methodology (engagement) must assume the mode of cultural criticism, social creativity, and political engagement in which we should resist commitment to any knowledge machinery that only works to understand the world but not to change it, and instead provoke moral development, and enact constituting and constituted social practices of human flourishing. An ethics faithful to the spirit of pentecostalism does not allow itself the luxury of bathing in the blithe air of the problematics and vocabulary of past eras and their spirits (specters), but must continuously work to invent its own analyses and language, to speak in new tongues.

This simply means that we must evade contemporary dominant social ethics. The originality of the new ethics does not lie only in going beyond the social ethics that came before, but also in doing ethics in new ways that are more concrete and historical (yet theoretically engaging and sensitive to structural dynamics) than what exists now.[66] Put differently, the evasion of ethics means a refusal to discuss dominant ethical theories and ethical questions abstractly, seeking universally valid principles. Pentecostal ethics

---

65. Ralph Waldo Emerson, "Circles," in *Nature,* p. 296.

66. My idea of evading ethics is indebted to Cornel West, *The American Evasion of Philosophy: A Genealogy of Pragmatism* (Madison: University of Wisconsin Press, 1989).

has to transition from abstract, epistemology-centered ethics to the more contextual approach of comparative and social-problem-focused ethics. In this light, social ethics is about identifying concrete problems that threaten the moral fabric of a community and seeking to address them with the best of theological, philosophical, and social scientific resources.

One of the ways pentecostal ethics at the grassroots level deals with social issues concretely is to relate them to the resources of the faith and to cultivate a life in the Spirit. In most cultural contexts in which pentecostalism finds itself it attempts to answer the interior questions raised by primal (inherited) worldviews and existential issues by applying biblical resources and by interpreting the work of the Holy Spirit in specific cultures. Pentecostal pastors, especially those in Africa, use language very reminiscent of Paul Tillich's theological "method of correlation." They also go beyond Tillich's correlation method to that of Theodor W. Adorno. Like Adorno, they use "theological concepts to interrupt and question society."[67] At the scholarly level pentecostal ethics should similarly aim at cultivating a life in the Spirit and relate the questions asked in the interior of contemporary cultures to the resources of the Christian faith and to the radical openness of the world to divine surprises. In addition, they should engage contemporary cultures with questions raised in the interior of theology and when necessary challenge the very questions posed by contemporary cultures, showing them as either inaccurate or distorted.

Pentecostal ethics should also engage the creative role of feeling in ethical work without being pejoratively ideological and sentimental. There are five reasons for engaging the creative role of feeling in pentecostal ethics. First, emotions shape the landscape of the pentecostal encounter with the divine, the conduct of its worship service, and the expressions of personal oceanic feeling. From inception pentecostals have not shied away — to use Martha Nussbaum's words — from the messy material of joy and ecstasy, fear and grief, love and compassion in their social, religious, mental, and personal lives. Emotions have formed part of their discernment process of the spiritual presence in their midst, have been integral to their deep awareness of their divine depths, and are inseparable from the sheer physicality of their religiosity. Nussbaum remarks that there can be no adequate ethical theory without an adequate theory of

67. Christopher Craig Brittain, "Tillich and Adorno: Two Approaches to a Theology of Correlation," *Bulletin of the North American Paul Tillich Society* 36, no. 3 (Summer 2010): 36-41; quote on pp. 36-37.

emotions. This is, perhaps, more so for pentecostal ethics than for mainstream ethics.[68]

Second, emotions are connected to human thoughts, inextricably mixed with our intelligence, and feature importantly in our ethical reasoning and judgment about the good and just. A cognitive/evaluative understanding of emotions rather than viewing them as mere animal spirits (energies, impulses) shows them to involve a cognitive appraisal or evaluation of situations, to have eudaimonistic relevance, and to highlight the salience of *external* persons (things, objects) in human flourishing. Emotions are forms of value judgment and thought.[69] Nussbaum is thus on the mark when she writes,

> Instead of viewing morality as a system of principles to be grasped by the detached intellect, and emotions as motivations that either support or subvert our choice to act according to principle, we will have to consider emotions as part and parcel of the system of ethical reasoning. We cannot plausibly omit them, once we acknowledge that emotions include in their content judgments that can be true or false, good or bad guides to ethical choice.[70]

Third, the creative process is a very emotional one. The longing for excellence, the intense feeling to see, hear, smell, taste, touch, or create the object of desire, the furtive search in the darkness for the loose end of Being's fabric that will unwrap its hidden breach of *novum*, and the *thymos*[71] that drives human beings to seek recognition, they all lie at the heart of human creativity.

Fourth, pentecostal ethics or theology of culture has a duty to develop an adequate protocol (criteriological work) for differentiating the spiritual presence from Durkheimian collective effervescence. Durkheim's theory of the spirit purports to show how humans can become generators of their own social spirit in the unfolding process of creativity present in the richness and varieties of human cooperative practices. In this process emotional energies play a key role. Pentecostal theology of culture needs to de-

---

68. Martha C. Nussbaum, *Upheavals of Thought: The Intelligence of Emotions* (Cambridge: Cambridge University Press, 2001).

69. Nussbaum, *Upheavals of Thought*, pp. 3-16.

70. Nussbaum, *Upheavals of Thought*, p. 1.

71. For an excellent discussion of *thymos* in philosophy see Francis Fukuyama, *The End of History and the Last Man* (New York: Avon, 1992), pp. 162-98.

velop the protocol to help us know the difference or intersection between the social spirit and the divine spirit and how to mobilize the (emotional) support of one or both for abetting human flourishing and resisting injustice and human degradation.

Finally, the eros for justice and political engagement in all concrete relational contexts requires some passion. It is prophetic to show solidarity with suffering and oppressed people and to allow anguish over such to nourish one's intellectual work. Such feeling must not only be anchored to the history of injustice, discrimination, and suffering, but must also be grounded in a vision of love, hope, equality, and justice to facilitate the re-creation of the finite moral world. It is pentecostal to set one's sight on possible new alternatives and lean toward the unexpected. The pentecostal principle is the capacity to begin. It encapsulates the notion that no finite or conditioned reality can claim to have reached its destiny. And it calls for an ethical methodology in new spirit.

ℵ What Is Pentecostal Spirit?

This chapter has been designed to help us answer the question, what is pentecostal spirit? (The term is used in a rather special sense as in the "spirit of a civilization.") Now that we have come to the end of the chapter, how do we answer the question? A people gives itself its spirit in its lived actuality of existence.[72] The spirit is created as a result of the people's effort and struggle; it works out from the people's actualized self-determination and thus symbolizes their existence, "what it is that they are as a people."[73] It is the shadow *(teme)*[74] of Being in a specific existential spatiality and temporality. The spirit arises and ceases as the people appears and ceases. A people's spirit has no goal outside itself. It is not even its own end. It is pure means, a pure mediality.

The pentecostal spirit is the consolidation of actualized pentecostal principle. It is, in other words, the summation of the struggle to grasp and be grasped by the pentecostal principle: a group's self-determination to actualize and live in constant

---

72. My summary of spirit in this section is indebted to Tsenay Serequeberhan, *Our Heritage: The Past in the Present of African-American and African Existence* (Lanham, MD: Rowman & Littlefield, 2000), pp. 16-19, 21, and to Hans-Georg Gadamer, *Truth and Method* (London: Continuum, 1989), p. 13.

73. Serequeberhan, *Our Heritage*, p. 17.

74. *Teme* is a Kalabari (Niger Delta) word for shadow and spirit. See Nimi Wariboko, *The Depth and Destiny of Work: An African Theological Interpretation* (Trenton: Africa World Press, 2008), pp. 5, 68-72.

possibility of achieving this very principle. Pentecostal ethics is the critical and systematic reflection and interpretative exploration of the future, progress, and problems and concerns deriving from the history, lived antecedents, and concrete actuality of the pentecostal spirit. The source of the need for the reflection and exploration is the diremption between the lived actuality and the hoped-for ideality of the principle.

Helping ourselves with a Hegelian rhetorical flourish, we dare to say that hitherto pentecostal ethics has not found its method; *it regarded with envy* the biblical, fundamentalist ethics and borrowed or had recourse to the method of general social ethics which is only an amalgam of social sciences, philosophy and liberal theology — *or even crude rejection of all intellectual rigor*, methodological sophistication, and interdisciplinarity. *However, the exposition of what alone can be the true method*[75] of pentecostal ethics falls within the treatment of the pentecostal principle itself; for the method is the exposition of the ideals and lived actuality of a community in which the pentecostal spirit dwells.

The method is about movement of the principle, how the community understands and names the pentecostal principle, how it interprets its identity and morality in terms of the principle, and how it sees its place in the world, and evaluates its culture's relation to the Divine. This method takes as its point of departure the willingness of the ethicist to approach social existence, social organization, and institutions to be taught by them. This is not, however, in "the character of a pupil," "but of an appointed judge" compelling them to answer questions about the human capacity to initiate the new, to seek alternatives to current arrangements that promote human flourishing, and to bring heaven on earth.

This chapter began with the aim of apprehending the spirit of pentecostalism as a social movement. One of the major insights that emerged in the process of investigating the pentecostal spirit is the playful character of pentecostalism. This is an important insight that requires further reflection. Our understanding of the pentecostal spirit will be inadequate if we do not examine the festival (pentecost) nature of the pentecostal movement. Chapter 5 will investigate the connections between the pentecostal principle, the quest for actualization of potentials, and a "theology of play" as a radicalization of grace. I will press for a new understanding of play as a theological-philosophical orientation to point pentecostalism to the fulfillment of its historic task.

75. The flourish is taken from Hegel, *Science of Logic*, trans. A. V. Miller (New York: Humanities Press, 1976), p. 53. Quoted in Serequeberhan, *Our Heritage*, p. 28. In following the flourish I have italicized direct phrases from Hegel.

5 The Promise of the Pentecostal Principle

Religion as Play

I think the pentecostal penchant for playfulness, which we have already seen in several portions of this book, has the potential to change the regnant understanding of religion in the twenty-first century. We need to pay some attention to the connections between the pentecostal principle, the human quest for actualization of potentials, and "religion as play" to demonstrate how this study points us to areas of further research in philosophical theology. Indeed, our understanding of the pentecostal spirit will be extremely impoverished if we do not reckon with its festival nature, the playful character of pentecostalism as a whole. Named after a festival (the Day of Pentecost), the pentecostal movement has the element of play in its core. I will now explore the nature of its playful character and locate it within the pentecostal principle itself. As I indicated earlier, play is the gift of grace. Play is an expression of the freedom of the spirit. Play is the courage to be surprised.

To approach religion playfully — as pure means — is to view it as an expression of freedom, a positive assurance that God will make our worship, prayers, and services what he wills. For instance, what gives worship meaning for pentecostals is not measured by its ability to achieve any goal or celebrate any purpose. It is judged by the Holy Spirit's involvement in it and it is the Spirit alone who can make it meaningful and fruitful. As we read in Psalm 127:1, "Unless the Lord builds the house, those who build it labor in vain." True worship is the work of God *(opus Dei)*. God will make of it what he wills. This "impractical" approach to religion stands as a divine gift and a challenge to a world caught in the vortex of crass cost-benefit utilitarianism and managerialism. Playfulness opens believers to the facets of the divine-human relation that are surprising or wonder-inspiring. According to theologian Brian Brock,

> Playfulness suggests that [religion] that is comfortable in following divine leading will exhibit a willingness to and facility in taking risks in the course of serving or preparing to serve others. This ethos embraces the drama and fragility of human efforts that fly in the face of a risk-averse society terrorized by the risk it aspires wholly to overcome. Playful [religion] confidently embraces what appears to the world as risk not in order to secure its own benefit, but as an act of following God of surprises who assaults modern sensibilities about financial prudence and cost-benefit decision making. Truly playful [religion] may not even recognize, or may only recognize after the fact, what the world labels risk.[1]

Let me now indicate how the argument of this chapter will unfold. I will start by showing how the logic of play is connected to the logics of grace and the pentecostal principle. This I will do by engaging with the works of two pentecostal theologians, Jean-Jacques Suurmond and Wolfgang Vondey, who have identified the playful character of pentecostalism and argued for play as the organizing principle for theological thinking. Their argument is strengthened and advanced as I develop the notion of religion as play. Next I will show that a proper understanding of religion as play can only come from a perspective that radicalizes grace, as is happening in pentecostalism. The notion of religion as play will be carefully developed along a pathway that connects potentiality (both potentiality and im-potentiality), the pentecostal principle, and "first-philosophical" analysis of play.

The radicalization of grace engenders a problematic for pentecostals. The logic of radicalization of grace is somewhat imbricated with desires for instant blessings, miracles, and the abolition of time. At the transversal intersection of theology, psychoanalysis, philosophy, and sociology, I will investigate what the desires for miracles tell us about the secularization process that is at the heart of pentecostalism. This takes us to the heart of the chapter, where I examine the relationship between grace, law, and play.

---

1. The word replaced by what is in the brackets is "work." Brock is here analyzing one of Karl Barth's characteristics of human work undertaken in reliance on God: playfulness. I have adapted Brock's meditation on the playfulness of work to my purpose here. See Brian Brock, *Christian Ethics in a Technological Age* (Grand Rapids: Eerdmans, 2010), p. 315.

Under grace we have a playful relation to the law and this opens up a space where we can fulfill the demands of the law under the figure of love.

Finally, I argue that this radical understanding of grace as play and hence true religion also as play is at the core of pentecostalism. Pentecostalism displays the structure of aesthetic categories and logic of play. I end it all with a restatement of the idea of the pentecostal in a way that takes into the account the insights we have gained so far in this study.

Theology of/as Play: Upended or Unended?

Earlier writers like Jean-Jacques Suurmond, who rightly identified the playful character of pentecostalism, did not situate it within the "essence" of the pentecostal principle,[2] the human quest for actualization of potentialities, and the context of sin-salvation-grace. In addition, the notion of play they used is at best pure end (play as an end in itself), and not pure means.[3] Yet this book's notion of play is not just about play as an unended

2. Play as the connectivity of order, dynamics, and indeterminacy represents the capacity for something new, the creative possibilities of new beginnings, and surprising shifts to different levels of flourishing. To this insight let us add that of Plato. In the *Laws* dialogue, he not only argues that grace denotes the pleasures of the purposeless game, but also that the grateful soul is ready for playfulness. See also Jean-Jacques Suurmond, *Word and Spirit at Play* (Grand Rapids: Eerdmans, 1994), p. 59; and Arthur J. Jacobson, "Origins of the Game Theory of Law and the Limits of Harmony in Plato's Law," *Cardozo Law Review* 20 (May-July 1999): 1335-1400.

3. After I had concluded the writing of this book, on November 13, 2010, I came across John Milbank's notion of the church as a "pure means." Unfortunately, he does not expatiate on how and why he regards the church as a pure means. He has relied on the thoughts of Agamben and Benjamin, as I have done, to reach this conclusion. Let me quote the passage in which he characterized the church as pure means:

> This order then composes a higher organism, the resurrected body of Christ collectively participated in. This *ekklēsia* is undying because it is not composed of sacrifices in the face of death for the sake of the endurance of a finite edifice that must one day collapse. Rather, in Benjamin's and Agamben's terms, it is composed only of "pure means," of ecstatic living offerings of divinized bodies according to a "logical worship" (*logikē latreia*, Rom. 12:1), whose superfluous potential can always be resumed, in any circumstance. . . . God, who is the ultimate goal-beyond-goal of all human life, surpassing all contrasts between ends and means. (John Milbank, "Paul Against Biopolitics," in *Paul's New Moment: Continental Philosophy and the Future of Christian Theology*, ed. John Milbank, Slavoj Žižek, and Creston Davies [Grand Rapids: Brazos, 2010], p. 46)

action. There are five key aspects to the notion of play in this book that separate it from the thought of Suurmond. First, in this book play is not conceptualized as a counterpoint to work, the problem of leisure, or seriousness (although these are not denied), but as a deactivation of law and radicalization of saving grace. Second, play is conceptualized as a pure means, purposelessness. Play is regarded as having the structure of aesthetic judgment — an unended action. Third, play is considered *profanatory* behavior. Fourth, play is seen as exhibiting non-zero-sum dynamics, which is key to understanding the inherent dynamism of the relationality of human socialities and growth of social complexity. Finally, play is conceived as freely evolving potentialities. It is the eros toward open future, the to-come as the quest for potentials. Play is the mode of being of potentiality itself.

ℵ Play and Non-Zero-Sumness

One perspective from which to understand play as a possible exemplar of the pentecostal principle is to situate it in the context of human cooperative act, complexity, and interdependence. One of the fundamental impulses that drive human creativity and interactions to approximate catholicity and to express an openness to and straining and stretching toward their divine depths is the energy of non-zero-sumness, according to Robert Wright in his book *Nonzero*,[4] in which he develops a logic of non-zero-sumness and applies it to moral imagination. Non-zero-sumness is the kind of transactional payoff that animates history and human sociality and moves human existence to increasing communality and building and sustenance of communal structures. Where does non-zero-sumness come from? It is human cooperativeness (the process of mutuality and reciprocity) that produces and sustains non-zero-sumness. Play is a paradigmatic form of cooperation and it is a suitable metaphor or even a reflection of the dynamic creativity and participation that drive existents to *act,* to actualize themselves by exchanging resources with one another in the process of mutuality and reciprocity. And play in this way points beyond itself to the theonomous depth of human culture. I take the thrust of a theonomous connection of human creativity with divine depths to be the exercise that encourages the building of communal relationships and deepening of relationality.

Wright's specific theory of human cooperativeness is an invitation for theologians and ethicists to undertake a theological analysis of non-zero-sumness and

---

4. Robert Wright, *Nonzero: The Logic of Human Destiny* (New York: Vintage, 2001). See also his *The Evolution of God* (New York: Little, Brown, and Company, 2009).

the materialist ideas that undergird it. Let me suggest some theological resources that we can possibly draw upon to aid reflection on some of them. First, the idea of cooperativeness conduces to theological analysis of freedom. The ability to cooperate with others to achieve one's purpose not only supervenes freedom, but it is also constitutive of it. Cooperativeness is one dimension of human relationality which is crucial for self-consciousness, self-identity, and self-actualization. Second, because of the importance of interdependence, surplus, and cooperativeness, we need to shift the grounding of our ethics of love from self-sacrifice and atonement to themes of mutuality. Third, in the world of adaptive autopoietic complexity, a world without end, "redemption" may need to be redefined so as to occur inside the systemic cooperative process and not to come from outside at the end of time. Perhaps justice of the processual here and now has become more important than an end-time giant settling of accounts. Finally, Wright's theory of non-zero-sumness is a key to understanding the intensification of social life in today's global political economy. Wright grounds his theory on the biological notion of genes: as in his idea of social structures built into human genes. But the theory may be better grounded in the pentecostal principle; that is, in the diffusive ebullience of fundamental relationality (aspects of which are communality, participation, and possibilities) that the pentecostal principle calls for in human existence.

In his recent book *Beyond Pentecostalism* (2010), pentecostal theologian Wolfgang Vondey substantially elevates the discourse of theology as play. Despite suffering from some of the same weaknesses as Suurmond's work, Vondey's book seems to me to be the most sophisticated treatment of theology as play available today. He uses play as the organizing principle for the ambitious project of reconstructing the global theological agenda along the insights of pentecostal theology. His "approach seeks to join together play and theology in a manner not widely established in theological discourse. . . . More precisely, the integration of the idea of play in the theological landscape has been carried out generally by offering a theology *of* play rather than by seeking an understanding of how theology itself may proceed *as* play."[5] Yet in a sense, Vondey is guilty of the same accusation he levies against fellow theologians. His book does not offer a critical analysis of play as a proper image for human existence and for the divine-human relationship. While he has given us an understanding of how to perceive theology itself as play, his work does not help us to understand the dy-

5. Wolfgang Vondey, *Beyond Pentecostalism: The Crisis of Global Christianity and the Renewal of the Theological Agenda* (Grand Rapids: Eerdmans, 2010), pp. 171-72. Italics in original.

namic principle that is moving pentecostalism to become religion as pure means.

The notion of pure means is a helpful lens for interpreting the extreme phase of capitalism, the general tendency of the twenty-first century, and its pentecostalism as a concrete social reality. In this study we are seeking to address the issue of the social ontological truth of the concrete religio-cultural order of historical expressions of pentecostalism. We are endeavoring to lay bare the "inner greatness," the "historical-ontological essence" of pentecostalism as a phenomenon of our epoch without conferring ontological dignity on any pentecostal movement. How do we philosophically understand the religion of a people who like Origen believe that "[it] is always the Day of Pentecost"?[6] Or even understand them in the light of what Moltmann (commenting on Joachim's "concept of the age of the Spirit") says about the nature of the kingdom of the Spirit which is not subsumed in either the age of grace or that of glory.

> The kingdom of the Spirit is experienced in the gift conferred on the people liberated by the Son — the gift of the Holy Spirit's energies. . . . In the powers of the Spirit, the energies of new creation are experienced. . . . In the Spirit, that new community comes into being which is without privileges and subjection, the community of the free. In the Spirit, the new creation in the kingdom of glory is anticipated.[7]

We are in an era governed by the worship of bold, rapid, abundant energies. From gushing oil wells to chain reactions of atomic explosions, from race cars to space shuttles, from action movies to bungee jumping, from the supersonic chats of cell-phone text messaging to the profound, instantaneous, and infinite speed of the Internet, everything is in the mode of explosion and detonation. As Peter Sloterdijk puts it, we are all "fanatical adherents of explosions, worshippers of that rapid release of a large quantity of energy."[8] Pentecostalism, in its fury, abundant energy, and

6. Origen, *Contra Celsum*, trans. Henry Chadwick (Cambridge: Cambridge University Press, 1953), VIII, 22, p. 468.

7. Jürgen Moltmann, *The Trinity and the Kingdom*, trans. Margaret Kohl (Minneapolis: Fortress, 1993), p. 211.

8. Peter Sloterdijk, "Conversation with Fabrice Bousteau and Jonathan Chauveau," in "Vies Mode D'Emploi," *Special Issue, Beaux Arts Magazine* (2004): 192, quoted in Nicolas Bourriaud, *The Radicant*, trans. James Gussen and Lili Porten (New York: Lukas and Sternberg Press, 2009), p. 177.

rapid growth, is the religious archetype of the impetus of our age. Energy is a pure means and pure endedness, if not actually only a pure means (pure mediality).

The notion of energy as a pure means opens up another perspective for comprehending our epoch: economy, politics, and religion. The Italian philosopher Giorgio Agamben argues that the current phase of capitalism is "a gigantic apparatus for capturing pure means, that is, profanatory behaviors."[9] Politics does not operate as pure means; it principally refers to activities determined by the preset ends of late capitalism. It has been reduced to debates about the efficient means to accomplish closed ends. Today's politics (co-opted and emasculated by late capitalism) is about the administration of projects and the maintenance of order and not about creating and sustaining a platform for debating and contesting different ends; it is not a means toward an open end.[10] Pentecostalism portrays religion as pure means, a pathway of profanatory behaviors. Religion as a sphere of openness, pure means, is profoundly and qualitatively different from religion as an end. Vondey's conceptualization of play and even his theology *as* play fail to relate his thesis to the nature of pentecostalism as a pure means and to its connection with the impetus of our age.

But let us return to Vondey's primary focus, which is on theology *as* play. Even here, what he means by theology *as* play is not always very clear. Does he mean that in the midst of the global epistemic crisis theology can only find its capacity to consist "as play"? What exactly does the "as" mean? Does he want theology to behave "as if it were" play, or does theology as a body of knowledge and potentialities at work in it now have to be incorporated into or live in another body, that of play? What is the process by which theology determines the place of play with respect to its existence? Without laying a good foundation of understanding about religion and play, how can theology as play appear as the normative (acceptable) structure of order that assigns degrees of lesser and greater intensity of playfulness to objects of theological domains? What being supports its appearing? Theology as play, as *being-there*, must evoke its being; in philosophical terms, if it aspires to be logics, logical organization, or transcendental organization which sorts the intensities of playfulness according to its criteria of truth, it must first let us know its being.

---

9. Giorgio Agamben, *Profanations*, trans. Jeff Fort (New York: Zone Books, 2007), p. 87.

10. Giorgio Agamben, *Means without Ends: Notes on Politics*, trans. Vincenzo Benetti and Cesare Casarino (Minneapolis: University of Minnesota Press, 2000), pp. 115-17.

Unlike Vondey, I explain play's link to theology within a larger framework which can be summarized as "existence = human action = religion = play."[11] The task of theological ethics is to inquire into, understand, and evaluate this network of interactive spheres of human activities and practices and help it toward flourishing and its theonomous divine depths. So we say that our theology as play is not a mere imposition of a metaphor or heuristic device on a set of collective practices, but is to say something revelatory about human existence and its re-presentation as a form of thought. I do not treat play as a metaphor, but substantialize it. Here we are neither dealing with play as an addition (the play perspective as simple supplement to other ways of doing theology) nor as a synthesis (play as self-revelation of a theology seized by pentecostalism). Play is the "what-there-is" of religion — that which makes up the structure of religion. Theology is the local region of the thought process, life in the mind, thinking exercises that unfold the implications of this "what-there-is" and the pa-

---

11. The sign "=" does not here mean strict equivalence. What it is gesturing toward is something like this: Existence is expressed in human actions (in the Arendtian sense of the word). Action, in a deep sense, is actualization of potential, the pursuit of excellence, as I have argued in my book *The Principle of Excellence: A Framework for Social Ethics* (Lanham, MD: Lexington Books, 2009), and it is religious in character. Religion is human action, the human search for wholeness and meaning. It is an expression of what it means to be human. Anyone who has examined modern life's pursuit of excellence, the persistent need to ferret out and actualize possibilities in all facets of existential life, will also recognize its "religious" quality. This is all the more so if one juxtaposes passion for excellence vis-à-vis Alfred North Whitehead's definition of religion. The word "excellence" can replace the word "religion" in his definition and it could well be an adequate characterization of excellence. Whitehead characterizes religion in this way:

> Religion is the vision of something which stands beyond, behind, and within, the passing flux of immediate things; something which is real, and yet waiting to be realized; something which is a remote possibility, and yet the greatest of present facts; something that gives meaning to all that passes, and yet eludes apprehension; something whose possession is the final good, and yet is beyond all reach; something which is the ultimate ideal, and the hopeless quest. (Whitehead, *Science and the Modern World* [New York: Macmillan, 1926], p. 275)

Finally, religion has been shown in this study to be a play; it has the "play element" in its core.

The "=" sign also gestures to the fact that what is on the right of it embraces what is on the left, encompasses it, and yet symbolizes it. The right symbolizes the left by not only pointing to the left, but by also participating in it. In another sense, the right is the signature of the left. The right is always implicated in the multiplicative (expressive) composition of the left.

rameters of its correlative "being-there" for human flourishing as a point of play. This conception of the task of theology in effect demands the subordination of theology (theological ethics) to the affirmation of subjects[12] faithful to the pentecostal principle, which is beyond pentecostalism. Vondey's book is a necessary and welcome effort in this direction insofar as it deftly detects, beneath the crises, discordant voices, the disorder of multiplicity of approaches, the logic of play that should hold together theology. This logic also holds together the concrete collective practices that theology re-presents as an exercise in thinking.

Vondey's conceptualization of theology as play and his practical deployment of it as an *apparatus* that strategically organizes the domains of theology in the urgent task of addressing the global theological crisis presupposes what, for lack of a better term, I will call a play-fully ordered religion. The existence of the playful character in religion is not in question from the beginning of his book. Theology is simply to reflect this character and theologizing is organized from the presence of this character in pentecostalism. What Vondey succeeds in doing is at best to show the nature of theology *as* play, and not the existence of play (playfulness) in the nature of religion and existence. Without this foundation in religion and without an engagement with the ethnography of real practices on the ground, theology *as* play stands the risk of being a pure activity of theologizing.

Another problem with Vondey's otherwise commendable approach is that it does not work out the nature and necessity of the play (or the play metaphor) from the inner dynamics of grace, from the dynamics that underlie and define pentecostalism within the world-historical process, or as an expression of the general will of existence. In my understanding, insights on play emerge from the logic and dynamic of the pentecostal principle. This chapter will further show that the logic of play is the logic of grace, and the logic of the pentecostal principle. It is the logic of Paul's "as not" (1 Cor. 7). It is the logic of "as-if" and the logic of aesthetics of tongues-speech as seen in chapter 1. Play in this book not only names and expresses the particular pentecostal spirituality, but also offers an understanding of the pneumatic existence of human life and sociality in interaction with their divine depths.

The pentecostal principle as play is "pure self-presentation," to use Hans-Georg Gadamer's phrase. Play is the mode of being in which the

---

12. Refer to the discussions at the end of this chapter for the treatment of subject and subjectivation.

principle is actualized. Play's essence, as Gadamer informs us, is in its movement, transcending ended action and instrumental pursuit.[13] The actuality of play is the free evolving potentialities that do not (often) conform to the roles, rules, and rhythms of the given world. Play's freedom of expression and its character of pure means, spontaneity, improvisation, enthusiasm, and relationality are central to understanding the free, unbounded movement of the pentecostal principle. In fact, we will show below that the movement of the pentecostal principle is play itself; it is the perichoretic dance of potentiality and existence at its forward and backward movements of being-in communion.

We opened our engagement with Vondey's work by noting the way he distances his theology from the theology of play. But let us take a moment to examine whether he actually escapes the grip of the mindset he critiques. Theology of play interprets play life as freedom from the tyranny of work and seriousness. This perspective also sets an external distinction between play and theology as the job of understanding how play can ease life and religious seriousness. The person who interprets play as freedom from work can only be free at the cost of work. Theology as play only "internalized" this external distinction into its working paradigm, transferring it to an inward necessity, impulse, or dynamics. Theology itself must be seen as play and embrace a methodology that explicitly thinks through and out of the reality of play. From this point of view, Vondey's notion of play still belongs to theology and religion only exteriorly.

But true play is community, a relationship between subjects, and subjects and their divine depths; the subjects' mutual participation in the freely evolving potentialities of existence and the interpretation of such. In its nature of purposelessness, play transcends the present, the given world in the direction of possibilities and not yet defined potentialities. "Seen theologically, this is the special dimension given by the experience of the Spirit. In the Spirit we transcend the present in the direction of God's future, for the Spirit is the 'earnest' or 'pledge of glory.'"[14]

In this sense, the relationship between play and theology cannot be interpreted as that between subject and object (theology of play); and play is not a leaven within the theological dough as it ferments its way out of cri-

---

13. Hans-Georg Gadamer, *Truth and Method,* trans. Joel Weinsheimer and Donald G. Marshall (London: Continuum, 2004), p. 94.

14. Jürgen Moltmann, *The Trinity and the Kingdom,* trans. Margaret Kohl (Minneapolis: Fortress, 1993), p. 214.

sis (theology as play, a means to an end, an organizing metaphor). Rather, play as pure means is constitutive of theology itself (theology *en* play, if you like). Play is not synonymous with theology; play interpenetrates every part of the nature (dough) of theology and extends beyond it as well. Theology does not need to posit itself as play to un-conceal its truth. It only needs to take off its scholastic and other pedantic accretions, undress without shame, and trample on its purple garments with the feet of children and to behold the potentiality and im-potentiality of grace and play.[15] This should not be construed to mean that theologians can tap into an original state of theology before its decoupling from the playfulness of existence itself, but only to nudge them to engage with the deactivation of law (work, seriousness, instrumentality) and the radicalization of grace.

Thus, Vondey's ideas are significant and worthy of much attention. Yet as currently formulated they cannot provide us with a pentecostal framework for thinking beyond Pentecostalism. We need a beyond that presupposes the pentecostal spirit and takes "pentecostal" as a predicate, and not a name. Theology-as-play as a methodological paradigm and pentecostal resource of the global theological agenda must grow up out of a solid understanding of the pentecostal principle. Otherwise, it is not truly pentecostal. And as I have argued from the beginning of this book, being pentecostal is not the same thing as pentecostalism. The pentecostal principle cuts into pentecostalism, the Protestant principle, and the Catholic substance — and exceeds them. Vondey's book develops a sophisticated notion of theology as play, but this book not only develops a notion of religion as play, but also crafts a kind of ontological (or "first-philosophical") analysis of play that can undergird his project. By also showing how religion as play develops from a perspective that radicalizes grace, this book opens up another resource of pentecostalism for the global Christian theology project that Vondey is nudging the theological academy to take on in this second decade of the twenty-first century.

---

15. Here I am making a playful allusion to the apocryphal Gospel of Thomas: "His disciples asked: 'When will you reveal yourself to us, and when will we see you?' Jesus answered: 'When you undress without shame, when you take off your clothes and trample on them with your feet like children; then you will behold the Son of the living God, and you will have no fear.'"

From Potentials to Pentecostal Principle to Play

I have already demonstrated that the pentecostal principle is about the realization of potentials, about actualizing the capacity to do something new. For this reason let us try to understand what we mean by potentiality. Potential, as we learned earlier from Aristotle, is both potentiality and impotentiality *(adynamia)*. Potentiality (whether to be or to do) is capable of not passing into actuality. Potentiality can actualize itself, succumb to the urge of fulfillment; but in doing so it does not exhaust itself. It is always in play. As Aristotle put it, "What is potential can both be and not be. For the same is potential as much with respect to being as to not being."[16] A potential can pass into an actualization whose conditions of actuality demand that the creative actualization cannot exhaust the potentiality or destroy the im-potentiality. It means that a potentiality doubles as both potentiality and potentiality not to be, that at every moment of realization, pure actuality is indistinguishable from pure potentiality. We might call these two sides or dimensions of potentiality "fulfillment" and "im-potentiality."

I am tempted to derive the same idea from a modified version of Alain Badiou's philosophy. That is, we could begin by saying that potential, as far as human socialities are concerned, is the infinite multitude of what presents itself, that which is given. At the level of potentiality all that are present are not symbolically structured and cannot spontaneously move and tend to their own independent goal. Yet "their" is not quite the right word here, for technically speaking there is no "their" and no "ones," because the multiple of experience is not structured. The structuring which enables us to count the "ones," to signify them as relevant to our own flourishing, to move them toward actualization and fulfillment, is the law. Here law stands both for the moral imperative of a person to become what she is essentially and the symbolic structure that defines the state of things, the state of existing sociopolitical relations.

Before this determination or structuring occurs, the preceding multiple of the given appears essentially as nothing, as a void. The determination, however, cannot exhaust the pure multiple. It cannot completely encode, "gentrify," all possibilities. Each state of affairs excludes some possibilities. There are always excluded possibilities that actually belong to

---

16. Aristotle, *Metaphysics*, 1050b, 10. The quotation above uses the translation in Giorgio Agamben, *Homo Sacer: Sovereign Power and Bare Life*, trans. Daniel Heller-Roazen (Stanford: Stanford University Press, 1998), p. 45.

the state of affairs. From time to time and in a totally unexpected way, one or more of the excluded possibilities pops up and reconfigures the order of being. All the knowledge of the existing order cannot enable us to predict ahead of time when an event will occur. But note that this event, this surprise, the underivable new, is not coming from outside. It is something within the state of being, from within the given multiple, which attaches itself to the state of being as its inherent inconstancy and/or its excess. Let us call this event that appears *ex nihilo* grace. Grace is what opens the (excluded) possibilities for exchange, for pushing pass (past) limits in any given system. It is a symbol of its constitutive incompleteness. So our earlier fulfillment and im-potentiality become law and grace. Before I take up the line of thought that this last sentence provokes, let us approach grace from a more theological perspective in the aside (ℵ) below, with a play on Heidegger's "waiting *for*" and "waiting *upon*" as elucidated in his *Gelassenheit* ("Discourse on Thinking"), where he speaks about the nature of existential meaning.[17]

ℵ THE RADICALIZATION OF GRACE

We receive grace *for* our transgressions. It is something that provides us with what we need to reconcile our broken relationship with God, with other human beings, and with creation. But when grace is radicalized it becomes grace *upon* us. We receive this kind of grace; we wait for this grace, without knowing what we are waiting for, without waiting for anything. Grace now has a reference beyond any calculative reference. Grace is left completely open. In contrast to grace *for*, it is grace which allows no preconceived purpose, new rather than old meaning, to emerge within the *awareness* of one's acceptance by God — one's redemptive indwelling by the Holy Spirit — and authentic *releasement* to the pleasures of such. This is grace open to purposelessness, open to what is given. Play begins with an awareness of this kind. Play must arise out from the ground of grace and bloom into the ether of openness to the mystery of pneumatic existence and letting-be of things. We stand at once within the realm of potentialities that actualizes itself and holds back itself in actualization. Martin Heidegger writes, "that which shows itself and at the same time withdraws is the essential trait of what we call mystery."[18] And the words of theologian David L. Miller in his *Gods and Games: Toward a Theology of Play* confirms:

17. Martin Heidegger, *Discourse on Thinking: A Translation of Gelassenheit*, trans. John M. Anderson and E. Hans Freund (New York: Harper & Row, 1966).

18. Heidegger, *Discourse on Thinking*, p. 55.

What is implied by this is that man's noblest and most profound destiny lies in making the central purpose of his life a kind of purposelessness. For to have as one's goal a preconceived purpose is to be caught in the idealistic trap of "waiting for" an ego-projection of anxiety laden destiny. The authentic purpose of man's therapeutic condition, therefore, would be the reverse; it would be the purposelessness which is *letting-be* of life and meaning.[19]

We can also draw the connection between grace and play via another perspective. Let us start by stating that grace is a meaningful and not a necessary act of God. If it is necessary then God is not "free." On the other hand, if it is accidental then God is capricious. And grace cannot be grounded on itself. So the only conclusion left for us is that grace is grounded on God's good will or pleasure. Hence grace is "God's play, a play on his groundless and inscrutable wisdom."[20] And the wisdom of God is playful: "I was daily his delight, playing [*sahaq*] before him always" (Prov. 8:30).

In a very broad sense, we can even say that play is at the core of our understanding of who God is. The mutual indwelling of God, the Father, the Son, and the Holy Spirit is described in classical theological terms as a dance, *perichoresis* (*chorein* in Greek is dance or step). In other words, the triune God is an eternal dance, a playful companionship. Dance, as Johan Huizinga informs us in his now classic book *Homo Ludens,* is a perfect form of play.[21]

Law and Guilt: A Psychoanalysis of Desire for Miracles

Let us return to the idea, inspired by Badiou, that law and grace can stand in for fulfillment and im-potentiality. The law determines what works within a given framework of relations. As the ultimate horizon of knowledge and acceptable action, it determines what is possible. The finite law is (falsely) posited as the truth of the potential itself. So when a law speaks it is not the law which is speaking, it is potential itself which speaks through it.[22] Grace is about the impossible, doing the impossible; it changes the very framework of how the possible, the acceptable is determined. As "part of no part" of the existing framework or order of being, it stands in for the

19. David L. Miller, *Gods and Games: Toward a Theology of Play* (New York: Word Publishing Company, 1970), p. 151.

20. Jürgen Moltmann, *Theology of Play,* trans. Reinhard Ulrich (New York: Harper & Row, 1972), p. 17.

21. Johan Huizinga, *Homo Ludens: A Study of the Play Element in Culture,* trans. R. F. C. Hull (Boston: Beacon, 1995), pp. 164-65.

22. See the small-type section below.

true universality of the entire network of included and excluded possibilities, the entire social space, the totality of relations, and also undermines it. Any individual or group can be touched by grace as it has no determinate content. It is an empty signifier. Grace, unlike the law, accepts its simple subordination to potential, as belonging to potential. Many particulars, many actualized potentials, many laws, or many religious forms will strive to hegemonize the empty signifier, that is, a particular content claiming to function as its stand-in, its representative.[23] But because grace is a "part of no part," is devoid of positive, particular content, and can never be full or exhausted, there will always be a constitutive gap, a lack in the particular form hegemonizing it and presenting itself as the universal. "Do we not encounter here the paradoxical logic of *desire* as the constitutively *impossible*, sustained by a constitutive lack (the absence of fullness of the empty signifier) that can never be supplied by any positive object . . . ?"[24]

א Law Speaks as Potential Itself

I stated above that the finite law is (falsely) posited as the truth of the potential itself. So when a law speaks it is not the law which is speaking, it is potential itself which speaks through it. Needless to say, this is not a true picture of the law as the symbolic structure that defines the state of things, the state of existing sociopolitical relations. One of the ways law exercises power in any society is its ability to separate people from their potentiality, from what they can do, and thus to render them impotent. But more importantly, it can sever them from their impotentiality. And herein lies one of the major threats of law to the fundamental character of the pentecostal principle. As an excursus, let us think about what is happening in modern democratic society. According to Agamben, modern democratic powers and state structures increasingly prefer to act on the im-potentiality of their citizens. As he puts it:

> It is on this other, more obscure, face of potentiality that today the power one ironically defines as "democratic" prefers to act. It separates humans not only and not so much from what they can do but primarily and for the most part from

23. The moment a sociality, institution, or religious form pretends to fully realize potential, to have passed from the spectral im-potentiality, that which is to come, into final actual fulfillment, it has calcified the human capacity to bring something new into ongoing existence. The pentecostal principle has turned into a monster, a terror in that institution. Any claim of its ultimate success is always a catastrophe, an ultimate failure.

24. Slavoj Žižek, *The Ticklish Subject: The Absent Center of Political Ontology* (London: Verso, 2008), p. 216. Italics in original.

what they can not do. Separated from his impotentiality, deprived of the experience of what he can not do, today's man believes himself capable of everything, and so he repeats his jovial "no problem," and his irresponsible "I can do it," precisely when he should instead realize that he has been consigned in unheard of measure to forces and processes over which he has lost all control. He has become blind not to his capacities but to his incapacities, not to what he can do but to what he cannot, or can not, do.[25]

Now that we have translated potential into law and grace and uncovered the latter's shared logic with desire we will be able to examine pentecostals' desire for instant blessings, miracles, and abolition of time in terms of the intersection of theology, psychoanalysis, and sociology. We must address this question: What does the desire for miracles tell us about the secularization process within the heart of pentecostalism?

Desire in pentecostalism is doubled-edge. It is both about what I the pentecostal desire and what the Other desires from me. It is about "what I really want" and "what the Other really wants from me." These two types of desires often coincide. Take for instance 3 John 2: "Beloved, I pray that you may prosper in all things and be in health, just as your soul prospers" (NKJV). This is one of the proof texts, if not *the* proof text, for the wealth, health, and name-and-claim-it movement. I want what the Other wants from me. My desire is ultimately God's desire.

Every form of pentecostalism is a "representation of desire" looking at us. Each is "the representative of a desire in the image [of God]."[26] For pentecostalism is a way of seeing the world. It is "a kind of aesthetics, a way of looking at the world that produces and is produced by a certain kind of desire."[27] If the "eye" that sees us is an eye of desire, what then is reflected back to us? What is represented in the pupils of the world, of us that are *seen,* and the image staring at us? It is desire, or rather the aestheticization of desire.[28]

25. Giorgio Agamben, *Nudities,* trans. David Kishik and Stefan Pedatella (Stanford: Stanford University Press, 2011), p. 44.

26. For quotes see Nicolas Bourriaud, *Relational Aesthetics* (Paris: Les presses du réel, 2002), p. 23.

27. William T. Cavanaugh, *Being Consumed: Economics and Christian Desire* (Grand Rapids: Eerdmans 2008), p. xi.

28. Desires cut off from their proper end. Alas, in many a pentecostal circle the desires are tied to a negative view of freedom (absence of external constraints or obstacles to happiness; it is freedom *from*) and not to positive freedom (common end such as communion with others or increasing attachment to God, freedom *to*).

And it is "an image of the reality of the connection" between pentecostalism and postmodernism and the logic of late capitalism.[29]

The representation of desire is driven more by expectation than by memory or remembrance. It is not the fact of natality, cognition of spiritual life, or internal affections for the kingdom of God that is at issue here, but "the felicity of this life." The journey of the desire starts in the imagination. Imagination is the first internal moment of the generation and representation of desires; it is the site of the struggle between the conflicting forces of being-toward-birth (which is accompanied by gratitude) and being-toward-death (which elicits fear, anxiety, and inadequacy). In pentecostalism one is invited to not only pneumatologically imagine the uniqueness of one's natality (in all its various forms), but also ignite the right affections for the eschatological kingdom, and cultivate ~~wild bold~~ right expectations as a desiring being. Pentecostalism brings to life and develops the "condensed" emotion, promise, and dignity in the image of God through a fractal dialogue of imitative creativity and play — and does all this as a social interstice.[30]

One of the desires of pentecostals is for a timeless universe or to enjoy time, the now, as having no heirs and children, never running out, and too impotent to separate wish from its fulfillment. Pentecostalism wants all the kingdoms of the world and kingdom of God in a moment of time — and God is petitioned to fulfill this wish without delay. Herein lies its deepest ambiguity: reliance on the comforts of eternity (divine rescue and assistance) and usurpation (longing) of divine prerogative (transcendence over the passage of time).

29. See Martha Nussbaum, *The Fragility of Goodness: Luck and Ethics in Greek Tragedy and Philosophy* (Cambridge: Cambridge University Press, 2001), p. 412. My use of the eye metaphor is informed by her analysis of Euripides' *Hecuba,* the scene where Hecuba blinds Polymestor.

30. According to Nicolas Bourriaud, "The term [*interstice*] was used by Karl Marx to describe trading communities that elude the capitalist economic context by being removed from the law of profit: barter, merchandising, autarkic types of production, etc. The interstice is a space in human relations which fits more or less harmoniously and openly into the overall system, but suggests other trading possibilities than those in effect within this system." *Relational Aesthetics,* p. 16.

This is the precise nature of pentecostalism within Christianity. It fits in but suggests other possibilities of inter-human and human-divine relations that are not readily accepted in the mainstream churches. The contexts of the mainline churches create spaces and time spans that are planned to the end; whose rhythms restrict the possibilities of fluid, flexible relations. The pentecostal way also stands in contrast to the rhythms that structure everyday life in the postindustrial society.

In this very space that we find the ambiguity there also lies a nagging paradox, "pleasure-in-pain." The pentecostal knows that miracle (divine surprise) is not the end, that she has an immortal soul whose salvation does not depend on signs and wonders. But she cannot pay the exorbitant price of abandoning the pursuit of miracles, turning away from the pleasures of divine rescues, and working only for salvation and sanctification. And she wants to believe that miracle is not the end, that there is an unconditional salvation of her soul which is not affected by the aesthetic pleasures of the miracles (prosperity) she pursues. So we have a Christian who desperately wants to have eternal life, but knows that she cannot exclusively focus on it, since she is condemned to the desire to achieve *jouissance* whose ultimate satisfaction eludes her. This state of nonsatisfaction, not the crucified life-form in the midst of all the worldly temptations, not the fear of hell in the Beyond, becomes the ultimate Kierkegaardian horror. This is sickness unto miracle!

Perhaps the agony of living with the painful awareness of this paradox can be best illumined in the Pauline language of Romans 7. Is salvation the sin? Has it become death to me? Certainly not! Yet I only know insatiable longing, desire by means of salvation. Really, I would not have the idea to long after materials and miracles if the Savior had not said: "Thou shall not covet. An evil and adulterous generation seeks after signs and wonders." But the longing was producing in me all manner of evil desire, covetousness thanks to the Master's prohibition, for without the prohibition the longing was dead. I was once alive without the prohibition. But when prohibition appeared the longing revived, and I met my death. Now it is no longer I who is coveting, but the longing that dwells in me. And for me, the salvation that was supposed to lead me to crucified, sanctified life, to swerve me away from hell, is bringing me into captivity of longing. The world found a way with me thanks to insatiable longing that seduced me; through it I came to be dominated by the law of sin and death. I now desire death. Who will deliver from this body of death?

Sociologically speaking, the pentecostals' attitude toward miracle tells us a great deal about their general orientation toward time. The pursuit of miracles can be partly interpreted as a struggle against time, as the strange Other which can be pitted against the big Other. Their not wanting to suffer or endure the ravages of the passage of time, demanding divine rescues which save people from the consequence of their actions, and also divine surprises which abolish the time gap between wish and wish-fulfillment inform us about this ongoing struggle. This orientation toward time demands or elicits different existential attitudes to the world within pentecostalism. It is very religious in its insistence on romantic temporizing, certainty of divine rescue, and de-differentiation of religion and society. It is at the same time radically secular. This is visible in the abandonment of the past, passing summary judgment on it, the rejection of all debts to the past and the future by collapsing the future and the past into the now (present), and the "unscrupulousness" toward the sacred. Where do all these leave us?

> One is left with a Christian faith that urges the individual to "let the dead bury the dead," to abandon traditional obligations, to subordinate ritualized observances to the needs of the moment, and to replace pious waiting with insistence on readiness at all times and places to make the most of opportunities for wholeness.[31]

This connection between salvation and guilt that we have described above is something that is inscribed into the processes of the pentecostal principle, the working of potentiality and im-potentiality in social existence. In the outworking of the principle, fall and redemption, law and grace, coincide.[32] We do not first fall into guilt in order to have the need for grace. Redemption does not come after the fall. Rather, they are identical; in itself one is the other. The increased possibilities for freedom and for the realization of potentialities which is the very nature of redemption, grace, is what the fall is about. The fall is existence and grace is existence retroactively igniting itself.[33]

Let us further explore this process or coincidence. We have earlier stated that potential is fulfillment and im-potentiality, law and grace. What is the law of fulfillment? It is the moral imperative. This is the idea that a person becomes what actually he or she is essentially and therefore potentially. Becoming a true person is thus a moral imperative. Thus, it is

31. Richard Fenn, *The Return of the Primitive: A New Sociological Theory of Religion* (Aldershot: Ashgate, 2001), pp. 121-22.

32. Please note that here I do not have in mind the biblical notions of fall and redemption. The use of these terms is confined to the philosophy of the pentecostal principle developed so far in this book and the terms are best interpreted in the light of the immediately preceding paragraphs of this chapter.

33. See Slavoj Žižek, *The Puppet and the Dwarf: The Perverse Core of Christianity* (Cambridge, MA: MIT Press, 2003), p. 118.

deemed immoral not to do and actualize what one is essentially and potentially capable of doing. According to Tillich,

> The moral imperative is the demand to become actually what one is essentially and therefore potentially. It is the power of man's being, given to him by nature, which he shall actualize in time and space. His true being shall become his actual being — this is the moral imperative. And since his true being is the being of a person in a community of persons, the moral imperative has this content: to become a person. Every moral act is an act in which the individual self establishes itself as a person.[34]

Every moral act is also an act in which the community and the individual work together to establish the individual as a person capable of answering to the demand of life as the process of actualization of potentialities for the sake of the individual and the community. This involves not only giving to each person her due, but also the relevant communal institutional forms in which person-to-person encounters happen and increase life.

What is the source of the moral imperative? According to Tillich, the source is the essential being. The imperative is the law of our essential nature, the unconditional demand to actualize our potentialities. This demand is experienced as "the silent voice of our being" which echoes the split between the human essential nature and its actual life. It is because of this estrangement that humans encounter the moral law, that is, the law of their essential nature, as an imperative for action. This law that is experienced as an imperative is not what human beings impose upon themselves as autonomous selves or is heteronomously imposed on them by a power outside the self, but it is the theonomous law of God. It is the will of God for the good of the essential being. As Tillich puts it,

> The "Will of God" for us is precisely our essential being with all its potentialities, our created nature declared as "very good" by God, as, in terms of the Creation myth, He "saw everything that he made." For us the "Will of God" is manifest in our essential being; and only because of this can we accept the moral imperative as valid. It is not a strange law

---

34. Paul Tillich, *Morality and Beyond* (Louisville: Westminster John Knox, 1963), p. 20. See also Galen Guengerich's rendering of the same idea and a study of Tillich's conception of justice in his "Comprehensive Commitments and the Public World: Tillich, Rawls, and Whitehead on the Nature of Justice" (Ph.D. diss., University of Chicago, 2004).

that demands our obedience, but the "silent voice" of our own nature as man, and as man with an individual character.[35]

The will of God is theonomously imperative not because it is God's command, and not because it dovetails with our essential nature. Tillich says that the will becomes unconditional and theonomously so when a person chooses to affirm his or her own essential nature.[36]

We have established that the moral imperative is the requirement to fulfill one's potential. Now let us explore how guilt is "ex-timate" in the process. When a person is working out her potentialities to be what she is essentially, to actualize her potentials, the whole of existence is not open to her. There are always a socially determined role and symbolic matrix that set the ideal (the ego-ideal) which she follows. This generates a fundamental guilt for betraying her more fundamental desire. In psychoanalytic terms it is the superego that generates the pressures of the guilt for the betrayal. According to Slavoj Žižek, "the superego manipulates the subject's actual betrayal of [her] fundamental 'passionate attachment' as the price [she] had to pay for entering the socio-symbolic space, and assuming a predetermined place within it."[37]

There is more to the guilt of actualizing one's potential. In liberal circles, one notion of "sin" is that it involves human beings not accepting their irreducible finitude. The proper ethical thing to do is to heroically assume this finitude, this constitutive lack of our finite context. The pentecostal answer is that absolute, unconditional acts do occur in the believer's life. They occur not because the believer fully intends them or can perform them. They occur as totally unpredictable events, miraculous acts that overshadow their lives. The display or experience of unconditional, transfinite acts is one of the crucial ways the divine dimension is enacted, presented, and acknowledged in their lives. And thus true sin is not a person believing that he can overcome his condition of finitude and act as God, but rather the sinner is the individual who denies, rejects this divine dimension of life and reduces all of human living to the constraints of finitude and has "reduced himself to just another finite mortal being." So the pentecostal subject believes that in actualizing their potentials individuals

35. Tillich, *Morality and Beyond*, p. 24.

36. Tillich, *Morality and Beyond*, p. 24.

37. Slavoj Žižek, *The Ticklish Subject: The Absent Center of Political Ontology* (London: Verso, 2008), p. 319.

should be bold to enact an act that stands for the gesture of breaking out of the constraints of finitude; this becomes a kind of "vanishing mediator" between finitude and act-event of God.[38]

In this attempt to be bold, to test the limit of finitude, is the call of the pentecostal principle (and even the Protestant principle) to resist any finite form claiming infinite status, any form of actualization claiming to have exhausted potentiality (im-potentiality), and to contest particular religious form striving to hegemonize the empty signifier, the universal. But the principle also arises to punish transgression of the limits of finitude in the actualization of potentialities, in the very obedience of this law. It appears the principle or the moral imperative needs (or has to have) the transgression to assert itself. More precisely, it is law, the moral imperative, that commands actualization to generate the transgression. The law incites its own violation — through hubris, a temptation to cut straight to the infinitude — that the principle forbids and "desires" for its self-assertion. Under the command of the moral imperative, sin is a failure to actualize one's potentials, a deliberate refusal to advance one's potential. It is to avoid this sin, which is a transgression of the command, that the law itself entices a transgression of finitude, hence hubris.

Can we resort to pure potentiality, untouched by human hubris, free from the touch of human finitude, and deprived of religious passions in order to escape or transcend the guilt of transgression? The moral imperative in its pure form, our potentiality in its pure form even condemns us to guilt in its function as the abstract *Sollen,* which reverberates as an empty "do this" of a command. An abstract injunction like this makes all of us "guilty precisely because we don't know what we are guilty of. . . ."[39] There is no pure fulfillment of human potentialities except human fulfillment. Yet one has to conceive of the whole of human fulfillment as part and its remainder. The part sustains the existence of the whole (the universal) with a minimal gap between it and the whole. It is this remainder, the "part of no part" that holds the place of universal fulfillment. It is what calls us to the explosion of actualization without the excitement of transgression. It is the openness of a new beginning. Its other name is grace. Unlike the concept of pure potentiality, the notion of grace does not hold that the potential can never be properly actualized. It does not

38. The comparison of a different conception of sin is inspired by Žižek, *Ticklish Subject,* pp. 462-63.
    39. Žižek, *Puppet and the Dwarf,* p. 110.

claim full realization of potentialities in the present, but it only says the event of actualization has already occurred, the fulfillment is accomplished and yet the gap remains (the quest for potentials that sustains all movement toward actualization).[40] If we write fulfillment as a circle, grace "is the cut that prevents the full closure of the circle." In grace as a remainder "possibility and impossibility, positive and negative coincide": it accomplishes the full ~~realization~~ eventalization of potentials precisely insofar as it hinders its exhaustion.[41]

Grace and Play

Grace is a negation of work. But play is its style of negation: subversion and repetition. The work of negation is a critique of grace by grace. Grace does not just work from the outside; it inhabits the form of work and its medium and transforms them from within. Grace upon grace, life upon life, here a little, there a little, inside upon outside. Repetition is the creative process of grace. The greatest proof of divine graciousness is that grace is repeated again and again. For those under grace, for every act, every day it is available. This repetitive excess is the abounding vitality and vitality of life, pneumatic existence.

Grace (God's *self-giving*) by definition is a genuine gift and not a secretly instrumentalized one.[42] Freely it is given and freely it is received. It has no purpose. No self-addressed envelope from the giver to send something in return. No post office to help you return it even if you want to. It is a pure means of relations between the believer and God. It is play, not because it is trivial and worthless, but because it has no end, an unended action. Play is

40. Žižek, *Puppet and the Dwarf*, pp. 140-41. Here it is important to mention a key difference between the pentecostal principle and the Protestant principle. While the latter has its eyes on the reaction of the infinite to any claim of a finite institution that it has realized full actualization of potential, the former focuses on the quest for potential.

41. For quotes see Žižek, *Puppet and the Dwarf*, p. 162.

42. As the pentecostal theologian Frank D. Macchia put it while discussing Jean-Luc Marion's notion of God's gift:

> [T]he gift is rooted ultimately in God's *self-giving*. The giftedness is preserved, since no comparable or adequate reciprocation or description is possible. Thus, "the novelty, mystery, unexpectedness, and uniqueness of the gift" are always preserved. (Macchia, *Justified in the Spirit: Creation, Redemption, and the Triune* [Grand Rapids: Eerdmans, 2010], p. 167. Emphasis in original.)

the essential character of spirituality governed by the grace-principle rather than the work-principle. It is the state of religion that is deprived of the spur of necessity, want, and purpose — human-divine relationship reorganized in the spirit of play. Jesus said, "unless you change and become like children, you will never enter the kingdom of heaven" (Matt. 18:3).

Under grace we have a playful relation to the law which counteracts the inherent "violence," "transgression," and instrumentality of the law. The law is not abolished, but "deactivated," rendered inoperative. Under grace, the law "would correspond to an action as pure means, which shows only itself [and is experienced] without any relation to an end,"[43] such as eternal condemnation. The activity of grace is play, free from work, disengaged from the serious business of the law. Play functions at best as a means without ends and at worst as pure means (pure mediality) and pure endedness (that is, has an end in itself). It is within this space opened by a playful relation to the law that we "then fulfill and recapitulate the law in the figure of the love."[44] The law is now a "playful thing"; for grace has severed the nexus between violence and law, between law and desire for transgression.

The law under grace is not some other law, more lenient and gracious, more sanctified and spiritual; it is the law itself, "at the moment when inoperativity removes the spell from it and opens it up to a new possible common use."[45] The law enters in this way into its second, final nature "which is nothing other than the truth of its former nature."[46] Insofar as the former law has potentiality, its use is not for condemnation, violence, and guilt, but for common love, for a different way of acting and living, for wresting religion from its usual "economy," its usual aims, reasons, and utilitarian movements. This transformation, this "disclosedness," this opening of the truth of the law, manifests when grace disposes it toward a new use without abolishing it.

Indeed, grace places the inoperativity of the law into a separate sphere where a permanent new use for the law is found. It places the law in a single sphere for both exercise and inoperativity, function and suspension. The law's function and its suspension are held in tension within grace.

43. Giorgio Agamben, *State of Exception*, trans. Kevin Attell (Chicago: University of Chicago Press, 2005), p. 88.

44. Giorgio Agamben, *The Time That Remains: A Commentary on the Letter to the Romans*, trans. Patricia Dailey (Stanford: Stanford University Press, 2005), p. 108.

45. Agamben, *Nudities*, p. 103.

46. Agamben, *Nudities*, p. 103.

This is because inoperativity is not inert; on the contrary, it allows the very potentiality that has manifested itself in the act to appear. It is not potentiality that is deactivated in inoperativity but only the aims and modalities into which its exercise had been inscribed and separated. And it is this potentiality that can now become the [source] of new possible use, [the law whose violence and function have] been suspended and rendered inoperative.

To use [law under grace], and to make it serve as an instrument for a particular purpose, are not the same thing. Nor are we dealing here with a simple and insipid absence of purpose, which often leads to a confusion of ethics and beauty. Rather, at stake here is the rendering inoperative of any activity directed toward an end, in order to then dispose it toward a new use, one that does not abolish the old use but persists in it and exhibits it.[47]

Pentecostals are already reasonably good at treating the law as deactivated, inoperative. They are used to carving out fragments and creating forms that suit their needs, sometimes inventing new uses for the law within their own *assemblage*[48] of fragments. They invent, create, or carve pathways among the laws. For their ability to navigate the landscape of laws, we might call pentecostals *lawnauts* (law + *naut, nautos,* navigation).[49] Each pentecostal group carves different pathways depending on its roots, its starting cultural identity, and worldview. But these are not roots that are static and reified; instead they are adaptive, dynamic, searching for other roots to establish connections and to be transformed. Pentecostals have roots that work as routes. Pentecostals are *radicants,* to use the neologism of French philosopher Nicolas Bourriaud for today's "postproduction" artists. He writes that a radicant

47. Agamben, *Nudities*, p. 102.

48. Quoting French authors Louis Althusser and Gilles Deleuze, Nicolas Bourriaud defines assemblage *(agencement)* as "a multiplicity which is made up of many heterogeneous terms and which establishes liaisons, relations between them. . . . Thus the assemblage's only unity is that of co-functioning: it is a symbiosis, a 'sympathy.'" Bourriaud, *The Radicant,* trans. James Gussen and Lili Porten (New York: Lukas and Sternberg, 2009), p. 155.

49. This name is inspired by Bourriaud, who calls today's artists *semionauts* for their ability to invent pathways among signs. See his *Radicant*, pp. 39, 53, 102. See also Bourriaud, *Postproduction Culture as Screenplay: How Art Reprograms the World,* trans. Jeanine Herman (New York: Lukas and Sternberg, 2002).

is a term designating an organism that grows its roots and adds new ones as it advances. To be radicant means setting one's roots in motion, staging them in heterogeneous contexts and formats, denying them the power to completely define one's identity, translating ideas, transcoding images, transplanting behaviors, exchanging rather than imposing.[50]

The radical understanding of grace as play and hence true religion also as play is at the core of pentecostalism. The historic task of pentecostalism is to abandon the institutional form it has built over this essence and let Christianity as pure means, as play, emerge as a gift to all of humanity. This is its ultimate heroic gesture. Every generation of Christian renewal must, out of relative imagination, discover its playful core, and fulfill it or betray it.

As we have already noted in chapters 2, 4, and the preceding sections of this chapter, pentecostalism displays the structure of aesthetic categories and the "logic" of play. Pentecostalism is the sacred in a playful mode. The pentecostal principle is about existence unfolding in a mode of play. This is to say existence may be viewed *sub specie ludi,* from the point of view of its eros toward the polymorphous play and dis-play of freely evolving potentialities. Pentecostalism is a dogged (fevered) pursuit of play in the struggle to recover a lost (or not yet reached) vision of freedom or to attain a portion of that freedom whose very elements, perhaps, belong to art alone. The future of the current pentecostal recovery (revision) is a *vita aesthetica.*

Play is the signature of all things. It is the signature of creativity, resistance to social formatting, and struggle against any finite form claiming the status of the infinite. There are five features that easily define play — especially children at play. They are purposelessness, timelessness,[51] novelty, non-zero-sum dynamics, and enthusiasm *(en-theos).* True play has no end — it is non-instrumentalized.[52] It is a pure means, totally given to its freely evolving potentialities.[53] It demands total engrossment (its focus is on the here and now) and in so doing creates its own time. Its imaginative construct, freshness, flexibility, and relational aesthetics give our actions new potentials. It has capacity to put us in touch with our divine depths (milieu).

---

50. Bourriaud, *Radicant,* p. 22. See also his *Postproduction,* pp. 51-53.

51. See Robert K. Johnson, *The Christian at Play* (Grand Rapids: Eerdmans, 1983), pp. 35-36.

52. Gadamer, *Truth and Method,* pp. 102-30.

53. Herbert Marcuse, *Eros and Civilization: A Philosophical Inquiry into Freud* (London: Sphere Books, 1969), p. 157.

The pentecostal principle is the tracing of the lines of this signature in all forms of human coexistence as a social-ontological dynamic. It captures the terms of engagement of human existence and social life in play. The pentecostal principle is about existence as a pure means, the movements of unended action. In this study, we have attempted to grasp its nature and that of the playful character of pentecostalism. The purpose is to move theological ethics into a new key that can play with the regnant impetus of our age.

We have moved over from the theology of work (law) to the theology of grace. Perhaps it is now time to move over to the theology of religion as play, which is about the deactivation of law and radicalization of grace in the age of the Spirit. Pentecostalism appears to be playing the role of a "vanishing mediator" between the theology of grace and that of play. The divine act of grace is a purely abyssal act of free decision ungrounded in any positive content, positive reasons, actual properties, qualifications, deserts, and acts of its beneficiaries. Play is a radicalization of grace. It is a necessary outcome of the innermost possibility, inner dynamics of grace insofar as grace resists assimilation into the calculated purposefulness and rational tradition of work theology. The saved person hears the divine melody of salvation not in the clanging cymbals of hard-working bones, nor in the pious chants of servility, but in the transformation of a sinful life into the joyful play of eternal redemption and regeneration.

I began this book as a project of ethical methodology. But as I worked to develop the pentecostal principle to anchor my thought it appeared to me that play is at the root of cosmic unfolding and in the interplay of finitude and natality in human existence. Existence unfolds in a mode of play and any theology that takes seriously human existence, human flourishing, and the progress of life must find a way of anchoring its project to play. Thus, in its finished form this book explores the pentecostal principle and takes preliminary steps toward a theology of religion as play. In this regard, it interprets pentecostalism as play — as the replication of and reply to earlier (future) mode of play in the divine-human relations.

The Idea of the Pentecostal

Christianity has two sources: the "Jesus event" and the experience of the Spirit — Easter [resurrection] and pentecost. The two events are intimately bound up with one another, but neither can absorb or re-duce the other. There was one Easter; there are millions of Pentecosts.

José Comblin, *The Holy Spirit and Liberation*[54]

Beginnings can . . . be measured by the re-beginnings they autho-rize. . . . An event is the creation of new possibilities. It is located not merely at the level of objective possibilities but at the level of the pos-sibility of possibilities.

Alain Badiou, *The Communist Hypothesis*[55]

The resurrection is always the finitude of possibility of possibilities, and the pentecost is its infinitization.[56]

---

54. José Comblin, *The Holy Spirit and Liberation*, trans. Paul Burns (Maryknoll, NY: Orbis, 1989), p. 184.

55. Alain Badiou, *The Communist Hypothesis* (London: Verso, 2010), pp. 219, 242-43.

56. This statement is mine. Let me unpack this notion of infinitization of Pentecost in a sermonic way. Later in this chapter we will take a more philosophical approach to opening up the meaning of the whole of this very compact sentence. Unlike Easter, there are millions of Pentecosts. This is so because while Easter is unique and unrepeatable, Pentecost is not. Pentecost as the event of receiving the Holy Spirit occurs many times in the New Testament and it is still occurring today. For instance, in the New Testament, we have such an event re-corded in John 20:21-23. (The Johannine version of the Pentecost reminds us of the creative breath that Adam receives from God in Gen. 2:7.) Then we also have the more famous re-cords in the book of Acts (chapters 2, 8, 10) and arguably the case of speaking in tongues in 1 Corinthians 14. The Spirit is still being poured out on all flesh as in the past.

Pentecost also symbolizes new birth, new creation, being born again. There is always a new beginning and this occurs continuously. There is always a little more required of us to perfect God's justice on earth, to actualize our God-given gifts and potentials.

Pentecost is the fruit of Easter; the "tree" of Good Friday and resurrection will go on bearing fruits. Let us not forget, Pentecost was a festival of harvest on the fiftieth day from Passover. To continue with the harvest metaphor, we may state that Pentecost points to the perpetual harvest or showing of the fruit of the Spirit in the life of the born-again as re-corded in Galatians 5:22-25. (Note here how Paul connects crucifixion and Easter to the fruit. See also Gal. 2:20.) Pentecost may be also likened to the perpetual bringing of souls into God's kingdom. The Acts 2 Pentecost involved the harvest of 3000 souls coming to Christ.

The Acts 2 Pentecost also recorded the disciples speaking in many tongues such that all those gathered heard the message in their own languages. Pentecost is about translation. Any time someone translates the gospel, the Word of God, and its promises of love, justice, and shalom into new languages (not only spoken language, but also languages of new ages, times, and areas and spheres of life) and into terms people in other religions may under-stand and come to Christ, Pentecost is repeated, reborn.

We have come a very long way to this point and crossed many disciplinary boundaries and thus it seems appropriate to present the argument of this book *in nuce*. This book formulates the pentecostal principle — the capacity of social existence to begin something new — as a synthesis of both the Protestant principle and the Catholic substance and the animating force toward a theonomous connection of culture with the divine depth of existence (more on this synthesis in a moment). The pentecostal principle serves as a framework for interpreting history and as a methodological approach to social ethics. Based on a rigorous elucidation and defense of the pentecostal principle, this study formulates a method of ethics that explicitly thinks through and out of the pentecostal reality. It shows how pentecostal experience and spirituality can be brought into the field of ethical methodology with a serious engagement with major conversational partners at the vanguard of public theology, social ethics, political theology, and philosophy.

א The Nature of the Synthesis

This synthesis is not a mere higher unity (no dialectical overcoming, and the Protestant principle and Catholic substance are not canceling themselves out), but a redefinition (displacement, destabilization) of the frame within which the opposition between the two is understood. The synthesis that is the pentecostal principle comes about, amid other factors, by deactivation of the law and the radicalization of grace.

The pentecostal principle cannot be located in the development of Protestantism or in the surpassing of Catholicism. It has to be located in the very core, the very beginning of the Christian movement. The community of the believers is the symbol of the love of the Holy Spirit and the Spirit is the bond of the community of the believers. We have the pentecostal principle because we (the church) are pneumatic creatures rather than the other way around. We have a pneumatic life engendering intensification of social life, putting life's centers of gravity in life itself, and refusing to define existing life against death. Pneumatic life is lived in the expectation of the new, and not in the fear of the subsuming of life by death.

The pentecostal principle directs attention to the theology of the third article, urging us to make pneumatology (the third article theology) the starting point for theology. The third article is about the Spirit of God that harbors and undergirds the possibility that brings the real into emergent being. The pentecostal principle is a synthesis because it is the passion for existence, for the new, for the actualization of potentialities, and for unearthing of the hidden potentialities of past actualities which grounds, connects, and exceeds both the Catholic substance and the Protestant principle.

As a historical movement, pentecostalism emerged from the gaps within the finite, but also non-totalizable order of being defined by the coordinates of Catholicism and Protestanism. The synthesis that is pentecostalism "refers to the gap itself — that is to say, the synthesis between [them] represents a shift toward accepting the very gap between them."[57] This gap works on the nisus of the pentecostal principle. Or put differently, the pentecostal principle inhabits this gap or reflects its logic. Catholicism, Protestantism, and pentecostalism can never fully correspond to or overtake the pentecostal principle.

This book is first and foremost an engaged pentecostal-theological intervention in the methodology of social ethics. This intervention begins with the critique of Paul Tillich's Protestant principle and its transformation into the pentecostal principle. The Protestant principle is transformed into a principle of creative restlessness, of emergent creativity in the fabric of life, and of the pneumatological dynamic in social existence. Next, the Day of Pentecost is deployed as a symbol of not only the irreducibly pluralistic nature of existence, but also as an affirmation of the capacity to begin, the articulation of natality as theorized by Hannah Arendt.

The study then engages with the thought of Italian philosopher Giorgio Agamben. His notion of ethics/politics as pure means is used to shed light on ecstatic speech. Tongues-speech is considered as an aesthetic of pure means and thus offers a perspective to counter the instrumental logic of mainstream religious ethics. The interpretation of tongues-speech also engages with Agamben's theory of sovereign exception with a view to opening up a new discursive space for pentecostal political theologies.

Following philosopher Steven G. Smith's notion of the spiritual as first philosophy and theologian D. Lyle Dabney's concept of the Holy Spirit as the Spirit of possibility, the theory of the pentecostal principle posits the central focus of social ethics and ethical methodology to be the concern for possibilities and surprises, the freely evolving actualization of potentialities. Its orientation to society's ethical project is shot through with the meaning of resistance and forward movement into the not-yet, the development of being qua human being. The concept of the pentecostal principle is not about maintaining order, but about disrupting and interrogating orders in the name of a new and better human development and future.

---

57. Adam Kotsko, *Žižek and Theology* (London: T. & T. Clark, 2008), p. 50. This interpretation of the synthesis is indebted to Žižek's reinterpretation of the Hegelian notion as provided in this book.

The pentecostal principle is about openness to the unfinishedness of life and the emergence of new alternatives. This leads us to the exploration of nature's emergence (the science of emergence) to aid our thinking in the development of a new ethics that is in line with the pentecostal principle. We examine creative emergence and its possible implications for social ethics, outlining a form of social ethics that is necessary for citizens to cope with the nature of a social world increasingly characterized by contingency and possibilities. We argue that a commitment to "emergentist worldview" obliges us to embrace the prophetic-pentecostal spirit; and that citizens should rely on the spirit rather than on rules and predetermined ethical codes for navigating what is and what must be a bewildering world.

The analysis of emergence shows that there is no one complete ethical code or comprehensive system of values and calculations to guide the working of the pentecostal principle in any complex society. This insight demands that leaders and public theologians of complex societies need to emphasize pluralism in order to properly harness the dispersed knowledge necessary for collective flourishing. The argument for pluralism is further supported by the thesis that the many tongues of pentecost call for many voices in public debate and that those informed by the pentecostal principle need to master the form of argumentation suitable for public theology. To this end we develop an explicit procedural method of ethical analysis relevant to public policy decision-making in the era of irreducible pluralism.

The various demands that the pentecostal principle makes on the ethical organization of any complex society call for a special way of being if that society is to properly harness its resources. What should be the mode of creative, moral self-interpretation of a historical community of persons who are (or who think they are) the bearers of the principle? We respond to this pertinent question by formulating a notion of the spirit that not only fits the pentecostal principle, but also is duly informed by the current pentecostal movement.

One of the major insights that emerges from our discussion of the pentecostal spirit is the playful character of pentecostalism. Our understanding of the pentecostal spirit will be inadequate if we do not reckon with the festival (Pentecost) nature of the pentecostal movement. The playful character of pentecostalism is analyzed within the context of the connections between the pentecostal principle, the quest for actualization of potentials, and play as the signature of all things. We show that the "logic of play" is the inner dynamics of both the pentecostal principle and the pentecostal spirit.

Overall we attempt to grasp the nature of the pentecostal principle and that of the playful character of pentecostalism and to use the knowledge so gained to craft an ethical methodology in a new spirit. The crafting of this methodology is done in the shadow of a nagging question: Are pentecostals the true, authentic, and faithful bearers of the pentecostal principle? The true bearers will be those who are vocationally conscious of the principle and are willing to interpret and transform their society (and religion) in its light. The pentecostal principle as an *existentiell* procedure (the capacity to do something new, the choice or neglect of possibilities that open new paths, the capacity of *eventalization* of existence) requires both historical and subjective elements. If it is to be inscribed as a historical orientation of general human becoming, its truth projected into a world, then there is a decision that an individual has to make to become part of the truth, to become a bearer of the principle. The person incorporates him- or herself into this truth (grasping it and being claimed, grasped, by it), into the interplay between the truth and history (its historical manifestation). This is the process of becoming a bearer, a subject; a process French philosopher Alain Badiou calls subjectivation:

> a subjectivation is always the process whereby an individual determines the place of a truth with respect to his or her own existence and to the world in which this existence is lived out.[58]

Pentecostals are yet to rise to this level of commitment and fidelity to the principle whose name they bear. They arguably have the form of the principle but are yet to consciously grasp and express the substance. The pentecostal principle is pentecostal not in the sense of primal spirituality or pneumatic resources of any religion, but rather in the sense of the ethical ideal that arises from the tension between the symbol of the "is" (what is already) and the "ought" (what ought to be realized) in the directness of communal structures (meaning-fulfilling, existential relationships) toward better future alternatives, toward freedom.[59] The pentecostal principle can be found in the power to begin something really new, and it ex-

---

58. Badiou, *Communist Hypothesis*, p. 235.

59. By freedom I mean not *free will* but the belief (demand) that something new could be realized through acting agents.

presses itself in the unbounded freedom that pneumatic existence and pneumatological imagination represent; it is recognizable in the forward impulses of unfolding human history, and it is legible in its rejection of any claim of finishedness by any existential form or configuration. The pentecostal principle goes beyond pentecostalism. It transcends the religious and confessional character of pentecostals. The pentecostal principle is a power that stands beyond all concrete realization and goes beyond pentecostalism as a religious or cultural form. It is the dynamic power in the current worldwide pentecostalism, but of necessity goes beyond it. It is present in Catholicism and Protestantism, but transcends them. It is available in things that want to go beyond themselves to their depth, to dynamic ontological creativity, to the Spirit of creation and new creation. It is available in all forms of existence as the resident power of continuous outworking of possibilities and potentialities.

א THE RESURRECTION IS ALWAYS THE FINITUDE OF POSSIBILITY OF POSSIBILITIES, AND THE PENTECOST IS ITS INFINITIZATION.

Let me unpack this statement. So far it is only Jesus who is believed to have resurrected and we therefore argue that the possibility (or the experience) of resurrection in the human race, in history, before the eschaton, is limited, particular, and finite. But the Day of Pentecost is a replicable experience in history and there are millions of them in terms of the experience of Spirit baptism, in the experience of something new, in events, in the capacity to do something new. The argument so far has only shown the finite nature of one and the infinite character of the other. It is yet to demonstrate why Pentecost is an infinitization of the resurrection.

Resurrection created an open platform for something new in human relationships and in human-divine relation. In its proleptic, anticipatory nature, it offers the promise of future resurrection for all people. The platform it creates is the possibility of external life that anyone can access through a belief in Jesus Christ. As Paul argues in 1 Corinthians 15:12-24, without Christ's resurrection there is really no salvation: faith does not bring forgiveness, no future in the presence of God, and there is total destruction at death. On the contrary, the resurrection of Christ provides the guarantee of the resurrection of those who believe in him. The resurrection of Jesus of Nazareth is the preactualization of the resurrection of humankind and the new creation.

The resurrection of Christ did not only create a new platform, it is itself new because it had no potentiality in the old situation of life and death. It was an event — meaning it was not preceded by any potentiality that we can claim as its cause. Jesus Christ's resurrection had a universal singularity. We can only appropriate this singularity by faith ("an immediately subjective recognition of an event's singularity"[60]) and by a genuine fidelity to its declaration and the ensuing consequences that erase all distinctions between Jews and Greeks, men and women, slaves and free persons.

Pentecost exploits this platform for its positive network of externalities or possibilities. Pentecost and pentecosts (as specific works of the Holy Spirit) are the sinew between — and the nisus of — Jesus' resurrection and the future resurrection of humankind. If resurrection is the seed, pentecost is the harvest; if the one is the firstfruits, the other is the endless fruits that come after; one is the first installment that anticipates the whole, the other is the fullness.

In one sense the Pentecost appears to be *in* the future of resurrection. But in another, the future resurrection of humankind is both revealed in and is the ground of the past Pentecost and ongoing pentecosts. From one angle of vision, Christ's resurrection appears to work on pentecosts as an antecedent, efficient cause; from another it can be seen as working proleptically, teleologically. (At Easter the Pentecost appeared proleptically, appeared ahead of time. Besides, the future resurrection acts as a lure to past and present pentecosts.)

Now it is important to deepen our understanding of the economic work of the triune God as it relates to these things. In resurrection Christ is the key player and at Pentecost the Holy Ghost is the main actor. But in the lights of Romans 1:4 and 8:11, we are tempted to interpret Pentecost (the work of the Holy Spirit) as both revealed in and the ground of the resurrection. In sum, we are simply saying that both resurrection (the "one") and pentecost (the "many") were pneumatologically constituted and pneumatologically accomplished.

The language of one and many can be put in the terms of set theory. If resurrection is 1 (because it happens for only one person), then pentecost is 0. The one represents both the person and the act itself. The zero represents also the persons and the act. Pentecost is zero not only because it is not-resurrection (the not-yet resurrected), but also because it is the fecund multiple, the fount of possibilities, which the one symbolizes and points to. To be resurrected is to have a presence in heaven. It is to be "finite" in the particular sense we have used the word above. To

---

60. "[I]f there has been an event, and if truth consists in declaring it and then in being faithful to this declaration, two consequences ensue. First, since truth is evental, or of the order of what occurs, it is singular. It is neither structural, nor axiomatic, nor legal. No available generality can account for it, nor structure the subject who claims to follow in its wake. Consequently, there cannot be a law of truth. Second, truth being inscribed on the basis of a declaration that is in essence subjective, no preconstituted subset can support it; nothing communitarian or historically established can lend its substance to the process of truth. Truth is a diagonal relative to every communitarian subset; it neither claims authority from, nor (this is obviously the most delicate point) constitutes any identity. It is offered to all, or addressed to everyone, without a condition of belonging being able to limit this offer or this address." Alain Badiou, *Saint Paul* (Stanford: Stanford University Press, 2003), p. 14.

have zero is not to have a presence but to be marked by the boundary of presence; it is to be infinite, to represent pure potentiality, the generative null set. The zero, the void, is the absent "no-thing" upon which the Holy Spirit acts (intervenes) to present something, to invent something new, to constitute and transform new believers, and at the eschaton convert to tens of thousands upon tens of thousands of resurrections. The zero is the dynamic part of the 0 + 1 fabric whose threads, as Comblin intones, cannot be teased apart.

Resurrection as a beginning can be measured by the re-beginnings it authorizes, the new possibilities it creates. In the proleptic and teleological operativity of the Holy Spirit, the movement is not linear, not from beginnings to re-beginnings. There is the qualitative in-breaking of God's re-beginnings into beginning. More so, given the proleptic structure of Christian theology, Ted Peters argues, an event "begins the promise of the coming kingdom of God and the fulfillment of all creation that it will bring. It begins with the future and works back to the present."[61]

The resurrection-to-pentecost movement is a *recapitulatio*. It is to begin, to open up *(be-ginnan)* the iterative dynamic of becoming "life-in-the-Spirit" itself, to stir up the matrix of possibilities again. That a beginning of beginning be made resurrection was effected. That beginnings be made pentecost came. (On the Day of Pentecost, Saint Peter preached that the last days are the first days; that the end of days opens up a new beginning.) The beginning of resurrection is guaranteed by each pentecost, each new Spirit baptism, each repetition, each new relation. A relation is a (productive, rhythmic) repetition,[62] a *recapitulatio*. Every fresh relation comes from an initial relation that maps upon the new alternative pathways of excluded possibilities and novel immediacy. Relation is the supreme capacity of the interactivity of the Holy Spirit and human beings. In the "life-in-the-Spirit," they open it up, cut it open again and again, redesign, redirect, or repair relation's fluid dynamics as it carries believers deeper and deeper into their theonomous divine depths and spiritual healing.

It is germane to also think in the category of *pro* instead of *re*. If resurrection is a *re*volution then pentecost is a *pro*volution. As Moltmann puts it, "in *pro*volution, the human dream turned forward is combined with the new possibility of the future and begins consciously to direct the course of human history. . . ."[63] Thus, in a sense the experience of pentecost is part of the process of necessary subjectivation: the way of being that is faithful to the truth procedure of the resurrection (to use Badiousian terminology) and abiding in bearers of the pentecostal principle.

61. Ted Peters, *God: The World's Future* (Minneapolis: Fortress, 2000), p. 378.

62. "A repetition is by definition never the 'same' as that which it repeats. It is always already other. In its iterations it becomes readable, a code." Catherine Keller, *Face of the Deep: A Theology of Becoming* (New York: Routledge, 2003), p. 186.

63. Jürgen Moltmann, *Religion, Revolution, and the Future* (New York: Scribners, 1969), p. 32, quoted in Peters, *God*, p. 380.

Epilogue

The End Which Is to Come

Beginning is the unpredictability of grace.[1]

One of the great things I did when I left college and finished my one-year national service in Nigeria was to read the war speeches of Sir Winston Churchill. I memorized one of his sentences: "It is not the end, nor the beginning of the end, but the beginning of the beginning." I have had this quote in my head since 1985 and as I was writing this paragraph in the midsummer of 2010, I decided to check it for accuracy. To my surprise I found that the last phrase actually reads, "the end of the beginning." Well, it does not matter now; the twenty-three-year-old young man who believed Churchill, that every end is a new beginning, still does. So let us start at the beginning again.

1. This statement has been in my head since 2005. I am no longer certain how it came about. I am not sure if it jumped out of the head fully formed as Athena did out of Zeus. Sometimes I think it might have originated as some curious mixture of the ideas of the prophet Jeremiah, Hannah Arendt's *The Human Condition* (Chicago: University of Chicago Press, 1958), and Jonathan Sacks's *The Dignity of Difference: How to Avoid the Clash of Civilizations* (London: Continuum, 2002). Sacks himself is referring to Arendt's idea of forgiveness when he writes, "Forgiveness . . . introduces into the logic of interpersonal encounter the unpredictability of grace," p. 179. I first read Arendt's and Sacks's books in 2005. In the notes for a sermon (delivered July 31, 2005, titled "It Is a New Beginning" with the main text drawn from Gen. 1:1), where I first wrote this statement down, my next fragment of thought — on the same line with it — was Lam. 3:23: "They are new every morning; Great is your faithfulness." Alternatively, it might have also jumped into my head, fully formed, out of a long forgotten text.

The pentecostal principle is the capacity to begin. It encapsulates the notion that no finite or conditioned reality can claim to have reached its destiny. The movement of every existent to its destiny, to the full realization of its potentialities, remains ever incompletable because it is "rooted" in the abyss of divine freedom. Every end has only one option: to be a new beginning. Hannah Arendt once put it this way:

> Beginning, before it becomes a historical event, is the supreme capacity of man; politically, it is identical with man's freedom. *Initium ut esset homo creatus est* — "that a beginning be made man was created," said Augustine.[2]

Because of the demand of new beginning, more is expected from every moment and every life, and there is a radical openness to alternatives and surprises. The restlessness of all en-spirited life is recognized, understood, and grasped.

Now that we have seen that the beginning of this text has become its end or the beginning of its end, let us now proceed to make its end a new beginning. Let us examine the end that is only a beginning for new thought. We have stated that the pentecostal principle not only captures the dynamics of the Spirit as the power and logic of history, but also drives individual lives and cultural forms and functions to their divine depths or the ~~eschatological~~[3] future of God. It works not only going from past to present as material and efficient causes, but also teleologically[4] (proleptically). For driving potentiality and im-potentiality to actualization and for its theonomic operations on culture it is the signature of the "preactualization of the future consummation of all things in Jesus Christ," to borrow the words of Ted Peters.[5]

---

2. Hannah Arendt, *The Origins of Totalitarianism* (New York: Schocken Books, 2004), p. 616.

3. See the discussion of "messianic now" to learn why eschatology is under erasure here.

4. Teleology here does not refer to final causes or fixed essences. The laws of nature are regarded as habitual, dynamic, and general in C. S. Peirce's sense of them. This perspective allows us to perceive them as law possibilities and tendencies opened to interactions between creaturely freedom and the messianic now (eschatological presence of God, if you like) through the dynamic relations of reality that is the Holy Spirit. See Amos Yong, *Spirit of Creation* (Grand Rapids: Eerdmans, 2011).

5. Ted Peters, *God: The World's Future* (Minneapolis: Fortress, 2000), p. xi.

This consummation is not a closure, but further dis/closure, an open-ended process. It seems the future, a temporal mode, will not come to a close and there will always be a relevant open future. The future of God is an openness of the divine to grant potentiality for the reality of the world (earth) to transform itself and the opening of a gap in the present where the future, the to-come dwells.[6] Consummation, at least as I interpret it, does not mean bringing the temporal mode of the future to a close. Rather, it is a recapitulation and an anticipation. Consummation is a form of figuration wherein the cumulative human achievements (ingathering) in the New Jerusalem come together in a disfiguration with the not-yet to form a new constellation. Figuration is always a dialectics in deferral. But this deferral is not infinite as the unconsumed potentiality soon turns back on itself, fulfilling (bringing forth to increased legibility, recognizability) the figuration and deactivating the dialectics at a standstill.

It is also germane to mention that the future I have in mind is a proleptic anticipation and as such is not in linear terms and not necessarily an in-breaking of God's future into the "present," but rather a kind of "messianic now," a gap between past infinity and future infinity of time.

Many academic theologians, even pentecostal ones, are too quick to ascribe eschatological time ("the end of time," "final end," "the end perpetually deferred," or a general orientation to the future) to pentecostalism, disregarding the "messianic and miraculous [that] encapsulate . . . [the pentecostal] sense of time and history." Following Giorgio Agamben's analysis of Paul's concept of the messianic now *("ho nyn kairos"),* one can say pentecostals are not merely oriented to the future, but are also involved in a "recapitulation of the past" — that is, in passing summary judgment on the past. The significance of the judgment is to enable a critical engagement with the present and a redemption of the past at the same time.[7]

---

6. On the issue of dynamic eschatology, doctrine of everlasting progress, *epectasis,* see Gregory of Nyssa, *Commentary on the Song of Songs,* trans. Casmir McCambley (Brookline, MA: Hellenic College Press, 1987), and Amos Yong, *Theology and Down Syndrome: Reimagining Disability in Late Modernity* (Waco: Baylor University Press, 2007), pp. 274-82. For more on openness and transformation, see Jürgen Moltmann, *God in Creation: A New Theology of Creation and the Spirit of God,* trans. Margaret Kohl (Minneapolis: Fortress, 1993), p. 165; and Peters, *God,* pp. 321, 331.

7. See Giorgio Agamben, *The Time That Remains: A Commentary on the Letter to the Romans,* trans. Patricia Dailey (Stanford: Stanford University Press, 2005), pp. 75-77; and Ruth Marshall, *Political Spiritualities: The Pentecostal Revolution in Nigeria* (Chicago: University of Chicago Press, 2009), pp. 66-67.

Ruth Marshall has recently combined ethnographic description and astute philosophical analysis to shed light on the pentecostal conception of time. She admirably extends Agamben's philosophical exploration of messianism to born-agains and forces a rethinking of the "automatic" categorization of the pentecostal conception of time as eschatological:

> In the messianic conception of time, the arrival of the messiah may be accomplished "at any instant," in the very heart of history, pulverizing the coherence and continuity of historical time into innumerable messianic instants in which the radically new becomes possible. . . . [The messianic time, "the time of the now"] is not the time of the end and should not be confused with the apocalypse; rather, it is the time *before* the end, which is not simply another period of chronological time, but a time that "begins to end," that "contracts itself." It is not a time separate from chronological time, which for Paul spans from creation to the messianic event of resurrection, but rather *the time that remains* within chronological time, between that event and the *parousia*, the full presence of the messiah, and arrival of *eschaton,* or the end. Rather than staging a perpetual deferment of the *eschaton,* messianic time is the incorporation of *parousia* into every instant of chronological time, implying a transformation in the actual experience of time. . . . In a certain limited sense, Pentecostalism is more messianic than it is eschatological. . . . [M]essianic time is staged in Pentecostalism as an operational time, as a time *within* the present time. This is evidenced by the experience of faith as a total openness to the presence of *(parousia)* of the Holy Spirit; the centrality of miracles; and the fact that the urgency of evangelism and conversion lies not only in preparing believers and the world for *parousia* and the *eschaton,* but also in fulfilling God's plan and *hastening* this fulfillment.[8]

א The Messianic Now

The messianic now implies the neutralization of the various binaries of time, whether secular/sacred, present/end, end/future, or the Jewish *olam hazzeh/olam habba.*[9] In the messianic now the temporal-segmentary-factical property of time

---

8. Marshall, *Political Spiritualities,* p. 66. Emphasis in original.

9. "The two ends of the *olam hazzeh* and the *olam habba* contract into each other without coinciding; this face to face, this contraction is messianic time, and nothing else. Once

is expropriated and what is left is its "generic potentiality" which can be used in the form of *as not*. In this way, old divisions are rendered inoperative. Yet they are not necessarily replaced with new ones; rather, through pentecostals' actions of commitment to parousia and fidelity to the resurrection, they act as if such divisions do not exist. When time is short, when time has contracted itself, what is, is "as not," as Paul points out in 1 Corinthians 7.

The pentecostal conception of temporal orientation places time between this world and the future world. It is a movement of immanence that goes over every moment of chronological time but never goes beyond. It is time moving within time, as if it were hovering over a breach within. Time seems to have transformatively contracted (shortened itself) into a concentration, and the act of experiencing the arrival of Christ is at any instant.

The eschatological end, set in relation to itself via the messianic now, is "not replaced by something else, but rendered inoperative." The eschatological future, invested by messianic now, is not negated with regard to hope and fulfillment, "but it is taken up again and transposed, while remaining unchanged," to a zone of time that is neither past nor future but subtracted from the present and remains as a cut, a breach of pure praxis.[10] This breach gestures to "an outside in the very intimacy of an inside." Time is exposed to itself. The messianic now "keeps open a space, a spacing within immanence."[11] Pentecostals incarnate (or are supposed to incarnate) this split and unconceal it. Without this unconcealment, without this exposition, the gap will not exist. In this breach they deal with the things, statuses, and accomplishments of this world but hollow and nullify them through the form of the as-not (Paul's *hōs mē* in 1 Corinthians 7:29-32).

This cut is not only subtracted from the present, it also does not coincide with the already and not-yet. It is not exterior to them either, "but divides the division itself."[12] The division of division engenders a tension within time itself. With the messianic cut into time it is no longer possible for any part of the earlier divisions to coincide with itself or with any other.[13] The messianic cut is "the time that remains," "the time that remains between time and its end,"[14] and it necessarily situ-

---

again, for Paul, the messianic is not a third eon situated between two times; but rather, it is a caesura that divides the division between times and introduces a remnant, a zone of undecidability, in which the past is dislocated into the present and the present is extended into the past." Agamben, *Time That Remains*, p. 74.

   10. Agamben, *Time That Remains*, pp. 28, 5-6, 23, 25.

   11. Jean-Luc Nancy, *The Inoperative Community*, trans. Peter Connor, Lisa Garbus, Michael Holland, and Simona Sawhney (Minneapolis: University of Minnesota Press, 1991), pp. xxxvii, 58, 30.

   12. Giorgio Agamben, *The Signature of All Things: On Method* (New York: Zone Books, 2009), p. 49.

   13. Agamben, *Signature of All Things*, pp. 55-57.

   14. Agamben, *Signature of All Things*, p. 62.

ates the messianic remnant (as in Romans 11:5: "In the time of the now a remnant is produced") in the gap.[15]

א Spirit Messianism

Pentecostals inhabit this gap and keep it open by a different form of messianism, that of Spirit messianism. In the midst of concrete social existence, they try to not let the messianic now close either by quenching (grieving) the Spirit or by the operations of satanic forces. Spirit messianism is the theory of action and subjectivation in the messianic now. The messianism of pentecostalism as a form of social practice is, strictly speaking, not a messianism of the Son, though it came forth from it. The messianism of the Son, founded, as Paul believes, on the event of the resurrection, is a negation of negation (death). The messianism of the Spirit is "an affirmation without preliminary negation."[16] It is what comes to the believer in the caesura of the messianic now. It is what comes as he or she excavates the breach and the grace supernumerary to it for new possibilities of concrete life in the here and now. It is the name of what happens universally when the center of gravity of life becomes an iterative encounter with the immanentization of the transcendent Spirit. The messianism of the Son only becomes a dimension of the subject, processes of subjectivation, and a subtraction from the path of death.

Let us look at the idea of the messianism of the Spirit from another perspective and develop it further. Both Alain Badiou and Giorgio Agamben in their separate studies of Paul show that he was careful to portray himself as an apostle, not a prophet, philosopher, or mystic. The preference is linked either to Paul's understanding of the messianic now or to his rejection of the discourse of signs which is in the purview of prophets and law. For Agamben, who focuses on the time structure opened up by the event of the resurrection of Jesus as the Messiah (the messianic now), Paul rejected calling himself a prophet because prophets are defined by their relation to the future:

> Each time the prophets announce the coming of the Messiah, the message is always about a time to come, a time not yet present. This is what marks the difference between the prophet and the apostle. The apostle speaks forth from the arrival of the Messiah. At this point prophecy must keep silent, for now prophecy is fulfilled. . . . The word passes on to the apostle, to the emissary of the Messiah, whose time is no longer the future, but the present. This is why Paul's technical

---

15. Agamben, *Signature of All Things*, p. 53.

16. Alain Badiou, *Saint Paul: The Foundation of Universalism* (Stanford: Stanford University Press, 2003), pp. 65, 66.

term for the messianic event is *ho nyn kairos,* "the time of the now"; this is why Paul is an apostle and not a prophet.[17]

Badiou looks at Paul as a subject who declares the founding event of the resurrection and who is faithful to it as a universal singularity (1 Cor. 2:1-5). The truth of this event and its regime of discourse, which Paul institutes, is opposed to the schemas of discourse based on signs, deciphering miracles which are beyond the natural order (language of prophets) and based on wisdom (how to live in the right order with cosmic, natural totality; the language of philosophy). These two discourses legitimate themselves either on the basis of the cosmos (natural totality) or on the power of exception.

In opposition to these regimes of discourses, Paul institutes the apostolic or Christian discourse of intervention that ruptures history. Paul's apostolic discourse, while not denying the existence of miracles and even occasionally boasting that he could perform some, never relied on miracles for his message or authority (2 Cor. 12:1-11). This discourse also subtracts itself from prophetic (law) discourse and philosophical (Sophia) discourse to name the possibility of the event of resurrection (1 Cor. 1:17-29). According to Badiou, the discourse of the apostle is

> one of pure fidelity to the possibility opened by the event. . . . The philosopher knows eternal truths; the prophet knows the univocal sense of what will come (even if he delivers it through figures, through signs). The apostle [is one] who declares an unheard-of possibility, one dependent on an evental grace. . . .[18]

Paul in declaring the event of the resurrection and being faithful to it never relied on any other form of discourse to emphasize the messianic now: not of power or wisdom because God has chosen the foolish and weak things of the world to confound the wise and the powerful. Simply, Christ is what happens to the Christian subject and represents his or her pure beginning. Paul "presents himself as deploying a subjective figure that has been subtracted from both [signs and wisdom], which means that neither miracles, nor the rational exegesis of prophecies, nor order of the world have any value when it comes to instituting the Christian subject."[19]

Pentecostalism has not only adopted Paul's messianic now, but also inscribed into this space the discourse and practices of signs and miracles which are manifestations of the Spirit. The space of the messianic now becomes space for "prophetic actualization of God's plan," "actualization of potentialities, providentially given within a divine plan," and the "realization of a providential prediction."[20]

17. Agamben, *Time That Remains,* p. 61.

18. Badiou, *Saint Paul,* p. 45.

19. Badiou, *Saint Paul,* p. 50.

20. Ruth Marshall, "The Sovereignty of Miracles: Pentecostal Political Theology in Nigeria," *Constellations* 17, no. 2 (2010): 206, 207, 213.

Today's pentecostals, with their preoccupation with signs and fulfilled prophecies have synthetically inscribed the discourse of (miraculous) exception within the space of the messianic now, thereby subordinating it to the mystical[21] or to the law, which are two aspects of the same thing. "For the miraculous exception of the sign is only the 'minus-one,' the point of incoherence [of whole of natural laws], which the cosmic totality requires in order to sustain itself."[22] To put it differently, pentecostals have dialectically turned Paul's withdrawal of mediation (the bypassing of law, sign, and wisdom to reach the divine) into signs that manifest the sacred as im-mediate.

The opening of God to humankind (to use Heideggerian language) is *here,* on the surface of what is. If Paul cut the figure of time to produce the messianic now (as Agamben informs us), for pentecostals the sacred is dispersed into multiple sites of encounter (space is cut so that the "trans" of transcendence is not a "cross over or going beyond," but a tracing of being-with) and each *here* is an im-mediate manifestation that is an (invisible) revelation of the Spirit. This is the here-and-now of pentecostal conviction. (And the social practice of pentecostalism is the reception and articulation of this conviction.)[23]

It is this re-inscription into Paul's discourse, this glorification of the logic of signs and proofs, this return of private meanings, this retreat from the language of naked event, that I am naming as Spirit messianism.

What is the point of contesting or supplementing the regnant eschatological perspective on the pentecostal orientation to time? After all, the eschatological perspective emphasizes possibilities and the *novum* as the pentecostal principle. The issue here is not whether the regnant theological explorations of eschatological future ignore possibilities and the radically new, but is how best to combine this with the radical openness to the Holy Spirit (God) and the orientation to surprises and miracles that are characteristic of the pentecostal worldview as we have argued earlier. It is true to say that the pentecostal worldview does not deny Leibniz's *"omne possibile exigit existere,"* but it is truer to say that it is more at home with Agamben's *"omne existens exigit possibilitatem suam."*[24]

To better understand the notion that the pentecostal principle bridges efficient and teleological causes, let us remind ourselves of some of the key

21. Badiou, *Saint Paul,* pp. 51-52.

22. Badiou, *Saint Paul,* p. 42.

23. This paragraph is inspired by Christopher Fynsk's analysis of Jean-Luc Nancy's work in the foreword to *Inoperative Community,* pp. vii-xxxv.

24. Agamben, *Time That Remains,* p. 39.

points we have made in the preceding five chapters and introduction. The pentecostal principle captures the restlessness that is characteristic of the infinite fabric of life. This relates to the material and efficient causes in collective transformation of existence. It also offers a lure to all transformation in the reality of world insofar as it relates to potentiality and impotentiality. It has power of lure that draws forward the infinite fabric of life to full actualization, its destiny of asymptotic full realization and closeness to God who is perfect actuality. As Thomas Aquinas tells us, the actualization of human potentialities (personal and cultural) is for the sake of that good which perfects and completes them, that is, God, the uncreated goodness.

God is concerned with human flourishing, which involves the fullest realization of personal capacities, potentialities of coexistence, and happiness of others; this kind of flourishing draws us to itself. Human creativity undergirded and lured by divine ontological creativity is the movedness of human flourishing. This is so because human creativity is spirit-shaped communal practice. This perspective situates creativity in everyday practice in the communal life of the people and makes it a response to the spirit's active presence in the life of the community. In this view, creativity is about the everyday act of working together to reach the full stature of being transparent to divine creativity. A person is creative because the person is helping to build a certain kind of community and working to raise others to live a flourishing life. Creativity is the kind of practice that promotes an agapic community of citizens, a community where all can live in peace, prosperity, and vibrancy, realizing their full human potential. Persons engender theonomic connections between their work and the divine by not working alone but by being building blocks of their own communities.

For the fact that the pentecostal principle plays this crucial role of bridging efficient and teleological causes, I call it the signature of existence. Restlessness (considered as material and efficient causes) is the sign of life, and prolepsis (as teleological cause), the lure of God's future, is the sign of divine participation in history, of what I earlier described as immantrance, and a gap separates them (restlessness and prolepsis). The pentecostal principle is the signature of existence because, as Agamben once said, "signs do not speak unless signatures make them speak."[25]

The question of the restlessness of existence, like the question of semiotics, is about existence — whether it exists; and the question is eas-

---

25. Agamben, *Signature of All Things*, p. 61.

ily settled with a yes or no. But the issue of teleology is akin to that of semantic (one of the two planes of significance of language that Émile
Benveniste identified). The question here is not existence, but restlessness
as a producer of meaning or meaningfulness, and this meaning cannot be
easily reduced to individual life or a succession of concretions; it has to be
globally conceived. The teleological order, like the semantic order of language, is extracted from the universe of discourse and interpretations.
Generally scientists stay with the first, "semiotic" order of restlessness,
while theologians and ethicists stay with the "semantic" order of restlessness. In the terminology of linguistics, scientists stay with "the sign," and
theologians stay with "the speech," transforming the signs into discourse
of the restlessness; like the Psalmist, they want to know what the signs are
declaring about the glory of God. How do we move from sign to speech?
In these two orders we are "dealing with two distinct criteria of validity
that are required for the one and for the other. The semiotic . . . [order]
. . . must be recognized; the semantic . . . [order] must be understood."[26] I
am intuiting here that it is the virtue of the operations of the pentecostal
principle (at least as I have explained it here) that the signs pass into discourse. Without it, it appears that theology as a system of interpretation
of signs (of what is going on in the universe; theology is also a sign) is
paradoxically blocked by the very signs that call it into being. In
Agamben's terms, there will be "no passage from semiology to hermeneutics and we must situate signatures precisely in the 'gap' that separates
them. Signs do not speak unless signatures make them speak. But this
means that the theory of signification must be completed with a theory of
signatures."[27] The theorization of the pentecostal principle is an "attempt
to construct a bridge over that gap, to render thinkable the passage between the semiotic and the semantic."[28]

Another major theme (more precisely a sub-theme) that we handled
in the preceding chapters was emergence. We pursued it with regard to
deepening our understanding of the dynamic character of the pentecostal
principle. Creative emergence helps us to see how novel properties and behaviors can arise in a system, properties and behaviors that are not explicable by the lower parts or in terms of the sum of the parts. In a contingent,

26. Émile Benveniste, *Problèmes de linguistique générale*, vol. 2 (Paris: Gallimard, 1974),
p. 64, quoted in Agamben, *Signature of All Things*, p. 60.

27. Agamben, *Signature of All Things*, p. 61.

28. Agamben, *Signature of All Things*, p. 61.

emergentist world leaning to the real there will always be eruptions from the creative basis of relationality. There is always an excess which cannot be fully incorporated or suppressed by the extant system.

The import of understanding human social existence within the context of life's inherent dynamism, within the framework of creative emergence, impels us to ask how best we can fit the governance of socialities into the wider and more fundamental rhythm and impulse of pentecostal principle. The fundaments of the organization of society should lead to intensification of possibilities and potentialities at all levels as we deal with uncertainty while holding on to the expectation of new emergent qualities at any moment.

In the light of all this, a crucial task of social ethical thinking is to prepare citizens to deal with a world of increasing complexity, openness, possibilities, and uncertainty. It requires an ethos emphasizing that in the world we live in, potentialities or possibilities always exceed what has become. (This is the nature of the spirit of pentecostalism or the basic demand of the ~~protestant~~ pentecostal ethics.) We need a citizenry that can sense the unprecedented and is comfortable with surprises, can identify opportunities and threats, and can craft the appropriate responses rooted in their creative and prophetic power. We need to fashion an ethics that will enable individuals to cope with emergence, to rely on the spirit rather than on rules and predetermined ethical codes for navigating what is and what must be a world opened to surprises.

Chapter 3 makes an argument for an ethical methodology that takes pluralism very seriously. The phenomenon of glossolalic utterances on the Day of Pentecost as described in Acts 2 has pluralistic significance not only within the Christian communion, but also with respect to dialogue about scientific truths and between voices engaged in public theology and public policy. This chapter, grounded in methodologically pluralistic theology, lays out the "mechanics" for translation and interpretation of values, theological presuppositions, and languages from one side to another in debates about public policies. The chapter shows that a methodological approach that is analogically informed by the diverse glossolalic utterances described in Acts 2 can provide a framework for pentecostal engagement in public policy debates. And they can do this from a position distinctively informed by pentecostal spirituality without also denying others the right to be heard, and together with others attempt to discern what God is doing in the public space.

The ethical-analysis methodology developed in chapter 3 not only attempts to grasp the social analysis and empirical reality of problems, but also strives to plumb the depths of the presuppositions about human nature and community's understanding of God in the debates.

The reasons for developing the mechanics of ethical analysis for public policy engagement are twofold: first, there is a need to develop capabilities that address and guide the basic ordering of the common life in non-particularistic theological terms; and second, there is a need to present arguments that promote greater inclusiveness, greater justice, and higher levels of human flourishing that spur men and women to transformative praxis, to embrace and make ever more legible the pentecostal principle in how social life hangs together.

Then in chapter 4 we offered a reflection on the nature of the pentecostal spirit — the principle of self-consciousness or subjectivity of pentecostals, their creative self-interpretation of their moral life — to guide our overall orientation to pentecostal ethics, to develop an ethical methodology in a new key. The pentecostal spirit is a way of being that is radically open to divine surprises, always at work resisting obstacles to human flourishing, and committed to creating, broadening, and deepening new possibilities of life. We argued that its ethical methodology (engagement) must assume the mode of cultural criticism, social creativity, and political engagement in which we should resist commitment to any knowledge-machinery that only works to understand the world but not to change it, and at the same time provoking moral development, and enacting constituting and constituted social practices of human flourishing. An ethics faithful to the spirit of pentecostalism does not allow itself the luxury of bathing in the blithe air of the problematic and vocabulary of past eras and their spirits (specters), but must continuously work to invent its own analyses and language, to speak in new tongues. This is an ethics that is all about that which stands higher than actuality: the possibility that is in the human capacity to begin something new.

One of the major insights that emerged from chapter 4 is the playful character of pentecostalism. Our understanding of the pentecostal spirit will be inadequate if we do not reckon with the festival (Pentecost) nature of the pentecostal movement. Chapter 5 investigates the connections between the pentecostal principle, the quest for actualization of potentials, and playful character of pentecostalism. The result is a discussion of the major ethico-religious mission of pentecostalism and the "logic of play" as the inner dynamics of both the pentecostal principle and the pentecostal spirit.

The Roots That Route to the Pentecostal Principle

We have two issues to treat before bringing this book to a close. These issues will show how this study connects with my faith and scholarly work. First, I will relate this study to my early experience as a pentecostal Christian in Lagos, Nigeria. Second, I will take a little time to discuss how this project relates and fits into my oeuvre.

The definition and the theory of the pentecostal principle we have developed in this book are a refinement and distillation of my first impressions of born-again pentecostalism in September 1993. I became born again after obtaining my MBA in finance and accounting from Columbia University, New York, after working on Wall Street as an investment banker, and while doing corporate finance work for a local commercial bank in Lagos. I came to my first pentecostal meeting with a very analytical mind, but what struck me most at the very beginning was the emphasis on the human capacity for the new, to begin something new; not the health-and-wealth gospel. Having been used to working with accounting and financial principles and only days away from receiving copies of my first book, *Financial Statement Analysis,* I summed up my first impressions in terms of seven principles. These are what have been transformed into the pentecostal principle.

First, I felt that at the heart of the pentecostal movement is the belief that the Holy Spirit is moving anew upon human beings. Pentecost refers to a series of events: Acts 2, the experiences of the early apostles, and the continuing outpouring of the Holy Spirit on believers. I often heard from the brethren this refrain: "God is a God of new beginnings." Second, in the days and weeks that followed, those stronger and older in the faith repeatedly told me and other beginners that we could surpass our current form of existence and reach beyond what was formerly out of touch. There was a strong notion of self-transcendence because we served a God of surplus and possibility who could exceed our expectations (Eph. 3:20). The brethren often said to one another, "God has put us in a place of permanent advantage." One common prayer was that of exceeding ourselves, and being the head and not the tail. Third, all this is possible because we can do all things through Christ who strengthens us (Philippians 4:13). This was a call to strive harder to realize our God-given gifts and talents. We were told to actualize our potentialities, to die empty, to bless our generations as David blessed his (Acts 13:36). Like Paul (Phil. 3:12-14) we must always press forward. The one who is set free by Jesus Christ has all of her potentials come into play and they can freely evolve to bring glory to God as she is led by the Holy Spirit. I still remember a song we used to sing then: "Jehovah Jireh (Nissi, Shammah), He makes impossibility possible." Fourth, there was a focus on power too. "Ye are of God, little children, and have overcome them: because greater is he that is in you than he that is in the world" (1 John 4:4, NKJV). I was deeply impressed by the power of the Holy Spirit to assist believers. The power was available to energize human capacity to overcome, to push ahead and deepen and broaden being for human flourishing, and to improve existential life. Fifth, the members that I met in the pentecostal movement had a highly developed critical consciousness (2 Cor. 10:5-6). They were very critical of any human institution, project, or thought that elevates itself above God or even above a believer's personal human-God relationship. The freedom which the born-again has acquired to act on the level of the new humanity, to live the life in the Spirit, was seen as a capacity and a calling to resist human institutions that claim ultimacy. Sixth, the full realization of all the above qualities of the born-again life depends on the baptism (original and recursive new birth) of the Holy Spirit, holiness, grace, acknowledgement of divine guidance, and an openness to divine surprises, novelties, and liberation. Further, we were repeatedly advised that we had to cultivate ourselves to develop the right affections, pathos, love for the kingdom of God and the eschatological reign of Jesus Christ. All these were soaked within the context of worship, sermon, and teaching that had a joyous, playful character, that of exuberant children playing and "wasting" time before their heavenly Father.

Finally, God's grace is disruptive, stressing the patency of being and life. Grace enables creativity, removes blockages of passing and connecting such that reconciliation with God, realization of destiny, and reconstruction and re-creation of world occur. It erupts among human life-forms confined to the "zones of abandonment," marked by unrelenting vulnerability to death through poverty, and weighed down by socially imposed suffering. There were several eruptions in that Lagos setting of 1993. The eruptions came from both beyond and within the people: the collectively embodied spirit of survival erupting into the embrace of a transcendental impulse of disruption, the two congealing as the *contexture* of an individual's reception and working out of salvation.

To the people I worshiped with in the extremely poor neighborhood of Maroko, near the affluent Victoria Island, Lagos, grace was what was needed to lift off the burden of surplus suffering that has been politically imposed by the acts of the rulers of Nigeria and unseen spiritual agents.

Grace as an agent and a source of empowerment was a veritable ally in the struggle for survival. Grace was surplus power over personal and social sins. It was an excess beyond their surplus suffering and an intensification of life-enhancing, life-giving nourishment over the great vulnerability to death that was their lot. Having learned from them, I think of grace as God's act in that specific sense of Kant and Schelling:

> [It is] the point at which "eternity intervenes in time," at which the en-
> chainment of temporal causal succession is interrupted, at which
> "something emerges-intervenes out of nothing," at which something
> takes place which cannot be explained away as the outcome/result of the
> preceding chain (to put it in Kant's terms, the act designates the direct
> intervention of the noumenal dimension into phenomenality; to put it
> in Schelling's terms, the act designates the moment at which the abyssal/
> atemporal principle of identity — "I did it because I did it, for no par-
> ticular reason" — momentarily suspends the reign of the principle of
> sufficient reason).[29]

I turn finally to address how this book on methodology fits within my body of work on social ethics. This book exemplifies the third part of the trinitarian structure that informs my thinking on ethics, that is, ethics, metaethics, and methodology. I explored ethics with *God and Money: A Theology of Money in a Globalizing World* (2008). This book offers a reflection on the very concrete situation of the global monetary system. It makes claims on the structures of trade and payments and governments in order to promote flourishing lives for individuals and poor nations. It uses a conceptualization of the nature of the triune God (Paul Tillich's trinitarian principles) to point to alternatives and possibilities to the current global economic system.

My second book in this tripartite architecture explores the philosophy of possibilities, potentials, and alternatives. *The Principle of Excellence: A Framework for Social Ethics* (2009) proposes excellence (the continuous outworking of possibilities and potentialities) as the primary orientation or framework for social ethics. The unfinishedness of social existence and configuration, I argue, should be the starting point for metaethics. The argument here draws from the notion of Jesus Christ as the New Being. A

---

29. Slavoj Žižek, *The Fragile Absolute: Or, Why Is the Christian Legacy Worth Fighting For?* (London: Verso, 2008), p. 86.

Christology of excellence was developed as a way of pointing us to the need to imitate Jesus and to actualize our potentialities in spite of obstacles. In the language of systematic theologians of a bygone era, this book would be termed the doctrine, which usually sits between methodology and ethics.

What is fundamentally set forth in that book is pneumatological in nature. I understand this in two senses. First, the book's focus on actualization of potentials is one way of doing pneumatological-pentecostal ethics. Common grace, with the Holy Spirit as the dynamic element of God's providence, is the driving force behind the actualizing of the potentials of creation. The Spirit simultaneously nurtures and perfects, deepening the particularity of each person and connecting him or her to others, as it enables creation to actualize its God-given gifts.

Second, it is about the fluid, protean, and dynamic nature of human existence. I portray excellence as a transparent principle, not a stock of fine, laudable achievements. The principle dissolves the stock of achievements and renders it fluid, volatile, turning every end into a new beginning. This kind of understanding of the basic nature of human existence is a step toward answering this question: what is the energizing spirit behind the experimental nature of world-making? Is the openness, contingency, and revisability that is excellence powered by a transcendental, immanental, transimmanental, or immantranscendental spirit? The notion of pentecostal principle attempts to provide a response to these pertinent questions. One way it does this is to link the idea of creativity to kairos: kairos is the dynamic that has been given form by human creativity in concrete existence; it is the right time of spiritual presence (dimension of social life, of concentrated coexistence) which creates a nurturing space for unconcealment and communication of potentialities and possibilities that harness the potency of the future and forward-moving momentum of life in its concrete livingness.

The book you have in your hands un-conceals the methodology implicit in *God and Money*. It shows how both metaethics and concrete reflection (ethics) are made to work together and interpenetrate each other. Here the basic principles that guide the development of my ethical view — insofar as I am attempting to present a coherent system of thought — are laid bare. At one level, this book reveals the roots and fundamental character of my understanding of ethical reflection. At another, it is a form of thinking about the process and methods of my concrete ethical reflection on public theology engagement. It is not reflection itself; it is rather a way of seeking to understand the reflection and opening up its deepest symbols and presuppositions. The form of the discourse, or the seeking, is organized around the understanding of the Holy Spirit as the spirit of life and creation, and the dynamic power behind the emergence of the new.

The uniting subject matter of all parts of the tripartite structure is the quality of the relationship between human beings in social existence. This relationship is always unfinished, containing an excess which cannot be fully incorporated into it, and is ultimately driven by an eros toward the divine depths of existence. The turn to relationship is profoundly influenced by my interpretation of the triune Godhead as a relationality.

The manner in which all these are combined to present a coherent perspective is based on the theoretical framework of public theology. For me, public theology is the search for a form of social existence or particular cooperative enterprise in which individuality (a person's or group's intention or identity) is conserved at the same time that is transcended. It seeks a form of togetherness in which no individual identity is submerged into an overarching communion but is animated toward a larger body, a consummation of the aims of the individuals or groups for a higher level of concrete human flourishing, and a theonomous, eroticized commitment to excellence.

This is where I see public theology as a theology of possibilities, and the scent and ascent of possibilities keep me going and conditioning why I write what I write. I write to discern, identify, retrieve, parse, open up, move, create, and pursue possibilities in the various spheres human lives hang together. I call all that I write theology of possibility. It is the systematization and concentration of ideas for the enhancement of life in all forms of human sociality, and their articulation and unification with liberatory practices. It is both reflective and prescriptive. It begins with the practices of living institutions and then offers reflection on the presence, absence, and degree of opportunities and potentials for flourishing and inclusive human coexistence. It asks and responds to this basic question: Is there a creative alternative to current forms of sociality that can better serve the goals of justice, equity, participation, and communality? The answer is yes or soon there will be. All we need for this task is to deploy our imagination and show fidelity to the cause and course of justice.

The theology of possibility is not about the ideology of progress. It is, rather, about variation and alternative. The idea of possibility connotes a breakthrough that is not always a leap in progress. The actualization of potentials does not always run the Aristotelian vector of possibility to actuality. Often the vector runs from mere actuality to potentiality. There are times when actualization is about unearthing the emancipatory potentiality of the past (actuality) that was betrayed. There are situations where mere actuality retroactively ignites its hidden potentiality.[30] The idea of possibility is about putting persons at spaces where there are opportunities for going forward, potentials for pushing outwards the limits of life. It is the idea of starting and surpassing a future that is at the same time ending the limiting past in which that future is rooted. It is like the bend in the road. "You can stand at the bend and look back to where the road came from and then turn to see where it goes. But if you stand elsewhere on the road, you see either a straight line that ends at the bend or a straight line that began at the same bend. Only at the point of breakthrough can you see both directions at once. The future comes from the past, but not in a straight line."[31] Every human being has the right to stand at the bend of life that will fulfill him or her.

My understanding of the theology of possibility undergirds the who, what, where, when, how, and why of my theological reflections which I purposely locate at the bend of life and the life of the ethical mind.

Who: It is not done by elites for elites, but by all concerned about the involvement of institutions and major social practices in the less-than-flourishing life of poor people and poor nations. It is undertaken by and for all those who want to create better opportunities and possibilities in life for themselves and fellow human beings.

What: It is a reflection on ongoing realities of human coexistence that do not promote flourishing life for all in any given community. We write to bring hope, sustain justice, and promote healthy relationality so that all citizens can be all that they can be. It also involves making our bodies sites of resistance.

Where: It focuses on areas where both open and hidden transcripts of resistance to non-flourishing life are, and could be, enacted, enacted and sustained, enacted, sustained, and passed on in human sociality. Anywhere we see potentials for expanding possibilities for human flourishing we will make it a subject of radical inquiry.

---

30. See Slavoj Žižek, "Thinking Backward: Predestination and Apocalypse," in *Paul's New Moment: Continental Philosophy and the Future of Christian Theology*, ed. John Milbank, Slavoj Žižek, and Creston Davies (Grand Rapids: Brazos, 2010), p. 203. See also Žižek, *The Fragile Absolute*, pp. 80-83.

31. William Duggan, *Strategic Intuition: The Creative Spark in Human Achievement* (New York: Columbia Business School Publishing, 2007), pp. 15-16.

When: It happens when theology and ethics are united to release the marginalized, oppressed, and excluded from inhuman social constraints and launch them into a future of possibilities. We write so that we can offer practical solutions to institutions, leaders, and resisters to organize and re-organize communities for a more fulfilling and meaningful life.

How: Its orientation is to engage with the dominant and oppressive powers in their practices and in the ideas that undergird and sustain them with the purpose of changing them for the common good.

Why: We generate ideas and practices of resistance in order to change the world, combat oppression, and promote life more abundant. We firmly believe that our tomorrow should be better than our today. We are dedicated to keeping the supreme human capacity to being alive. We must not suffer from the given, the past, or the dead and must not permit it to seize the living. Let the dead bury their dead!

Those of us from Africa to whom the world has said there is no hope owe it to ourselves, and the rest of the world, to pursue the un-foreclosed and un-foreclosable option of existence. We owe it to our children and grandchildren to imagine what is beyond the horizon in our current phase of life and economic development. We have to think in terms of possibility — in possibilities only! For this reason, I am persuaded that pentecostal theology or philosophy should not be limited to the theology of the Holy Spirit. It should be broadened to include the pneumatological imagination, pneumatic existence, the pneumatological dynamics of existence, and the possibilities of human flourishing in theonomous relationship with the Spirit of God.

Bibliography

Agamben, Giorgio. *Nudities*. Translated by David Kishik and Stefan Padatella. Stanford: Stanford University Press, 2011.

———. *What Is Apparatus?* Translated by David Kishik and Stefan Padatella. Stanford: Stanford University Press, 2009.

———. *The Signature of All Things: On Method*. Translated by Luca di Santo with Kevin Attell. New York: Zone Books, 2009.

———. *Profanations*. Translated by Jeff Fort. New York: Zone Books, 2007.

———. *Infancy and History: On the Destruction of Experience*. London: Verso, 2007.

———. *The Time That Remains: A Commentary on the Letter to the Romans*. Translated by Patricia Dailey. Stanford: Stanford University Press, 2005.

———. *State of Exception*. Translated by Kevin Attell. Chicago: University of Chicago Press, 2005.

———. *Means without Ends: Notes on Politics*. Translated by Vincenzo Benetti and Cesare Casarino. Minneapolis: University of Minnesota Press, 2000.

———. *The Man without Content*. Translated by Georgia Albert. Stanford: Stanford University Press, 1999.

———. *Homo Sacer: Sovereign Power and Bare Life*. Translated by Daniel Heller-Roazen. Stanford: Stanford University Press, 1998.

———. *The Coming Community*. Translated by Michael Hardt. Minneapolis: University of Minnesota Press, 1993.

Anderson, Ben. "'Transcending without Transcendence': Utopianism and an Ethos of Hope." *Antipode* 38, no. 4 (2006): 691-710.

Arendt, Hannah. *The Origins of Totalitarianism*. New York: Schocken Books, 2004.

———. *The Life of the Mind*, Volume 1: *Thinking*. San Diego: Harcourt, 1978.

———. *Men in Dark Times*. San Diego: Harcourt Brace & Company, 1968.

————. *The Human Condition*. Chicago: University of Chicago Press, 1958.

Aristotle. *Nicomachean Ethics*. Translated by Martin Oswald. Indianapolis: Liberal Arts Press, 1962.

————. *Metaphysics*. Edited by Richard McKeon. New York: Random House, 1941.

Badiou, Alain. *The Communist Hypothesis*. Translated by David Macey and Steve Corcoran. London: Verso, 2010.

————. *Saint Paul: The Foundation of Universalism*. Stanford: Stanford University Press, 2003.

Begbie, Jeremy S. *Theology, Music, and Time*. Cambridge: Cambridge University Press, 2000.

Benjamin, Walter. "Critique of Violence." In *Selected Writings*, Vol. 1. Edited by Marcus Bullock and Michael Jennings. Translated by Edmund Jephcott. Cambridge, MA: Harvard University Press, 1996.

Birnbaum, David. *Summa Metaphysica II*. New York: J. Levine/Millennium, 2008.

Bloch, Ernst. *Literary Essays*. Translated by Andrew Joron. Stanford: Stanford University Press, 1998.

————. *The Principle of Hope*. Translated by Neville Plaice, Stephen Plaice, and Paul Knight. Cambridge, MA: MIT Press, 1986.

Bloch, Maurice. *Ritual, History and Power: Selected Papers in Anthropology*. New York: Berg, 1989.

Bloch, Maurice, and Jonathan Parry, eds. *Death and Regeneration of Life*. Cambridge: Cambridge University Press, 1982.

Bourriaud, Nicolas. *The Radicant*. Translated by James Gussen and Lili Porten. New York: Lukas and Sternberg, 2009.

————. *Relational Aesthetics*. Translated by Simon Pleasance, Fronza Woods, and Matthieu Copeland. Paris: Les Presses du Ráel, 2002.

————. *Postproduction Culture as Screenplay: How Art Reprograms the World*. Translated by Jeanine Herman. New York: Lukas and Sternberg, 2002.

Brittain, Christopher Craig. "Tillich and Adorno: Two Approaches to a Theology of Correlation." *Bulletin of the North American Paul Tillich Society* 36, no. 3 (Summer 2010): 36-41.

Brock, Brian. *Christian Ethics in a Technological Age*. Grand Rapids: Eerdmans, 2010.

Buber, Martin. *I and Thou*. Translated by Walter Kaufmann. New York: Charles Scribner's Sons, 1970.

Cavanaugh, William T. *Being Consumed: Economics and Christian Desire*. Grand Rapids: Eerdmans, 2008.

Chow, Rey. *The Protestant Ethnic and the Spirit of Capitalism*. New York: Columbia University Press, 2002.

Clayton, Philip. *Mind and Emergence: From Quantum to Consciousness*. Oxford: Oxford University Press, 2004.

Comblin, José. *The Holy Spirit and Liberation*. Maryknoll, NY: Orbis, 1989.

Cone, James H. *A Black Theology of Liberation.* Maryknoll, NY: Orbis, 1986.

Cox, Harvey. "Jazz and Pentecostalism." *Archives des sciences sociales des religions* 84, no. 4 (October-December 1993): 181-88.

Crichton, Michael. *Prey.* New York: Avon, 2002.

Dabney, D. Lyle. "The Nature of the Spirit: Creation as a Premonition of God." In *Starting with the Spirit.* Edited by Stephen Pickard and Gordon Preece. Hindmarsh: Australian Theological Forum, 2001.

―――. "Why Should the Last Be First? The Priority of Pneumatology in Recent Theological Discussion." In *Advents of the Spirit.* Edited by Bradford E. Hinze and D. Lyle Dabney. Milwaukee: Marquette University Press, 2001.

―――. "*Pneumatologia Crucis:* Reclaiming *Theologia Crucis* for a Theology of Spirit Today." *Scottish Journal of Theology* 53, no. 4 (2000): 511-24.

―――. "Otherwise Engaged in the Spirit: A First Theology for a Twenty-first Century." In *The Future of Theology: Essays in Honor of Jürgen Moltmann.* Edited by Miroslav Volf, Carmen Krieg, and Thomas Kucharz, 154-63. Grand Rapids: Eerdmans, 1996.

De Goede, Marieke. *Virtue, Fortune, and Faith: A Genealogy of Finance.* Minneapolis: University of Minnesota Press, 2005.

Derrida, Jacques. *Specters of Marx: The State of the Debt, the Work of Mourning, and the New International.* Translated by Peggy Kamuf. New York: Routledge, 1994.

Duggan, William. *Strategic Intuition: The Creative Spark in Human Achievement.* New York: Columbia Business School Publishing, 2007.

Eck, Diana L. "What Is Pluralism?" The Pluralism Project at Harvard University. Accessed August 3, 2010. http://pluralism.org/pages/pluralism/what_is_pluralism.

―――. "From Diversity to Pluralism." The Pluralism Project at Harvard University. Accessed August 3, 2010. http://pluralism.org/pages/pluralism/essay/from_diversity_to_pluralism.

Emerson, Ralph Waldo. *Nature: Selected Writings of Ralph Waldo Emerson.* Edited by William H. Gilman. New York: New American Library, 1965.

―――. "Circles." In *Selected Writings of Ralph Waldo Emerson.* Edited by William H. Gilman. New York: New American Library, 1965.

Erikson, Erik H. *Young Man Luther: A Study in Psychoanalysis and History.* New York: Norton, 1993.

Evans, James H., Jr. *Playing.* Minneapolis: Fortress, 2010.

Fenn, Richard. *The Return of the Primitive: A New Sociological Theory of Religion.* Aldershot: Ashgate, 2001.

―――. *Time Exposure: The Personal Experience of Time in Secular Societies.* Oxford: Oxford University Press, 2001.

―――. *The End of Time: Religion, Ritual, and the Forging of the Soul.* Cleveland: Pilgrim Press, 1997.

Fishbane, Michael. *Sacred Attunement: A Jewish Theology.* Chicago: University of Chicago Press, 2008.

Fukuyama, Francis. *The End of History and the Last Man.* New York: Avon Books, 1992.

Gadamer, Hans-Georg. *Truth and Method.* Translated by Joel Weinsheimer and Donald G. Marshall. London: Continuum, 2004.

Gregory of Nyssa. *Commentary on the Song of Songs.* Translated by Casmir McCambley. Brookline, MA: Hellenic College Press, 1987.

Guengerich, Galen. "Comprehensive Commitments and the Public World: Tillich, Rawls, and Whitehead on the Nature of Justice." Ph.D. Dissertation. Chicago: University of Chicago, 2004.

Hallward, Peter. *Badiou: A Subject to Truth.* Minneapolis: University of Minnesota Press, 2003.

Hardt, Michael, and Antonio Negri. *Multitude: War and Democracy in the Age of Empire.* New York: Penguin, 2004.

———. *Empire.* Cambridge, MA: Harvard University Press, 2000.

Hayek, Friedrich A. *Law, Legislation and Liberty,* Volume 2: *The Mirage of Social Justice.* Chicago: University of Chicago Press, 1976.

———. *The Road to Serfdom.* Chicago: University of Chicago Press, 1944.

Heidegger, Martin. *Discourse on Thinking: A Translation of* Gelassenheit. Translated by John M. Anderson and E. Hans Freund. New York: Harper & Row, 1966.

Heim, Mark. "A Cross-Section of Sin: The Mimetic Character of Human Nature in Biological and Theological Perspective." In *Evolution and Ethics: Human Morality in Biological and Religious Perspective.* Edited by Philip Clayton, 255-72. Grand Rapids: Eerdmans, 2004.

Huizinga, Johan. *Homo Ludens: A Study of the Play Element in Culture.* Translated by R. F. C. Hull. Boston: Beacon Press, 1995.

Jacobson, Arthur J. "Origins of the Game Theory of Law and the Limits of Harmony in Plato's Law." *Cardozo Law Review* 20 (May-July 1999): 1335-1400.

James, Ian. *The Fragmentary Demand: An Introduction to the Philosophy of Jean-Luc Nancy.* Stanford: Stanford University Press, 2006.

John XXIII. *Mater et Magistra.* Vatican City, 1961. Accessed online February 13, 2009. http://www.va/holy_father/john_xxxiii/encyclicals/documents/hf_jxxxiii_enc _15051961_mater_en.html.

Kalu, Ogbu. *African Pentecostalism: An Introduction.* Oxford: Oxford University Press, 2008.

Keller, Catherine. *On the Mystery: Discerning God in Process.* Minneapolis: Fortress, 2008.

———. *Face of the Deep: A Theology of Becoming.* New York: Routledge, 2003.

Kotsko, Adam. *Žižek and Theology.* London: T&T Clark, 2008.

Lamm, Julia A. "'Catholic Substance' Revisited: Reversals of Expectations in

Tillich's Doctrine of God." In *Paul Tillich: A Catholic Assessment*. Edited by Raymond F. Bulman and Frederick J. Parrella, 48-72. Collegeville, MN: Liturgical Press, 1994.

Land, Steven J. *Pentecostal Spirituality: A Passion for the Kingdom*. Sheffield: Sheffield Academic Press, 1993.

Lévi-Strauss, Claude. *The Savage Mind*. Chicago: University of Chicago Press, 1966.

Luhmann, Niklas. *Social Systems*. Stanford: Stanford University Press, 1995.

Macchia, Frank D. *Justified in the Spirit: Creation, Redemption, and the Triune God*. Grand Rapids: Eerdmans, 2010.

MacIntyre, Alasdair. *After Virtue: A Study in Moral Theory*. Notre Dame: University of Notre Dame Press, 1984.

Marcuse, Herbert. *Eros and Civilization: A Philosophical Inquiry into Freud*. London: Sphere Books, 1969.

Marshall, Ruth. "The Sovereignty of Miracles: Pentecostal Political Theology in Nigeria." *Constellations* 17, no. 2 (2010): 197-223.

———. *Political Spiritualities: The Pentecostal Revolution in Nigeria*. Chicago: University of Chicago Press, 2009.

Marx, Karl, and Friedrich Engels. *The Communist Manifesto*. Harmondsworth: Penguin, 1985.

Meillassoux, Quentin. *After Finitude: An Essay on the Necessity of Contingency*. Translated by Ray Brassier. London: Continuum, 2008.

Milbank, John, Slavoj Žižek, and Creston Davies. *Paul's New Moment: Continental Philosophy and the Future of Christian Theology*. Grand Rapids: Brazos Press, 2010.

Miller, David L. *Gods and Games: Toward a Theology of Play*. New York: Word, 1970.

Moltmann, Jürgen. *The Coming of God: Christian Eschatology*. Translated by Margaret Kohl. Minneapolis: Fortress, 1996.

———. *Theology of Hope: On the Ground and Implications of a Christian Eschatology*. Translated by James W. Leitch. Minneapolis: Fortress Press, 1996.

———. *God in Creation: A New Theology of Creation and the Spirit of God*. Translated by Margaret Kohl. Minneapolis: Fortress, 1993.

———. *The Trinity and the Kingdom*. Translated by Margaret Kohl. Minneapolis: Fortress, 1993.

———. *The Spirit of Life: A Universal Affirmation*. Translated by Margaret Kohl. Minneapolis: Fortress, 1992.

———. *Theology of Play*. Translated by Reinhard Ulrich. New York: Harper & Row, 1972.

Morgan, Benjamin. "Undoing Legal Violence: Walter Benjamin's and Giorgio Agamben's Aesthetics of Pure Means." *Journal of Law and Society* 34, no. 1 (March 2007): 46-64.

Morris, Simon Conway. *Life's Solution: Inevitable Humans in a Lonely Universe.* Cambridge: Cambridge University Press, 2003.

Nancy, Jean-Luc. *Being Singular Plural.* Translated by Robert D. Richardson and Anne E. O'Byrne. Stanford: Stanford University Press, 2000.

—————. *The Experience of Freedom.* Translated by Bridget McDonald. Stanford: Stanford University Press, 1993.

—————. *The Inoperative Community.* Translated by Peter Connor, Lisa Garbus, Michael Holland, and Simona Sawhney. Minneapolis: University of Minnesota Press, 1991.

Nussbaum, Martha C. *The Fragility of Goodness: Luck and Ethics in Greek Tragedy and Philosophy.* Cambridge: Cambridge University Press, 2001.

—————. *Upheavals of Thought: The Intelligence of Emotions.* Cambridge: Cambridge University Press, 2001.

O'Byrne, Anne. *Natality and Finitude.* Bloomington: University of Indiana Press, 2010.

O'Keeffe, Terrence M. "Ideology and the Protestant Principle." *Journal of the American Academy of Religion* 51, no. 2 (1983): 283-306.

Origen. *Contra Celsum.* Translated by Henry Chadwick. Cambridge: Cambridge University Press, 1953.

Paris, Peter J. *Black Religious Leaders.* Louisville: Westminster/John Knox, 1991.

Parry, Jonathan, and Maurice Bloch, eds. *Money and the Morality of Exchange.* Cambridge: Cambridge University Press, 1989.

Peters, Ted. *God — The World's Future.* Minneapolis: Augsburg Fortress, 2000.

Pixley, Jocelyn. *Emotions in Finance: Distrust and Uncertainty in Global Markets.* Cambridge: Cambridge University Press, 2004.

Sacks, Jonathan. *The Dignity of Difference: How to Avoid the Clash of Civilizations.* London: Continuum, 2002.

Schmitt, Carl. *Political Theology: Four Chapters on the Concept of Sovereignty.* Translated by George Schwab. Chicago: University of Chicago Press, 2006.

Serequeberhan, Tsenay. *Our Heritage: The Past in the Present of African-American and African Existence.* Lanham, MD: Rowman & Littlefield, 2000.

—————. *The Hermeneutics of African Philosophy: Horizon and Discourse.* New York: Routledge, 1994.

Smith, James K. A. *Thinking in Tongues: Pentecostal Contributions to Christian Philosophy.* Grand Rapids: Eerdmans, 2010.

Smith, James K. A., and Amos Yong. *Science and the Spirit: A Pentecostal Engagement with the Sciences.* Bloomington: Indiana University Press, 2010.

Smith, Steven G. *The Concept of the Spiritual: An Essay in First Philosophy.* Philadelphia: Temple University Press, 1988.

Sockness, Brent W. "Looking Behind the Social Teachings: Troeltsch's Methodological Reflections in 'Fundamental Problems of Ethics' (1902)." *The Annual Society of Christian Ethics* (1995): 221-46.

Solivan, Samuel. *The Spirit, Pathos, and Liberation: Toward an Hispanic Pentecostal Theology.* Sheffield: Sheffield Academic Press, 1998.

Stackhouse, Max. *God and Globalization,* Volume 4: *Globalization and Grace.* New York: Continuum, 2007.

Stackhouse, Max, Dennis P. McCann, and Shirley J. Roels, with Preston N. Williams, eds. *On Moral Business: Classical and Contemporary Resources for Ethics and Economic Life.* Grand Rapids: Eerdmans, 1995.

Stronstad, Roger. *The Prophethood of All Believers: A Study in Luke's Charismatic Theology.* Cleveland, TN: CPT Press, 2010.

Suurmond, Jean-Jacques. *Word and Spirit at Play.* Grand Rapids: Eerdmans, 1994.

Taylor, Mark C. *After God.* Chicago: The University of Chicago Press, 2007.

Taylor, Mark Lewis. "Tillich's Ethics: Between Politics and Ontology." In *The Cambridge Companion to Paul Tillich.* Edited by Russell Re Manning, 189-207. Cambridge: Cambridge University Press, 2009.

———. *Religion, Politics, and the Christian Right: Post 9/11 Powers and American Empire.* Minneapolis: Fortress, 2005.

———. *The Executed Gods: The Way of the Cross in Lockdown America.* Minneapolis: Fortress, 2001.

Thomas, Terrence. "On Another Boundary: Tillich's Encounter with World Religion." In *Theonomy and Autonomy: Studies in Paul Tillich's Engagement with Modern Culture.* Edited by John J. Carey, 193-211. Macon: Mercer University Press, 1984.

Tillich, Paul. *Dynamics of Faith.* New York: HarperCollins, 2001.

———. *The System of the Sciences According to Objects and Methods.* Translated by Paul Wiebe. East Brunswick, NJ: Associated University Press, 1982.

———. *Political Expectation.* New York: Harper and Row, 1971.

———. *Systematic Theology,* Volume 3: *Life and the Spirit; History and the Kingdom of God.* Chicago: University of Chicago Press, 1963.

———. *Morality and Beyond.* Louisville: Westminster John Knox, 1963.

———. *Systematic Theology,* Volume 2: *Existence and the Christ.* Chicago: University of Chicago Press, 1957.

———. *Love, Power, and Justice: Ontological Analyses and Ethical Applications.* Oxford: Oxford University Press, 1954.

———. *Systematic Theology,* Volume 1: *Reason and Revelation, Being and God.* Chicago: University of Chicago Press, 1951.

———. *The Protestant Era.* Chicago: University of Chicago Press, 1948.

———. *The Shaking of the Foundations.* New York: Charles Scribner's Sons, 1948.

———. *The Interpretation of History.* New York: Charles Scribner's Sons, 1936.

Tippett, Krista. *Einstein's God: Conversations about Science and the Human Spirit.* New York: Penguin, 2010.

Troeltsch, Ernst. *Religion in History.* Translated by James Luther Adams and Walter F. Bense. Eugene, OR: Wipf and Stock, 2002.

van Huyssteen, J. Wentzel. *Alone in the World? Human Consciousness in Science and Theology.* Grand Rapids: Eerdmans, 2006.

Volf, Miroslav. *Exclusion and Embrace: A Theological Exploration of Identity, Otherness, and Reconciliation.* Nashville: Abingdon, 1996.

Vondey, Wolfgang. *Beyond Pentecostalism: The Crisis of Global Christianity and the Renewal of the Theological Agenda.* Grand Rapids: Eerdmans, 2010.

Wall, John. "*Imitatio Creatoris:* The Hermeneutical Primordiality of Creativity in Moral Life." *The Journal of Religion* 87, no. 1 (January 2007): 21-42.

———. *Moral Creativity: Paul Ricoeur and the Poetics of Possibility.* New York: Oxford University Press, 2005.

Wariboko, Nimi. *Ethics and Time: Ethos of Temporal Orientation in Politics and Religion of the Niger Delta.* Lanham, MD: Lexington Books, 2010.

———. *The Principle of Excellence: A Framework for Social Ethics.* Lanham, MD: Lexington Books, 2009.

———. *God and Money: A Theology of Money in a Globalizing World.* Lanham, MD: Lexington Books, 2008.

———. *The Depth and Destiny of Work: An African Theological Interpretation.* Trenton: Africa World Press, 2008.

Weber, Max. *Economy and Society: An Outline of Interpretative Sociology.* Edited by Guenther Roth and Claus Wittich. Berkeley: University of California Press, 1978.

———. *The Protestant Ethic and the Spirit of Capitalism.* Translated by T. Parsons. London: Allen & Unwin, 1930.

West, Cornel. *Democracy Matters: Winning the Fight against Imperialism.* New York: Penguin, 2004.

———. *The American Evasion of Philosophy: A Genealogy of Pragmatism.* Madison: University of Wisconsin Press, 1989.

Whitehead, Alfred North. *Science and the Modern World.* 2nd ed. New York: Macmillan, 1926.

Wright, Robert. *The Evolution of God.* New York: Little, Brown, 2009.

———. *Nonzero: The Logic of Human Destiny.* New York: Vintage, 2001.

Yong, Amos. *Spirit of Creation.* Grand Rapids: Eerdmans, 2010.

———. *In the Days of Caesar: Pentecostalism and Political Theology.* Grand Rapids: Eerdmans, 2010.

———. *Theology and Down Syndrome: Reimagining Disability in Late Modernity.* Waco: Baylor University Press, 2007.

———. *Spirit-Word-Community: Theological Hermeneutics in Trinitarian Perspective.* Eugene, OR: Wipf and Stock, 2006.

———. *The Spirit Poured Out on All Flesh.* Grand Rapids: Baker Academic, 2005.

———. "A Theology of the Third Article? Hegel and the Contemporary Enterprise in First Philosophy and First Theology." In *Semper Reformandum:*

Studies in Honour of Clark H. Pinnock. Edited by Stanley E. Porter and Anthony R. Cross, 208-31. Carlisle: Paternoster, 2003.

Žižek, Slavoj. *The Ticklish Subject: The Absent Center of Political Ontology.* London: Verso, 2008.

—————. *The Fragile Absolute: Or, Why Is the Christian Legacy Worth Fighting For?* London: Verso, 2008.

—————. *The Puppet and the Dwarf: The Perverse Core of Christianity.* Cambridge, MA: MIT Press, 2003.

Zuckerkandl, Victor. *Sound and Symbol: Music and the External World.* London: Routledge and Kegan Paul, 1956.

Acknowledgments

There is no greater god than acknowledgment in scholarly writing. How unlike, how very unlike the writings of ordinary life! This difference weights against the former. The acknowledgment conveys the sense of fragility of all thoughts good and beautiful and points in a strange way to the loveliness of ordinary life. The reliance on others when they are both wrong and right forces the recognition that there is no real solid foundation to our thinking — all is revisable. Thought is the freedom we can never own, but use and interact with others because it precedes our will; too invisible to hand out on the market, and not possible apart from dwelling in its community. The freedom of infinite thought is chained to the necessity of reliance on those who come before you and those who stand ready to illumine your blind spots.

No one without friends and having his or her being in communion can bear the full impact of the *finitum capax infiniti* (the "finite gaining the capacity to bear the infinite") that serious thought imposes. In simpler language, I mean to say that we all need good persons to watch our backs as we charge forward to capture and intercourse with thought for the pleasure of the life of the mind. In the tryst with thought in that Arendtian temporal space between the infinite past and the infinite future that engendered this book that now is in your hands, the most encouraging and resourceful friend that watched my back is Amos Yong of Regent University. I benefited from his critical reading of the manuscript. He nudged me to include more works by pentecostal scholars in the manuscript and to set them into an extensive dialogue with outside voices. He also encouraged me to publish the manuscript under Eerdmans' Pentecostal Manifesto series, which he co-edits. I have thanked him already, but I urge you, the reader who is right at this moment benefiting from his labor of love, to thank him when you run into him in the concrete space of terra firma — not in the Arendtian temporal space of the thinking ego.

Special thanks are also due to Ruth Marshall of the University of Toronto, James K. A. Smith of Calvin College and another co-editor of the Pentecostal Manifesto series, and Jon Pott, Vice President and Editor-in-Chief of Eerdmans Publishing Company, and the extraordinary staff at Eerdmans (Linda Bieze, Vicky Fanning, and Jenny Hoffman), who guided the manuscript through the process of proposal, review, production, and publication.

The book was made possible by my precious family: my incomparable and loving wife, Wapaemi — a jewel of inestimable value — and our wonderful and supportive children, Nimi, Bele, and Favor. Their presence and inspiration in my life have made my life of the mind very productive, rewarding, and communal. I am grateful for their patience, support, and steadfastness. This book is dedicated to Wapaemi as she celebrates her fiftieth birthday in 2011 and as we celebrate our twenty-first wedding anniversary.

Thanks are due to the editors of the following journals for permission to reproduce my essays that form parts of chapters 2 and 3. Chapter 2 integrates "Emergence and Ethics: From Outline and Interpretation to Prophetic Spirit," first published in *Dharma Deepika* (July-December 2010): 50-64. And chapter 3 includes "Ethical Methodology: Between Public Theology and Public Policy." *Journal of Religion and Business Ethics* 1, no. 1 (Winter 2010).

Index